Who are the Evangelicals?

Tracing the roots
of the modern movements

DEREK J. TIDBALL

With Forewords by Clive Calver
and Mark A. Noll

MarshallPickering
An Imprint of HarperCollins*Publishers*

Marshall Pickering is an Imprint of
HarperCollins*Religious*
Part of HarperCollins*Publishers*
77-85 Fulham Palace Road, London W6 8JB

First published in Great Britain
in 1994 by Marshall Pickering

1   3   5   7   9   10   8   6   4   2

Copyright © 1994 Derek J. Tidball

Derek Tidball asserts the moral right to be
identified as the author of this work

A catalogue record for this book is
available from the British Library

ISBN 0 551 02503-4

Printed and bound in Great Britain by
HarperCollinsManufacturing Glasgow

Dedicated to
the staff and students of
London Bible College
on the occasion of
its jubilee.
In gratitude.

CONTENTS

PART TWO: **DOCTRINES**

FOREWORDS

The facts speak for themselves. The day has long passed when evangelicals could be glibly dismissed as a 'lunatic fringe', a tiny minority whose mindless ravings disturbed the tranquillity of normal church life. Now evangelicals are growing towards fifty per cent of Protestant church attenders in the United Kingdom. They have rapidly become a force to be reckoned with.

Today there are key denominational leaders who freely acknowledge their evangelical commitment. Independent Pentecostal and 'new' churches record rapid numerical growth. An evangelical festival – Spring Harvest – maintains over seventy thousand attenders each year. An Elim Pentecostal church is now the largest Christian congregation in the United Kingdom. Mainline denominations are forced to concede numerical decline, except in the evangelical wing, where numbers are increasing. And evangelicals are becoming involved again in areas like social responsibility and theological investigation which they had long neglected.

It is perhaps unsurprising that a secular commentator has been forced to conclude – 'Whatever one may think of them . . . tomorrow belongs to the evangelicals.'

This is, therefore, a book whose time has come. I freely confess that Ian Coffey and I had wanted to write it, yet Derek Tidball was ahead of us. I am thrilled that he was! For Derek brings to this volume the twin skills of the sociologist and the theologian.

He brings us a different kind of book. Instead of a triumphalistic résumé of evangelical virtues, the reader is presented with a personal analysis of who evangelicals are, and where they come from. Carefully dissecting many of the 'sacred cows' of evangelicalism, Derek seeks to explore the nature of true evangelical identity.

This is not always comfortable reading. In self-defence we may choose to argue that the author has no right to criticize. Yet a patient analysis of evangelical history, character, practices and theology provide the foundation of a powerful exposé. Often the temptation to self-congratulation is sacrificed on the altar of an honest assessment of present-day reality.

The result is a powerful picture of evangelicalism which does not always conform to the one that we would wish to have painted for us. This is, however, a reasonable portrait, and one which we should never glibly ignore. For there are many lessons to be learned from the paths followed by previous generations of evangelicals. Our theology merits careful analysis, and this the author has generously done.

It is my conviction that we owe a deep debt of gratitude to Derek Tidball for this book. A sincere, convinced evangelical himself, he brings a weight of personal experience to add to his considerable scholarship. The result is one that does not ignore our blemishes and weaknesses. At the same time it highlights both evangelical strengths and virtues, against the background of our story and the society in which we live.

If you believe, as I do, that evangelicals need to know who they are in order better to conform to our true identity, then this book is a must to be read. Be prepared to work at its contents, and be as blessed and encouraged as I am by the message it contains. Perhaps this book may present another milestone in the honest contemporary attempt to put evangelicals on the map, where surely in today's society they truly belong.

Clive Calver
General Director,
Evangelical Alliance of
the United Kingdom

All efforts to describe 'evangelicalism', whether historically or doctrinally, must fail, for the evangelical impulses of the last two and one-half centuries have been extraordinarily diverse, variegated beyond imagination, and constantly engaged in a process of division, recombination and reformation. If all such efforts fail, however, some are more successful failures than others. For its irenic tone, sage judgements, broad historical sweep and discerning ability to discriminate, Derek Tidball's attempt in *Who Are the Evangelicals?* is certainly one of the best. Not the least of this book's virtues is the care with which its author handles the very tricky matter of defining what he is talking about. A Rubik's Cube might not be the first material object we think of to assist in this knotty task, but for Tidball it works surprisingly well.

American evangelicals will be especially assisted by this book for the way in which it covers familiar territory with, so to speak, an English accent. Not only is it refreshing to read Tidball's summary of American evangelical history, especially for the chance to observe what an outsider to the United States thinks has been most important in our history. But in addition, Tidball has taken the time to read widely in American sources, and to situate debates over doctrine and practice among American evangelicals in the context of similar debates over similar issues in Great Britain. This trans-Atlantic perspective provides many specific points of illumination – for example, concerning parallel speculations on the return of Christ that took place in Britain and America in the nineteenth century, or concerning the reasons why 'battles for the Bible' take shape around different issues on either side of the Atlantic.

Informative as it is to hear about broad developments among evangelicals from a fresh perspective, the book is even more valuable for a discerning presentation of main evangelical convictions. Splendid chapters on the Bible, the doctrine and practice of conversion, the Second Coming of Christ, the church, social action, spirituality, and – best of all – the cross of Christ achieve several purposes. They outline simply, yet biblically, the essence of traditional evangelical belief. Then they examine variations, disputes, contentions, arguments and schisms that have divided evangelicals from each other in their apprehension of these matters. Finally, they engage in clear-eyed, gentle, but also courageous assessment of evangelical strengths and weaknesses. So carefully argued are these chapters that, by the time readers get to the last section of the last chapter, we are not shocked by Tidball's bold question, 'Would Jesus be an evangelical?' And we can understand why he answers as he does that, yes, Jesus would be an evangelical, but not without qualification.

For the rest, the book excels at its integration of early evangelical history from the era of John Wesley, Jonathan Edwards and Charles Simeon with a full range of contemporary developments. Of these the most important is Tidball's careful consideration of how the charismatic movement has – all at the same time – re-energized, diverted and perplexed historical evangelical movements. In defining how evangelicals *should* believe and act, Tidball follows the best authorities: Scripture first, then the noble worthies of the tradition like Edwards and Wesley, and finally the sanest evangelical voices today, especially John Stott. Readers may not agree in every particular with all of Tidball's conclusions, but, with that ordering of authorities, weighty and thought-provoking analysis is assured. Tidball also shows great insight into the heart of evangelicalism by putting to good use the hymns that have done so much to define its essence.

This book is especially welcome at a time when the world is shrinking rapidly. Its very recognition of how important the missionary movement has been to evangelicals testifies to Tidball's understanding of how believers in different corners of the world can draw encouragement from each other. For what it tells us about differences between American and British evangelicals, for what it tells us about the past and possible futures of evangelicalism, but most of all for what it tells us about the gracious God whom evangelicals seek (with all their sins, flaws and imperfections) to worship, I sincerely hope that this book will enjoy the wide readership it deserves.

Mark A. Noll
McManis Professor of
Christian Thought
Wheaton College, Illinois

INTRODUCTION

My grandparents, on my father's side, spent the early years of their Christian lives at Moody Tabernacle, Chicago. On returning to England, they joined the Salvation Army and, later, the Assemblies of God. My maternal grandparents were Baptists. For a reason I have never quite understood, when my Pentecostal father married my Baptist mother they decided the best way to resolve the situation was to join the Christian Brethren. So it was there, in an assembly once led by George Müller, that I was nurtured in the Christian faith and baptized as a believer. Soon afterwards our family moved and in our new town we transferred to the Baptists.

At University I became involved with the Christian Union, an active and loyal branch of the Inter-Varsity Fellowship, as it was then known, and revelled, week by week, in the excellent Bible teaching of the Anglicans, whom, until this point I had always regarded with some suspicion! This occasionally led me to stray from the Baptist chapel to worship at the lively Church of England in the centre of the city. On graduation I channelled much of my energies, both locally and nationally, into Youth for Christ, before entering the London Bible College for further training and subsequent ordination as a Baptist minister. To complete the picture, I later married a Baptist, from a Methodist family.

There is a common thread running through all these diverse churches and institutions: they were all evangelical. I have remained committed to evangelicalism and believe it to be the true biblical expression of the Christian faith. The commitment has remained firm despite subjecting it to the examination of wider theological and ecumenical criticisms. It has also remained firm knowing that contemporary evangelicalism is far from perfect and that its participants sometimes suffer from the besetting sins of narrowness and arrogance, for which, I believe, we should be profoundly penitent.

Evangelicalism is a significant movement within the history of the Church, which transcends national and denominational differences, and today enjoys considerable world-wide influence. Yet, it is frequently taken far less seriously by religious commentators than it deserves and is often known only to the wider world by caricature. Even evangelicals themselves have only a scanty knowledge of their own movement, often leading them to a narrowness of vision and judgment which is unnecessary.

To outsiders and insiders alike evangelicalism often appears a confusing jungle with indistinct boundaries. The purpose of this book is to provide an understanding of that jungle. It does so by seeking to set the present-day movement in the context of its history and by providing a map to some of the current issues and trends. My contention is that the contours of current evangelicalism can only be understood in reference to its past and, equally, that the past can greatly enrich our present understanding. Knowing where we have come from will, I believe, simultaneously both release and discipline today's evangelicals. Release is necessary since many suffer from the imposition of illegitimate strait-jackets and fail to appreciate the diversity and flexibility inherent in the movement – evangelicalism has always been a dynamic faith, never a static religion. Discipline is necessary because each new trend must be measured against its tradition to see whether it is an authentic expression of evangelicalism or not. The dynamic of the movement must be held in tension with the quest for authenticity.

Chapter 1 sets out to introduce evangelicalism both in its own right and by contrasting it to other streams of Christianity. Chapter 2 provides a way of understanding the diversity of evangelicalism and then maps the criticisms to which it is subject.

The next two chapters tell, in a brief form, the history of evangelicalism from its inception as a modern movement in the Evangelical Revival of the eighteenth century to the present day. Chapter 3 charts the story in Great Britain and Chapter 4 charts the parallel story in the United States of America. These chapters give a panoramic view which will be seen from more limited perspectives as key aspects of the movement are introduced in the rest of the book. To change the metaphor, these chapters are the theme music introduced in the prelude of a symphony only to be heard, in one form or another, again and again in what follows. The names, the events and the issues will, therefore, often be found more than once.

The topics chosen for introduction subsequently are: the Bible (Chapter 5), the atonement (Chapter 6), conversion (Chapter 7), the last things (Chapter 8), the church (Chapter 9), social action (Chapter 10) and spirituality (Chapter 11). Each sets out the evangelical view of the topic, draws on the historical perspective, maps the contemporary situation and raises pertinent questions about it.

The final chapter seeks to give an overall evaluation of contemporary evangelicalism and includes, more briefly, four additional topics where evangelicalism is currently re-evaluating its position in the light of contemporary trends and progressive revelation. These are the Holy Spirit; the role of women; the nature of the family and the nature of mission. Each of these deserves, and has received by others, full treatment in their own right.

Chapter titles have been selected from the lines (usually the first lines) of the great hymns of the evangelical faith. It is an acknowledgement that the evangelical faith has not only been inseparable from hymn-singing but that, both in the past and today, singing is often the primary channel through which doctrine is conveyed. The choice of classical hymns for this purpose is not to be taken to imply any dissatisfaction with contemporary evangelical hymn and song writing, although perhaps it is a hint of the richness to be found in the hymns of the past which present-day evangelicals are in danger of forgetting. The choice is consistent with the historical emphasis of the book. It is also, it has to be said, easier to quote those of the past than to negotiate the pitfalls of contemporary copyright laws. It would have been an interesting exercise to see if contemporary evangelical music could have supplied titles for the range of topics covered.

A word of explanation may be helpful about the bibliographical references which are so often ignored by the general reader. I have sought to keep these to a minimum but have used them in the following way. They acknowledge the source of any direct quotation and of many important ideas. But in doing so I have usually referred not to the primary source, which is often not easily available today, but to a secondary source which is much more accessible. So, for example, rather than citing the source in Wesley's *Journal* or Edwards' original, I have cited a modern author who quotes them. I have done so in the hope that readers of this book might be encouraged to follow up their interest by reading some of these recent books on the different leaders and themes of evangelicalism. The references for each chapter begin by highlighting a few books to which the reader could turn next.

One name occurs more frequently than most in the text and bibliography, that of John Stott. John Stott has made an enormous contribution to evangelicalism since the Second World War, serving as its foremost national advocate, leading international statesman and its chief apologist. In the latter role he has written an astonishing range of books setting out the evangelical viewpoint on many of its cardinal beliefs. He has been a model of how to combine biblical faithfulness with contemporary relevance. What is more, John Stott has done all this in a spirit of humility and graciousness, entirely free from the arrogance mentioned previously. Frequent reference to him has, therefore, been unavoidable. The significance of John Stott was gratifyingly confirmed a few years ago by one outside the tradition. David Edwards wrote of him that, apart from William Temple, who died as Archbishop of Canterbury in 1944, he is 'the most influential clergyman in the Church of England in the twentieth century.'[1] Evangelicals around the world, myself included, thank God for his life and ministry.

I wish to express my thanks to the Baptist Union of Great Britain for sabbatical leave in the summer of 1993 to write this book. Special thanks are due to my colleagues in the Mission Department, especially my secretary, Helen Kinsman, for whom that meant bearing extra responsibilities. I am also glad to express thanks to my friends Michael Parsons, who read virtually the whole manuscript and improved its grammar as well as making other helpful comments, and to Ian Randall, of Spurgeon's College, who read and commented on Chapters 3 and 4. I hope they feel I have done justice to their efforts. I am honoured by the generous forewords contributed by my friends Clive Calver and Mark Noll. I gladly admit the remaining faults and opinions to be my own. My thanks are also due to London Bible College for access to their excellent library. I am also grateful to my wife, Dianne, for her constant encouragement and willingness to spare me the hours to write.

The book was written in the summer of 1993 when the London Bible College was celebrating its jubilee. The college was established to be a centre of evangelical excellence, offering training and biblical and theological scholarship to a high standard, in the nation's capital. Since 1943, it has persistently achieved its goal. As a former student and member of staff, with many happy memories and associations, I express my gratitude in the dedication of this book to that college.

My hope is that those who are not evangelicals will find this book informative and discover that evangelicals are not quite as strange as they are often presented. My second, and even greater, hope is that evangelicals will be enriched by reading it and fired with renewed commitment to essential evangelical doctrines and practices, whilst shedding that which is peripheral, and demonstrating a determination to live out God's word in a way which is relevant to the culture in which we live.

Reference

1. David L. Edwards and John Stott, *Essentials: A Liberal-Evangelical Dialogue* London: Hodder & Stoughton, 1988, p. 1.

PART ONE

ORIGINS

1

BLEST BE THE TIE THAT BINDS

Introducing Evangelicalism

On 25th July 1990 the surprise announcement was made that Dr George Carey was to be the next Archbishop of Canterbury. It was a surprise because the announcement had not been expected for some time, and because Dr Carey was not considered by the commentators to be a serious contender. Two things stood against him. First, he had not long been a bishop and was considered inexperienced. Secondly, he was known to be an evangelical of the charismatic variety. If the first hindrance was not sufficient to prevent his elevation to Canterbury, the second certainly should have been. But Carey's appointment was a symptom of the growing significance of the evangelicalism he represented.

The Prime Minister of Great Britain at the time, but not for much longer, was Margaret Thatcher. She was known to have appointed a number of evangelicals to high positions, including her policy adviser, Brian Griffiths. She was aware of the growing strength of evangelicalism and gave it some recognition in the national life. Perhaps, too, she resonated with some of the supposed features of evangelicalism. The popular image of evangelicalism portrayed it as a 'conviction religion': moralistic in tone; conservative in moral views (and, therefore, it was assumed in political views); traditional in its attitude to the family; industrious in its work ethic (George Carey had risen from the disadvantaged East End of London and had not been through the privileged halls of Oxbridge which was the usual route to high office in the Church of England); popular in style and with a resolute, if simplistic, commitment to the Bible.

Popular images are often misleading and evangelicalism has often suffered from having ill-informed stereotypes imposed upon it. At least at one point Mrs Thatcher was right. Evangelicals were an increasingly significant group within the wider church and contemporary Christian faith can only be understood and rightly assessed if they are understood and rightly assessed.

The picture of evangelicalism today is very different than it was in the early years of this century. Then they could be described as 'hemmed in', 'small', 'in no state of health' and 'almost moribund'.[1]

In less flattering terms, around the same time, Bishop Hensley Henson described them, as 'an army of illiterates, generalled by octogenarians.'[2] But if that was the case it is so no longer.

The resurgence of evangelicalism

From the middle of the twentieth century onwards evangelicalism has undergone a remarkable resurgence in Britain, the United States and around the world. It is remarkable because it has happened at a time when most intelligent observers of religion were arguing that Christianity was in terminal decline and most sociologists were planning its funeral service. It is all the more remarkable because evangelicalism grew with tremendous vigour often outside the religious mainstream and in ways which were often unbecoming to conventional religion.

GREAT BRITAIN

In Britain evangelicalism has become a movement of enormous strength. The English Church Census,[3] conducted in 1989, revealed that of 3.9 million churchgoers 1,000,000 were evangelical. More significantly still, whilst the Catholic and broad/liberal wings of the church declined, evangelicals had grown by 3 per cent in the previous five years. A key element in this growth was the increase in numbers of charismatic evangelicals and new churches which were evangelical in ethos.

The Evangelical Alliance has become a movement to be reckoned with. Justifiably claiming to represent the one million evangelicals, it has adopted a pro-active stance and is now widely consulted by the Government and even more widely by the media in a way previously unknown, at least in its recent history. Intervention has borne fruit in the areas of Sunday trading, commercial advertising, religious TV, issues of religious liberty and a host of others.

Having long abdicated their responsibilities, preferring to channel their energies into local churches and the plethora of evangelical parachurch organizations, evangelicals have now come in from the cold and assumed positions of denominational leadership. The story of the Anglican, Methodist, Baptist and, to a lesser extent, the United Reformed Church, are noteworthy in` this regard. How evangelicals, for example, were to vote in the General Synod of the Church of England was considered the decisive factor in the outcome of the debate on the ordination of women. Evangelical voices are now heard with greater frequency in ecumenical circles. Evangelicalism can also claim a number of established and respected scholars in biblical and theological circles, such as F. F. Bruce, Donald Guthrie, I. Howard Marshall, R. T. France, Gordon Wenham, John Goldingay and Alister McGrath, to name but a few.

Evangelical enterprises also flourish. Spring Harvest, now over ten years old, continues to draw together some 70,000 Christians for its celebration and teaching weeks each Easter. Tear Fund (The Evangelical Alliance Relief Fund), established twenty-five years ago, now channels £20 million to the poor in the name of evangelicals each year. It has risen to become twenty-fifth largest charity in Great Britain, whilst it ranks fifth as far as committed covenanted givers are concerned. Theological colleges endorse the trend towards evangelicalism. Whilst many colleges are struggling to attract students, evangelical colleges are bursting at the seams. Christian bookshops sell £50 million of Christian books and other goods each year with a further £15 million being sold from other book retail outlets. Over half of these bookshops have been opened since 1975 and over three-quarters are independently owned and, it is probably safe to assume, evangelical. Publishers have noted the significance of the evangelical market in books.

THE UNITED STATES

The United States demonstrates the same patterns of growth and life – only the scale is different. Since 1965 liberal denominations have declined at a rate of 4.6 per cent every five years whilst evangelical denominations have increased by 8 per cent every five years.[4] In 1978–79, Gallup estimated between 40 and 50 million Americans to be evangelicals.[5]

Donald Bloesch[6] has documented the same signs of evangelical resurgence as in Great Britain. In the 1970s Gallup found 34 per cent of Americans claiming to be 'born again' and 42 per cent to believe that the Bible is the word of God and without mistakes in its statements or teaching. Evangelical theological seminaries have flourished, with many independent seminaries being founded. Evangelical student conferences have been attended in huge numbers. There has been an evangelical renewal within mainline denominations, and the take-over of many denominational institutions by evangelicals.[7] Evangelical publishing houses are lucrative businesses. In 1990 it was estimated that retail sales figures of Christian bookstores would reach $3.6 billion. 30,000 missionaries were serving overseas in 1980, eleven times more than the comparable number from liberal churches.[8]

Distinguishing marks of the American scene have been religious broadcasting, periodicals, independent Christian schools and political involvement. In 1985 there were 1,180 members of the

National Religious Broadcasters, a branch of the National Association of Evangelicals. Top shows could attract around two million viewers. Massive resources are invested to maintain broadcasting even though the evidence suggests their impact in influencing people either for Christ or for some moral or political position is extremely limited.[9]

Periodicals have been a major means of communication to the evangelical constituency and beyond with *Christianity Today*, founded in 1956, outstripping all others. By 1979 *Christianity Today* had twice the readership of the more established and mainline periodical *Christian Century*.[10]

There has been much greater enthusiasm to found Christian schools and colleges in the USA than in Great Britain, arising from a desire for evangelicals to socialise and educate their children in an atmosphere conducive to evangelical belief and free from the influences of secular humanism. It was estimated that in 1985, against a background of falling school rolls, there were between 17,000 and 18,000 Christian schools in the USA accounting for some two and a half million students.[11]

The political influence of evangelicals has recently been given high profile. Political views among evangelicals differ as recent history shows. Whilst Jimmy Carter, an evangelical, was elected President in 1976, it is the fundamentalist wing that has attracted most media attention with the rise and decline of the New Christian Right, as it is called. The two key names associated with the movement were Jerry Falwell and Pat Robertson, who himself made an abortive bid for the Presidency in 1988. A longer perspective is needed to determine what influence the 'moral majority' had on the Reagan and Bush administrations but even if, as the evidence suggests, their influence was not much in reality, the Republican presidential candidates at least saw the need to pay lip-service to them.

The cumulative evidence is that in recent years evangelicalism is a force to be reckoned with, a point noted by *Time* and *Newsweek* which declared 1976, the year the Southern Baptist, Jimmy Carter, entered the White House, to be the 'Year of the Evangelical'.

WORLD-WIDE

Evangelicalism is a global phenomenon. In Brazil the staggering growth of evangelicalism, especially of the Pentecostal variety, means that what was once a solidly Roman Catholic country is rapidly becoming an evangelical nation. 'The take-off came in the late sixties,' comments David Martin. 'At the beginning of this period evangelical Protestants counted some five million members, excluding children, and their wider constituency extended to some fifteen million. Two decades later the constituency extended to at least forty million, which is remarkable, even allowing for rapid growth in total population. It may even be the case that in parts of Latin America the number of Protestants regularly involved in worship and fellowship exceeds the number of Catholics.'[12]

In Korea, equally, there has been amazing evangelical church growth, which has resulted in 30 per cent of the population becoming Christian. Reports from China indicate even faster growth than that of Korea, although facts are hard to come by. The Philippines have seen a vigorous church growth programme and have now adopted an equally vigorous church planting programme. Elsewhere in Asia the story is different. Pakistan, Bangladesh, Malaysia and Sri Lanka have seen evangelical decline, mostly because of strong pressures from nationalism which is inextricably bound up with non-Christian religious allegiance.[13]

Africa, south of the Sahara, has long been the object of missionary interest and surveys there also point to the ascendancy of evangelicalism.

In the not too distant future evangelicalism will be led by those from the Two Thirds World and not as identified as in the past with the Western World.

What is evangelicalism?

So, evangelicalism is of significance. But what is evangelicalism? The word 'evangelical' comes from the Greek word for 'good news' which takes us to the heart of the matter. Evangelicals are 'gospel' people. Evangelicalism is the movement associated with the gospel. But such statements are deceptively simple. There is more to it than that.

Although used in the early days of the church, it was the Reformation which brought the word into more common circulation. John Wycliffe, a herald of the Reformation, was known as *doctor evangelicus* and wrote an unfinished book called *Opus Evangelicum* which laid considerable emphasis on the sufficiency of Scripture.

Martin Luther, horrified that his followers were being called by his name but realising that they needed to be called something more specific than Christians, made use of the term 'evangelical'. He wrote, in 1522, of 'this common evangelical cause'. He was engaged in nothing less than a gospel reformation. And so 'reformer' and 'evangelical' came to be used interchangeably. This usage of the word is still current. Churches of the European Continent still call themselves Evangelical in the sense in which elsewhere we would speak of them as Protestant, or, to be more precise, that branch of Protestantism associated with Luther rather than with the Reformed emphasis of Calvin.

Elsewhere, however, the word has taken on a different meaning. In line with its reformation heritage, from the eighteenth century onwards, 'evangelical' came to be the name applied to specific groups of Christians, irrespective of their denomination, who manifested a particular approach to the gospel and the Christian life. These were the people associated with the Evangelical Revival led by Wesley and Whitefield. Revivalism, of a different form, subsequently became a key characteristic of evangelicalism, especially in the United States. Two centuries later evangelicalism has grown to be an immense tree with all sorts of shoots and branches which often seem to have little in common, yet which clearly draw off the same roots.

Attempts at precise definitions are rather like attempts to pick up a slippery bar of soap with wet hands. Some are too narrow and exclude those who should be included. Such definitions often consist of a long doctrinal check-list. Some are so broad that they include those who patently should not be included, if the definition is to have any meaning. Some highlight one characteristic, such as evangelism, at the expense of other equally essential characteristics. Some are so vague that they do not help us to distinguish evangelicals from others. The debate has led many, for contradictory reasons, to suggest we erase the word from our religious dictionaries.[14] But there is something distinctive about evangelicalism. Abandoning the word would be like abandoning spectacles and would prevent us from bringing contemporary Christianity into any kind of focus.

John Stott's approach is to say that the two major distinguishing marks of evangelicals is that they are Bible people and they are gospel people.[15] Every definition draws attention to the central place given by evangelicals to the Bible. They count it as their supreme authority and though they may differ over theories of inspiration and methods of interpretation they believe it to be the trustworthy record of God's revelation of himself to humankind, having superior authority to any other means of direction in the church (such as tradition, reason or contemporary scholarship), sufficient for all the church's needs and to be treated with the utmost seriousness as a guide both to what we are to believe and how we are to live.

As gospel people, evangelicals stress that the heart of the gospel is the cross of Christ, usually insisting on that interpretation of the cross known as substitutionary atonement; that a personal response to Christ's work on the cross, usually called conversion, is necessary; that the fruits of the gospel should be subsequently seen in the believer's life and that the good news should be shared with all people through evangelism. John Stott's explanation of being a gospel people goes further than a narrow individualism, often thought to characterize evangelicals, and speaks of the good news having wider dimensions. It is good news for society and about a new world as well.

These are broad brush strokes. Much finer details will emerge. But all subsequent explorations about evangelicalism have these two affirmations as their starting point. Questions about the virgin birth, the historicity of the miracles of Christ, the sinfulness of humankind, the work of the Holy Spirit, views about the Second Coming of Christ, and heaven and hell, begin here; as do the more contentious issues of theories of inspiration, methods of interpretation, the place of biblical scholarship or wider contemporary scholarship, and which points are essential and which are of secondary importance and therefore permit diversity. Some of these will be explored in subsequent chapters.

Robert Johnston, writing of American evangelicalism, has aptly summarized evangelicalism like this: 'Evangelicals are those who believe the gospel is to be experienced personally, defined biblically and communicated passionately.'[16]

Johnston's statement that evangelicals communicate the gospel passionately gives us the clue to another essential feature of evangelicalism. Evangelicalism is as much about an ethos and an infrastructure, a complex network of transdenominational organisations, societies, events and paraphanalia, as about a doctrinal position. Evangelicals are great activists. Their religion is always a busy one, as their history amply demonstrates, and they have the superstructure to go with it.

They are always trying to convert people, to do good and to be growing in their understanding of the Bible and holiness. Hence evangelicalism spawns an army of evangelistic campaigns and associations, a riot of welfare agencies and reforming societies, a *smörgäsbord* of Bible conferences and mission conventions and an abundance of training instruments, and, since evangelicals have always been very modern in their approach to technology, these are all serviced by a further multiplicity of publishing and telecommunications businesses.

All this makes evangelicalism a subculture with its own ethos. Randall Balmer has caught it nicely in a recent, though somewhat dated, picture of his own experience. Being a Christian, he writes,

. . . meant immersing oneself in the evangelical subculture, affiliating with a local church (not just any church, but a church that 'preached the Bible'), eschewing 'worldliness' in its many insidious forms, hewing to strict codes of personal morality, sending the kids off to Sunday School, youth meetings and Bible camps, and, eventually, to a Bible School or a Christian college. It meant establishing a daily 'quiet time', a period of personal devotions characterized by reading the Bible, meditation and prayer. Being a *Christian* meant witnessing, 'sharing your faith' with non-Christians – that is, anyone who did not fit this definition. It also meant feeling very guilty if you failed to do any of the above, or if you failed to do it with sufficient rigor or enthusiasm, for there were always spiritual athletes around to shame you – pastors, travelling evangelists, godly matriarchs in any congregation whose personal piety served both as examples worthy of emulation and implicit rebukes to your own spiritual lethargy.[17]

This has led some, like Kenneth Myers, to argue that evangelicalism is really a subculture, more concerned about doing than knowing. It is, he says, behaviour patterns which are not even discussed in Scripture which are 'the tie that binds' rather than specific doctrines.[18] But that is to overstate the case. It is a subculture with its own behaviour patterns, values and heroes, particularly heroes and charismatic leaders, but it is equally a stream of Christianity bound by certain attitudes to the Bible and the Gospel.

After very detailed historical research, David Bebbington has suggested that there are four key features which characterise evangelicalism.[19] They are:

> Conversionism
> Activism
> Biblicism
> Crucicentrism

His suggestions have met with a ready response from across the spectrum of evangelicals and has quickly established itself as near to a consensus as we might ever expect to reach.

Contrasts to evangelicalism

It is often helpful to understand a movement by contrasting it to other movements. This brings its distinctives into sharp relief. Not only is it generally helpful to do so but, in this case, it is specifically legitimate to do so since evangelicalism often explicitly sees itself in these terms. There are two major tendencies in Christianity to which it stands in sharp relief: catholicism and liberalism.

CATHOLICISM

Catholicism is a brand of churchmanship, not exclusive to the Roman Catholic Church, which stresses the place of tradition, order, the oneness of the universal church and the objective aspects of the Christian faith.

Catholics argue that it is not possible to interpret the Bible as if the church had not already been doing so for the last two thousand years but that church tradition is the key to our understanding of it. Evangelical handling of the Bible, by contrast, often appears individualistic and immediate. Evangelicals would say that the Catholic approach in practice leads to a higher place being given to tradition than to the Bible; that tradition has often deposited on the church a great deal of baggage which does not arise from the Bible and that they themselves are not indifferent to the history of the church.

Evangelicalism appears to be the religion of free enterprise. In contrast, catholicism sees the value of the universal Church working in harmony together and safeguarding the tradition. One way of ensuring that harmony is to have a clear idea about authority and order. This leads to the acceptance of common liturgies, to the development of hierarchies and to the need for authorisation to act in the church.

Whereas evangelicalism stresses redemption as the central Christian truth, Catholicism tends to emphasize creation and incarnation. In doing so it leads to a far less intense religion, more at home in the world and with far less stress on the need for conversion. With that, the personal and subjective elements of the faith are weakened and the factual objective elements are strengthened. Hence, a catholic approach would argue that the sacraments of baptism or the mass were effective, because they bring about what God does irrespective of what a person feels. Evangelicalism, by contrast, majors on the need for personal faith if the sacraments are to be effective, and, in its worship, stresses the need for personal and genuine spiritual involvement. Evangelicalism is not the sacramentarian religion which is to be found in Catholicism.

LIBERALISM

Liberalism comes in many guises. Like evangelicalism it also is an ethos, a movement, and gives rise to institutions. Its central tenet is to stress freedom and liberation from all earthly authorities and closed systems.[20] As an open approach to the world it shuns dogmatism, questions tradition, espouses humility and constantly seeks to adapt the essence of the Christian faith to the modern world.[21] The commitment to freedom has led to many of its advocates taking a brave prophetic stance against the vested interests both of the world and the church.

To evangelicals, its stance often seems to be very uncertain about Christian basics. But the uncertainty which evangelicals regard as a vice is regarded by liberals as a virtue. At almost every point evangelicals and liberals are opposed. Liberals find it difficult to believe in the supernatural claims of the Bible or of the church down the centuries. Contemporary explanations in natural terms are preferred to miraculous explanations. Human nature is viewed optimistically and there is little acknowledgement of personal sin and still less of anything akin to a historic 'fall' of humankind. Divisions between 'saved' and 'unsaved' are unimportant. Jesus Christ is viewed with tremendous respect, but not necessarily as divine. More usually his humanity would eclipse his divinity, although there would be a recognition that he was more God-conscious or full of God than the rest of us. Views of the cross which interpret it in terms of punishment or substitution for sinners are rejected as unacceptable. But the cross remains important as an example and for the influence it brings to bear on humankind.

Underlying these viewpoints lies the liberal attitude to the Bible. The Bible is believed to be a human book rather than a divine revelation. Revelation comes rather through intuition or discovery. The Bible is a useful resource for Christians because it is the record of our forebears and their understanding of God, but it is one resource among many. As a human book there is no problem with saying that it is culture-bound and not necessarily a word for all times. Equally, apparent contradictions or mistakes present no difficulties. Contemporary scholarship can be brought to bear on it in such a way that the scholarship, rather than the Bible itself, becomes the arbiter of what is to be believed.

Recent years have seen a massive decline in liberal churches but liberalism has remained influential in universities and seminaries, which, of course, are responsible for the training of clergy and ministers. As a form of Christian faith, however, many would wonder whether liberalism is not inherently self-destructive, unless it is of a very sophisticated kind. The desire to accommodate the faith constantly to the world carries with it the almost inevitable threat that the faith loses all its distinctiveness. And if the faith has nothing distinctive to say, why bother with the faith?[22]

The question of fundamentalism

A particular Christian bedfellow of evangelicals which causes confusion and concern is fundamentalism. Whilst all fundamentalists are evangelical, not all evangelicals are fundamentalist. Fundamentalists have been described as evangelicals who are angry about something. Militancy is a major distinguishing mark of fundamentalism, but not of evangelicalism.[23]

But there are other significant differences between them even though most evangelicals would happily endorse the five other central points of fundamentalism; namely, the miracles of Christ, the virgin birth, the satisfaction view of the atonement, verbal inspiration and belief in bodily resurrection.

When the word 'fundamentalist' was coined it had a more neutral ring to it than it does today. The word derived from the writing of *The Fundamentals*, a series of papers published from 1910 onwards, covering sixty-five topics which were foundational to the faith. They were written in opposition to the modernist views of the Bible which were then gaining currency. But, both in the 20s and since the 50s the word has hardened in its usage and now, more accurately, describes a specific cultural expression of the faith predominantly to be found in the southern states of North America.

Today, many wrongly use the terms 'fundamentalist' and 'evangelical' interchangeably. But this is a serious misconception since there are some major differences between them. Eight differences have been highlighted by John Stott and affirmed by others.[24] To paraphrase, they are:

1 Fundamentalists are suspicious of scholarship which sometimes leads to a thoroughgoing anti-intellectualism. (Evangelicals are open to scholarship.)
2 Fundamentalists believe in the dictation theory of inspiration and deny the human and cultural dimensions of the Bible. (Evangelicals recognize the human and cultural elements of the Bible and so are committed to working at understanding its meaning in context.)
3 Fundamentalists revere the Authorised Version and mistrust other translations based on texts other than the *Textus Receptus*. (Evangelicals believe there are now more accurate translations.)
4 Fundamentalists interpret the Bible literally. (Evangelicals recognize the need for working at its interpretation and giving place both to its cultural context and the form of language it uses, such as metaphor, poetry and symbol.)

5 Fundamentalists believe in a separated church and distance themselves strongly from the ecumenical movement in all its forms. (Evangelicals usually have a much greater openness to other Christians and may have some involvement in the ecumenical movement.)

6 Fundamentalists allow their beliefs to be uncritically influenced by their culture, as demonstrated by their racial attitudes and attitude to prosperity. (Evangelicals are also influenced by their culture but seek to be critical of it from a Biblical viewpoint.)

7 Fundamentalists are often allied to a right-wing political stance and, other than through traditional philanthropy, are indifferent to social evils. (Evangelicals would be diverse politically and have become increasingly aware of the need for putting the social implications of the gospel into practice.)

8 Fundamentalists insist on premillennial views of the second coming. It has, in fact, been claimed to be their organising principle. (Evangelicals have always seen differences over the details of the second coming as legitimate.)

These distinctions, then, are the ties which bind an increasingly significant evangelicalism together – ties of the Bible and the gospel, of behaviour and of busyness. The ties which bind them together, diverse though they are, are also the ties that bind them apart from other groups within the church.

2

SWEETLY MAY WE ALL AGREEE

Evangelicalism's varieties and critics

The central tenets of evangelicalism bind together Brethren who go to Keswick, Pentecostals who celebrate in the Spirit, Anglicans who worship in mixed parish churches, Ghanaians who meet for warm fellowship in an alien culture, Koreans who meet in megachurches, Strict Baptists who adhere to Calvin and Methodist followers of the Arminian Mr Wesley, to name but a few! What sense can be made of such a variety? And, how can order be brought out of the mix of black gospel religion, Southern right-wing fundamentalism, Mennonite communities, world-involved evangelicals, holiness sects, Billy Graham evangelism and respectable, Reformed North Eastern theologians who all claim to be one and the same thing – 'evangelicals'?

This chapter seeks to explore the diversity of contemporary movements which find their 'sweet agreement' in evangelicalism and then to examine some of the critics of evangelicalism, both outside and in, which exhibit less than sweet agreement.

Varieties of Evangelicalism

In spite of the agreement about the Bible and the gospel, evangelicalism has always been characterised by variety. Throughout its history it has never been anything but a coalition of different groups subscribing to these two essentials. In its earliest days, for example, it was composed of Anglican evangelicals, Arminian evangelicals, represented by John Wesley, and reformed evangelicals, represented by George Whitefield. Given the diversity, it is not surprising that some have suggested the term should be abandoned. But that would be a mistake. The two essentials are powerful binding agents which do make evangelicalism a distinct entity in the wider church.

In seeking to make sense of those recognised as evangelicals a number of metaphors have been used which highlight the confusion. They are spoken of as an extended family; a twelve-ring circus in

which various different acts are performed; a coat of many colours;
a family tree with different branches drawing from the same roots;
a tribal system in which twelve or fourteen tribes are variously
identified;[1] a patchwork quilt; a mosaic and a kaleidoscope.

I believe it is more helpful to picture contemporary evangelicalism
as something like Rubik's Cube. Most of the above metaphors
assume that each branch of the family, tribe or act in the circus has
a consistency about it that, in my experience, is lacking. So, for
example, an Anglican evangelical may plug into the evangelical
network at very different places in terms of spirituality and go either
to Keswick, or to Renewal conferences, or to Puritan fraternals and
so on. A Baptist evangelical may be devoted to the King James Version
and be pietistic in spirituality or in touch with the latest trends,
familiar with the field of rock music and have a radical social
involvement. Evangelicals with similar labels will network with
very different people, plug into different events, support different
parachurch groups and, as a result, have a very different feel to their
evangelicalism from one another.

The Rubik Cube allows us to make distinctions on a number of
different dimensions and to create a variety of identikit pictures of
evangelicals. It is only an approach like this which makes sense of
the complexity of contemporary evangelicalism. My tentative
suggestion would be that the three most important dimensions are
attitudes to:

Church
Spirituality
World

The cube would then look like the diagram overleaf:

The details of the cube would be spelled out like this.

CHURCH

Established churches. In the UK this is the Church of England.
The USA has no equivalent because of the constitutional separation
of church and state. However, some churches, such as the Episcopal
church and, depending on the region, the Presbyterian, Methodist
and Lutheran churches, are near equivalents.

Denominational churches. In the UK this refers to Methodist,
Baptist and URC churches and a number of long-established groups
like the Salvation Army and Nazarenes. In the USA mainline
churches which are not in dominant positions in their communities
would be included.

Pentecostal churches refers to the classical Pentecostal churches

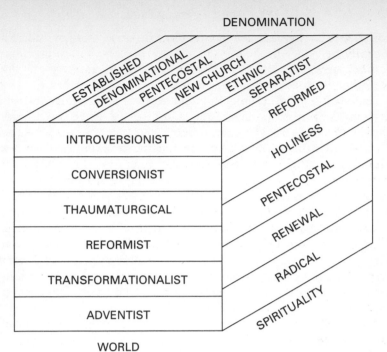

DENOMINATION

ESTABLISHED
DENOMINATIONAL
PENTECOSTAL
NEW CHURCH
ETHNIC
SEPARATIST

REFORMED
HOLINESS
PENTECOSTAL
RENEWAL
RADICAL
SPIRITUALITY

| INTROVERSIONIST |
| CONVERSIONIST |
| THAUMATURGICAL |
| REFORMIST |
| TRANSFORMATIONALIST |
| ADVENTIST |

WORLD

(such as the Assemblies of God, Elim, Apostolic churches, Church of God) and includes a number of independent pentecostal groups of a traditional kind, like that of Oral Roberts.

New churches includes those churches established out of Restorationism in the United Kingdom and which were, until recently, wrongly called 'House churches'. Among them are Ichthus, New Frontiers, Pioneer and Stream.

Ethnic churches are those churches formed on ethnic grounds, such as Black churches, Chinese churches, Korean, Malaysian or Spanish churches, most of which are evangelical in doctrine and practice.

Separatist churches are the independent evangelical churches which have little, if anything, to do with the wider church scene and are suspicious of ecumenism. Many will belong to a group in the UK such as the Fellowship of Independent Evangelical Churches but many will be entirely independent. The word 'separatist' is used to distinguish them from 'New' churches which are also largely independent. The Southern Baptists, for all their size, power and dominance in certain areas, fit within this category.

SPIRITUALITY

Although there may be a certan affinity between ecclesiastic position and spiritual orientation the relationship is anything but one-to-one.

Reformed evangelicalism owes much to Puritanism and emphasises the conflict which Christians must engage in against the world, the flesh and the devil, which regeneration makes possible. Its notable exponents have been Martyn Lloyd-Jones, Bishop J. C. Ryle, J. I. Packer, R. C. Sproul and C. H. Spurgeon. It finds its expression today in the Westminster Fellowship, the Proclamation Trust and the Banner of Truth in the UK and in such establishments as Wheaton, Trinity and Calvin Colleges, and Westminster Seminary in the USA and Regent College in Canada.

Holiness evangelicalism has its roots in the nineteenth century and John Wesley's teaching about perfect love. Arminian in orientation, it portrays a picture of the ideal Christian as in a serene personal relationship with God, it repudiates strenuous effort and works as a means of holiness and encourages Christians to obtain a second blessing as the way of holiness. This was the classical teaching of Cliff College and Keswick in the UK and of the camp meetings, Asbury College and higher life conferences in the USA. It is individualistic, sometimes even introverted, in perspective.

Pentecostal spirituality also speaks of a second blessing and has a close affinity to holiness teaching. But it is distinctive in its emphasis on the gifts of the Holy Spirit such as tongues, healing and prophecy. A central theme is that of power – for service to the body of Christ and witness to the world. In some strands of Pentecostalism, speaking in tongues is seen as evidence of having been baptised in the Holy Spirit, the crucial qualification for obtaining power.

Renewal spirituality picks up some of the themes of classical Pentecostalism but without the cultural baggage that goes with it. Having its origins in the charismatic movement it has gone through a number of permutations and may be found either in mainline denominations or in the newer restoration churches. It has, however, a much more positive attitude to the world than does its Pentecostal cousin and often has an acute social conscience. It finds its expression in the many celebrations and Bible weeks which are now held where some of the old evangelical taboos, for example, against drinking and dancing, are repudiated.

Radical spirituality lays its main stress on passionate social holiness, rather than individual holiness and personal morality. Arising from the radical wing of the reformation, in Anabaptism, it is seen today in groups like the Mennonites and the Sojourners Community, in the USA. Shades of it can be seen at the Greenbelt Festival in the UK and in *Third Way*. Commitment to holiness is measured in terms of commitment to the world and one's concern for moral, social and political justice.

WORLD

Again there is a link between spirituality and attitude to the world but, even so, it is worth isolating as a specific dimension. A scheme of analysis proposed by the sociologist Bryan Wilson[2] is helpful in this regard. Wilson analysed the way in which sects, that is, exclusive religious groups, related to the world. This is not to say evangelicals belong to sects, nor is it to say that evangelicals themselves can be neatly pigeon-holed. Even so the scheme can help us to understand orientations to the world which are found among evangelicals.

Introversionist. These have least to do with the world and believe that the Christian should be separate from it and withdraw as much as possible to prevent contamination by it. It can be seen in a thousand places where 'separation' from the world is taught strongly and active engagement in anything like politics or the arts is strenuously resisted.

Conversionist. The major point of contact with the world is in order to rescue people from it and save individuals from the inevitable path of doom on which it is set. This is the classic evangelicalism of the CSSM, Scripture Union, UCCF or IVCF, Campus Crusade and Youth With a Mission and of some of the missionary societies, like OMF and Wycliffe Bible Translators.

Thaumaturgical. The name derives from the Greek word for a wonder or miracle. Some evangelicals find the cure for the world's evils to lie in the working of miracles of physical or inner healing. Many pentecostal and independent churches would place their main emphasis here.

Reformist. These evangelicals believe it is right to influence the world for good and so are involved in it as salt and light. Their concern is wider than merely seeking for converts. They believe in doing good and working for justice for its own sake. Much classic evangelicalism spoken of under the conversationist heading would spill over into this category to one degree or another. Full-blown expressions would be found in Evangelical Christians for Social Action and in institutions like Fuller Seminary in the USA or London Bible College in the UK, where much use is made of contemporary biblical scholarship, as well as scholarship from other disciplines, such as, psychology or sociology, but from the standpoint of an evangelical commitment.

Transformationalist. More radical than the reformists, transformationalists usually have an active involvement with society. Yet, they see the church as the alternative society, the community of

God's Kingdom and seek to transform society prophetically and bring it into line with the Kingdom of God as much as possible. The writings of John Howard Yoder and Ron Sider would be examples of this together with other groups who are evangelical pacifists.

Adventist. Their basic orientation is a disinterest in this world and a preoccupation with the coming again of Jesus by which a new heaven and a new earth will be brought into being. This is often wrongly assumed to be authentic evangelicalism, perhaps because it was the form of evangelicalism most likely to capture public attention at the end of the last and early part of the present century. Premillennial in outlook, today it is associated with the Schofield Reference Bible, Moody Bible Institute and Dallas Theological Seminary in the USA and with movements like the Prophetic Witness Movement and various prayer groups for Israel in the UK.

Moving the individual pieces around on a Rubik's Cube will give all sorts of permutations. So it is with evangelicalism. As the individual pieces are moved, so a whole variety of different evangelical identities can be seen. It is those differences which will be explored in reference to a number of themes in the chapters which follow.

Critics of Evangelicalism

If there is disagreement among evangelicals, as illustrated by the diversity we have just outlined, it is of a limited nature whilst many outside the movement would dissent from agreement with evangelicals at fundamental points. One of the things which makes one suspect that evangelicalism is significant is the amount of criticism heaped upon it. If it was not significant it would not be worth criticising so much. The criticism comes from all quarters. We shall examine just four sources of criticism.

CULTURAL DESPISERS

Once some of the press discovered that the new Archbishop of Canterbury was a charismatic evangelical they adopted a very haughty tone. *The Times* spoke of the fears that Dr Carey 'might make the church look slightly dotty, or that he would flirt with religious fanaticism.' It further observed that, 'With their conviction that they (evangelicals) and only they possess the whole truth of Christianity they are a divisive presence in any denomination.'

The Daily Telegraph, in one of its more charitable pieces, similarly betrayed its ignorance of evangelicalism. It admitted that the church needed to rediscover its own sense of confidence and certainty but added, 'but to do this it should draw on the centuries of its own tradition rather than the psychologically manipulative techniques of modern American media evangelism.'

The Evening Standard was equally disdainful, remarking, 'The evangelical wing of the Church, to which he belongs, is notorious for packing them in with banjos, guitars, saxophones, synthesisers and dancing round the altar, but few of those who attend its ecclesiastical gigs are genuinely or lastingly converted to Christianity.' One wonders what research it had done to substantiate this remark.

In a recent essay[3] by Richard Holloway, Anglican Bishop of Edinburgh, a number of criticisms emerge which must be taken more seriously. He writes of the way in which the powerful evangelical student movement displays 'adolescent arrogance and intemperateness'. He accuses evangelicals of an inability to think in complex terms but of going for simple explanations and theories. He regrets their relative disregard for the theology of creation and the incarnation. He charges them most of all with moralism. And then, in a delightfully back-handed complement, he writes of the way in which they have been innovative in worship and concludes, 'It makes worship accessible to people in a way that the more developed liturgies do not. More people go to discos than to high opera, and one of the courageous things about evangelicals is their ability to embrace bad taste for the sake of the gospel.'

Perhaps evangelicals are forever condemned to suffer the verdict passed on many popular movements, that, since people respond to it and it works, it is not worth taking seriously and is fair game for target practice.

INTELLECTUAL DETRACTORS

Many intellectuals are equally dismissive of evangelicalism. The most thoroughgoing critique from within theology in recent years has come from James Barr, the Regius Professor of Hebrew at the University of Oxford, in his book *Fundamentalism*.[4]

Barr uses the terms 'fundamentalist' and 'conservative evangelical' as if they are virtually the same. 'Fundamentalism' refers more to a cast of mind and 'conservative evangelicalism' to an ecclesiastical position. But the one leads to the other. In Barr's opinion the three most important characteristics of fundamentalism are its emphasis on the inerrancy of the Bible, its hostility to modern theology and negativity to biblical criticism and its belief that those who do not share similar views are not really Christians.

In a series of essays he then sets out to unmask the poverty of fundamentalist views about the Bible, theology, miracles, doctrine, and ecumenism, inter-weaving throughout observations about the sectarian stance of evangelical culture. The religious experience of fundamentalism comes from the evangelical revivals and imposes something of a rigid spirituality on its adherents. So at no point are evangelicals encouraged to look beyond their own circles for any enlightenment.

On the Bible, he labours the point that the true fundamentalist believes in inerrancy and claims to interpret the Bible literally. The doctrine of inerrancy, he argues, prevents people from interpreting the Bible naturally. It is a notion which has its origin not in the Bible itself but in a particular philosophical rationalism and does not logically follow from the doctrine of inspiration. Fundamentalists are therefore inconsistent since, although they claim to be totally biblical, they build their faith in scripture on an extra-biblical foundation. Scripture itself does not teach inerrancy. Furthermore, the commitment to inerrancy leads to a preoccupation with harmonizing difference, explaining away difficulties and justifying the historicity of events. All this results in evangelical theology and biblical study being very unimaginative and lacking in originality.

Barr then argues that fundamentalists are not consistent for, in practice, they do not always interpret the Bible literally. They are often more concerned about imposing their own interpretive framework on Scripture than they are in seeing what the text actually says. One prime illustration of that is seen in the desire of evangelicals to produce their own 'sound' versions of the Bible which translate the original manuscripts in certain ways at key points to substantiate their chosen doctrines, such as, the virgin birth or substitutionary atonement. Another example is found in the Schofield Reference Bible, which, in his judgment, still exercises a major influence on evangelicalism, with its particular views of dispensational millennialism.

Professor Barr's critique of conservative evangelicalism is a serious one which expresses what many others feel but have not articulated. He exposes, often in language that is less temperate than one expects from a scholar, some of the naivety, rigidity and inner contradictions which have characterised evangelicalism. He touches a raw nerve in his argument that evangelicals do not, in fact, want the Bible to speak for itself but only allow it to speak with a predetermined voice.

But his critique is also a flawed one. My own reading of it gives me the impression of standing in a fairground's hall of mirrors. The picture is undoubtedly recognisable but distorted, and very distorted in parts. He achieves his thesis by a very careful selection of the evidence, mainly of a somewhat dated kind. He simply ignores that which is not convenient to his theory, such as much recent evangelical writing which does take a critical approach to the Bible into account. Consequently he has to absolve some, like F. F. Bruce and Donald Guthrie, who otherwise clearly belong in the evangelical camp from genuine membership of it, simply because they took modern scholarship seriously. He refuses to believe evangelicals are as open as they claim to be. He overrates some features of the evangelical family, such as millennialism, and underrates others, such as the charismatic movement. He shows little firsthand acquaintance with evangelicalism. He confuses fundamentalism, as many do, with conservative evangelicalism.

When challenged on these points by a number of critical reviews he has stoutly defended his position. Indeed, in the second edition of his book, he writes that where he is tempted to alter his views he would do so by passing an even more severe judgement on fundamentalism.

CHARISMATIC CRITICS

For a period, from the late 60s to the 80s 'evangelical' became a dirty word among those who might have been expected to be its friends and supporters. Although charismatic Christians often, but not always, had their origins in evangelical churches and shared still many of the standpoints and outlooks of evangelicalism, they turned on the home from which they felt alienated. To them, at the time, evangelicalism smacked of sterility. It was concerned with being sound in doctrine but was lifeless in worship, powerless in witness, loveless in relationships and empty in experience.

Michael Harper,[5] a man with an impeccable evangelical pedigree, for example, in telling the story of his baptism in the spirit is too gracious to denigrate evangelicalism but cannot disguise his unease with it when writing about his pre-charismatic days. So, he talks of his days in ministry before his charismatic experience as 'seven lean years' and his experience of the Spirit as 'transforming water into wine'. Others have been less restrained in their criticisms of evangelicalism.

Gerald Coates speaks for many in his implied criticism of evangelicalism, before it was affected by the life of the charismatic movement, in his enthusiastic use of a saying of P. T. Forsyth: 'I would rather be a part of a live heresy than a dead orthodoxy'.[6]

The late Arthur Wallis[7] reproaches evangelicalism for protesting against the Roman Catholic emphasis on tradition whilst it has plenty of traditions of its own, which not only make the movement hidebound but calls into question its commitment to the authority of the Bible which is sometimes very radical in its claims.

For a time this led to a major disruption of relationships. Divisions occurred and tracts were written against each other. A joint statement made by two opposing groups in 1977 admitted there had been misunderstandings, mistrust and polerisations between them.[8] Was it any more than a falling out within the family? Or was it, in fact, a time when a radically new form of Christianity was emerging which not only built on very different foundations than evangelicalism, and questioned some old evangelical taboos, but cut across the denominations in a new way and incorporated those, like Roman Catholics, whom many evangelicals could scarcely consider Christian?

More recently there has been reconciliation and a growing *rapprochement* between evangelicals and charismatics and a recognition that they can mutually enrich each other. Charismatics are rediscovering the centrality of the Bible, the importance of doctrine, the value of theology, of knowing history, of structures and even of liturgy.[9] Evangelicals have been warmed by the winds of the Spirit and have benefited from transformations in their worship; they have been freed from some rigidities and have discovered the value of the spontaneous and fresh understandings of spiritual gifts, as well as the need to bring back the Holy Spirit into their teaching and experience generally. The issues that divide remain real,[10] and any complete integration is unlikely, but it looks as if the evangelical tent is being enlarged to embrace charismatics as true members of the family.

EVANGELICAL DISSENTERS

The path taken by the charismatic movement brings into sharp focus debates going on within evangelicalism. Not all is well at home and there are a number of evangelicals who dissent from the current course of evangelicalism. They do so for a number of reasons.

John MacArthur, an influential American evangelical leader and Bible teacher, is one of those who would strongly dissent from the course of present-day evangelicalism because of its flirting with the charismatic movement. In a trenchant and wide-ranging critique[11] of the charismatic movement, which makes full use of its excesses, he argues that the basis for the charismatic movement is fundamentally different from that of evangelicalism. The foundation of evangelicalism has always been the Word of God, whereas the charismatic movement starts with experience. He quotes Robert K. Johnston with approval when he wrote that because of the influence of the charismatic movement evangelicals are reversing the approach of the Reformers and cutting loose from their heritage. Increasingly they are saying that 'theology must travel from Spirit to Word, not from Word to Spirit'.

He examines a comprehensive list of charismatics practices: prophecy is seen as crossing the line between a legitimate clarifying of Scripture and an illigitimate adding to it; charismatic interpretation of Scripture is found wanting; doctrine does not receive sufficient attention; tongues died out with the apostles; miracles had a special and exceptional place in apostolic times; people today are credulous; health and wealth gospels are false gospels; people are looking to Scripture as all-sufficient but looking beyond it for other means of health and growth.

In so far as evangelicalism is infected by these trends, John MacArthur is a strong dissenter.

Reg Burrows is a dissentient voice within Anglicanism. In his book *Dare to Contend*[12] he argues that present-day evangelicalism, which has taken the path marked out by major conferences at Keele (1967) and Nottingham (1977), stands in striking contrast to classic evangelicalism.

Classic evangelicalism, he argues, taught the Bible to be inerrant and the only authority. Contemporary evangelicalism speaks of the Bible only as authoritative, even if it affirms it as the first authority. Mission stressed evangelism, the uniqueness of Christ and the need for spiritual conversion. Now it is holistic, that is, involving both evangelism and social action, softer on the uniqueness of Christ and emphasises existential conversion. Once the catchword was 'separation'. Now it is 'involvement'. Classic evangelicalism was against ecumenism; contemporary evangelicalism is cautiously for it. Classic evangelicalism was for male headship and against the ordination of women. Present-day evangelicalism tends towards acceptance of the ordination of women. With prophetic passion Burrows calls the church back to classic evangelicalism.

He would not be alone in voicing some of his disquiet. John King in a recent article in the *Church of England Newspaper*[13] argued that the term evangelicalism belongs to history since what is thought of as evangelicalism today is so unlike the classic evangelicalism of the Victorian era when it was in its heyday. Nor is the unease confined to Anglicanism. Many independent evangelicals and those in other denominations would list the same issues as matters of concern.

Another voice which has set warning bells ringing is that of Leith Samuel, in his book *Time to Wake up.*[14] The book is sub-titled *Evangelical fantasy vs biblical realism*. Samuel was the much-respected minister of Above Bar Church, Southampton, for twenty-eight years and a noted Keswick Convention speaker. Samuel's work is to some extent written in reaction to the effect the charismatic movement has had on evangelicalism. In the light of the practice of prophecy he affirms the sole sufficiency of Scripture. As opposed to teaching baptism of the Spirit as a necessary experience, he affirms our greatest need to be that of a closer walk with God. In contrast to contemporary emphases on structural sin and the quest for power, Samuel affirms that personal sin and the need for pardon is the essence of the gospel. Healing, tongues and prosperity teaching are all critiqued before some wider issues of ecumenism and pluralism are introduced.

One fresh issue is introduced when Samuel examines the purpose of the church in the light of the trend, established by Bill Hybels and flowing from Willow Creek Community Church, Illinois, towards churches becoming 'seeker-friendly'. Whilst agreeing on the importance of evangelism he thinks the balance of the trend to be wrong. The church is there, first and foremost, for the glory of God – Father, Son and Holy Spirit – and for the edification of believers – new, mature and old alike. Then it is there for unbelievers as a springboard to faith. But the order of priorities is important and to put the unbeliever first and to produce some 'entertainment' so that they might hear the gospel is misplaced.

Power is seen by Michael Horton[15] and others as the central theme of much contemporary evangelicalism. They have mounted a sustained appraisal which censures contemporary evangelicalism for being based on false theological foundations. Whether it be in New Right politics, church growth, signs and wonders, pop psychology or personality cults, power is adjudged to be the central quest. Their analysis cannot be dismissed lightly and poses some serious biblical and theological questions about the present course of evangelicalism: questions which have increased in urgency as evangelicalism has increased in success. How true to the Lord, who was crucified in weakness, is an evangelicalism which spends its time questing for power?

Intellectually, the most sustained attack on contemporary evangelicalism comes from the pen of David Wells. In *No Place for Truth*[16] he asks whatever happened to evangelical theology? He accuses modern evangelicalism of being on too easy terms with the modern world and of having lost its capacity to dissent. Its piety has become a paltry thing, mirroring the self-fulfilment philosophies of the world. Its ministry has forsaken godly learning for success-orientated management. Its truth has become relativized and privatized. In all this, evangelicalism has been a thirsty partner as it has drunk deep at the wells of secularization. Evangelicalism, he pleads, is in need of urgent reform, a reform which must begin with 'the recovery of God'.

UNDERSTANDING CONTEMPORARY EVANGELICALISM

That much, but not all, of the criticism comes from the more conservative wing of evangelicalism shows how far evangelicalism has travelled since young evangelicals, like Richard Quebedeaux,[17] were arguing for a more progressive evangelicalism in the 1970s.

It also shows that evangelicalism is a living movement, always adapting to the culture which it inhabits and changing as the culture itself changes. It is this that some critics forget. Evangelicalism has never been the fixed and immutable entity that some would suggest. Its history demonstrates that, whilst holding on to essentials, evangelicalism has always appropriately adapted itself to its contemporary context. This is not to say that it is so fluid as to be an unprincipled movement. It is to say that just as a boy grows into a youth and subsequently into a man, and yet is manifestly the same person throughout, so evangelicalism maintaining its central core appositely develops to meet the new climate and circumstances, questions and challenges of its day, knowing where to adapt and where to resist.

If that is admitted, it becomes important to know evangelical history in order to help determine what is essential and non-negotiable and what is secondary and, therefore, perhaps permissible to change. Much of our present restlessness comes from not knowing that history and therefore not having a framework by which to understand contemporary developments. Bernard Ramm rightly points out that most evangelicals are deficient in their historical knowledge and that, to say the least, is unhealthy, if not positively disastrous.[18]

What follows, then, sets contemporary issues and raises questions about evangelicalism today in the unfolding of its story, in order that we might rejoice in legitimate diversity, whilst holding on to unity in essentials. At the same time, lessons can be learned from evangelicalism's successes and failures and note can be taken of telling criticisms, so that contemporary evangelicalism can face the future with maturity and humility.

3

ROCK OF AGES

The story of evangelicalism in Great Britain

One usually begins at the beginning. But in this case no one is quite sure where the beginning is. Some trace the origins of evangelicalism back to the Reformation, others to the separatist and Puritan churches which emerged in Elizabethan England. These and other times have a bearing on the story of evangelicalism in Great Britain. But evangelicalism became a more easily identified stream within the British church in the eighteenth century.[1]

The Eighteenth Century: The Evangelical Revival

The beginning of the eighteenth century saw religion at a low ebb. The nation was, for most, a rough and cruel place in which to live, with plenty of scope for immorality. Religion did not figure in people's minds. Addison observed that there was 'less appearance of religion in England than in any neighbouring state, Catholic or Protestant.'[2] Motesquieu commented, 'There was no religion and the subject, if mentioned, excites nothing but laughter.'[3]

The dignified and refined church did not touch the common people. Its clergy were in debate with deism, a rationalistic view which distanced God from His creation. But there was little spiritual vitality or even sense of responsibility. The Bishop of Llandaff, for example, was Rector of sixteen parishes simultaneously, as far flung as Leicester, Ely and Huntingdon.[4] The church was in serious decline.[5]

Then the tide turned. God began a new work, stirring people to vibrant and dynamic faith and employing the wider changes in society and thought, to produce an evangelical revival.

WESLEY AND WHITEFIELD
On 24th May 1738, John Wesley wrote, 'I felt my heart strangely warmed. I felt I did trust in Christ, Christ alone for my salvation; and an assurance was given me that He had taken away my sins, even mine . . .'[6] It was not an unprepared event. Wesley was an ordained

clergyman already who had been seeking assurance of salvation for over ten years. His quest had led him to membership of the Holy Club in Oxford, and to serve as a missionary to Georgia in 1738 for which his chief motive had been the salvation of his own soul. The attempt proved abortive but it had put him into contact with the Moravians who had prepared the soil which now bore fruit in Aldersgate Street, as he listened to Luther's preface to the Epistle to the Romans.

Nor was his conversion an isolated event. Howell Harris, a school master in Brecon, experienced an evangelical conversion in 1735. Daniel Rowlands, a curate in Carmarthenshire, was similarly converted the same year. So, too, was George Whitefield. No sooner had they been converted than they began itinerating with the gospel.

Whitefield, already noted for his eloquent preaching of the new birth,[7] began to preach in the open air to the heathen colliers of Kingswood, Bristol, in 1739. Day by day the crowds grew until they reached over 20,000. It was he who induced John Wesley to adopt 'this strange way of preaching in the field', to be 'more vile and proclaim in the highways the glad tidings of salvation' and to abandon the points of decency and order about which he was so scrupulous.

Both Wesley and Whitefield were to adopt 'a vagabond life' from then on, taking to the road as itinerant preachers. Their paths were to deviate, with Whitefield, supported by Selina, Countess of Huntingdon, spending much time preaching in America where, it is estimated, he spent between forty and fifty hours a week in dramatic pulpit oratory, not including travel. They were also to grow apart because of different doctrinal views; Whitefield being a Calvinist, believing in predestination, and Wesley opposing it.

Wesley spent fifty-one years itinerating, covering forty miles a day and stopping to preach in all the villages he passed through. Persecution was common and opposition from the clergy was frequent. Everywhere he went he set up cells for his followers to renew their assurance, stimulate their devotion, check sin and pursue holiness. Originally these cells were supplementary to worship in the parish church but the rift between the 'Methodists', as they were nicknamed, and the Church of England grew, especially after Wesley ordained his own ministers in 1784, until a separate Methodist church was formed.

DISSENT

The effect of the revival spilled over eventually into the dissenting churches. Many Baptist and Independent churches had become small and stagnant and not a few had taken the road to Unitarianism.

The remnant which was left was weak and concerned about maintenance. But new life came to them with, for example, a New Connexion of General Baptists being formed in Yorkshire in 1770. Many took up itinerancy and growth took place.[8] Not all were happy with these developments and as the century progressed not only did some complain of the divisive tendencies of the revival but others hardened, insisting that sterile truth was more important than living mission.

The roots of the revival, and of some of the revived dissenting bodies, go back a long way. John Bunyan, Joseph Alleine and Richard Baxter, Puritan writers of previous days, were influential to the Wesleys, as to others. Among the Baptists much new life came through a fresh evaluation of their Calvinistic roots by Andrew Fuller, in his *Gospel Worthy of All Acceptation* (1785). That work had an influence on William Carey and the formation of the Baptist Missionary Society, the first overseas missionary society, as well as on evangelism at home.

THE CHURCH OF ENGLAND

Evangelicalism in the Church of England also took its stand on justification by faith, assurance and holy living. But, whilst not isolated from the Methodist movement, it developed somewhat separately. Early developments took place unrelated to one another. Samuel Walker, of Truro, Cornwall, was converted in 1749 and within seven years 800 had asked him how they might experience the spiritual life they saw in their formerly pleasure-loving parson. William Grimshaw, of Haworth, Yorkshire, who was not converted through any single event, became a champion of the evangelical cause. He was so concerned with the moral reformation of his people that he drove them out of the public houses to attend church and stopped the races by praying for rain.[9]

In London, in the early days, the only evangelical in a parish was William Romaine, who had experienced a gradual evangelical conversion. His wardens refused to light the church for him to hold his lectures at St Dunstan's in the West. But crowds came none the less. John Fletcher ministered for twenty-five years in Madeley, Shropshire, and thought himself to be the sole evangelical in the county. When the King offered him preferment he replied, 'Tell his majesty that I want nothing but more grace'. John Berridge, of Everton, Bedfordshire, was converted late in life through studying the scriptures, but it had a remarkable effect on the numbers attending his church.

Attitudes to Methodism varied. Grimshaw intinerated and co-operated with them. But most evangelical churchmen opposed them or, like Henry Venn in Huddersfield, tried unhelpfully to control them. Evangelical clergy were too clerical, too fearful of emotion and too concerned about church order to encourage Methodism. They were moderate Calvinists doctrinally, owing much to their Puritan roots and underwent gradual, rather than sudden conversions. Wesley was aware of fifty or sixty evangelical clergymen by 1769 and wrote to them proposing co-operation. But only three replied.

As in Methodism, the Evangelical Revival spawned a new hymnody in the Church of England. It was centred on Olney, where the remarkably converted former slave ship captain, John Newton, was Curate. He, together with William Cowper, an occasional resident in the parishes, must have been responsible for spreading more evangelical doctrine through their hymns than preaching ever did. Among their hymns were 'Amazing Grace, how sweet the sound', 'Glorious things of thee are spoken', 'O for a closer walk with God' and 'There is a fountain filled with blood'. Elsewhere, a West Country evangelical clergyman, who was no lover of Methodism, Augustus Toplady, penned the hymn, 'Rock of Ages, cleft for me, let me hide myself in thee'. It expresses quintessential evangelical doctrine and it has been claimed that 'no other English hymn can be named which had laid so broad and firm a grasp upon the English-speaking world.'[10]

The achievements of evangelicals in the Church of England was remarkable. Without the support of bishops they raised the standards of ministry, brought new life and a new devotional spirit, engaged in philanthropy and greatly enhanced the quality of preaching. Some of this was done as they became increasingly aware of one another during the century, forming, for example, a Clerical Club in 1750 and the Eclectic Society in 1783.

For most of the century they lacked any real statesman, but one emerged towards the end in Charles Simeon,[11] who was appointed to Holy Trinity, Cambridge, in 1783, where he stayed until his death in 1836. For ten years he faced opposition in his own church despite many wishing to hear him preach. He influenced several generations of theological students in the direction of evangelical ministry, through his preaching, sermon classes and Friday evening conversation parties. He also had the foresight to see the importance of securing a succession of evangelical appointments to parishes and so set up a Trust to purchase available patronages to ensure that this would happen. He himself secured the loyalty of many evangelicals to the Church of England, who might otherwise have strayed to nonconformity. His influence touched many areas. Lord Macaulay spoke of it, probably rightly, as being far greater than any primate.

CHURCH OF SCOTLAND

Scotland, too, joined in the Evangelical Revival. Revival came to Cambuslang in 1742. A number of men in the Church of Scotland emerged as evangelical leaders including John Maclaurin (Glasgow), John Erskine (Edinburgh) and John Gillies (Glasgow). From 1761 onwards some churches opted out of the Church of Scotland and became known as 'Relief Churches' because they were unable to guarantee an evangelical succession to their pulpits within the established church and wanted relief from that restriction. Methodism, as such, never became widely established north of the border, but evangelical faith did.

PAN-EVANGELICALISM

In the 1790s evangelical co-operation across denominations began to emerge.[12] In spite of his reservations about Methodists, Samuel Walker had argued, 'It becomes all friends of the Gospel to bear with one another; and while they may differ in opinion and denomination, to unite in heart and endeavour for the support of the common cause.'[13] Allowing liberty of private judgement on secondary issues would permit them to combine for the sake of Christ's kingdom. The vision, shared by Wesley and Whitefield, came into reality in the work of home and overseas missions, notably in the founding of the London Missionary Society (1795), the British and Foreign Bible Society (1804) and the Religious Tract Society (1799).

Understanding eighteenth-century evangelicalism

Socially,[14] evangelicals were most effective in the emerging towns and scattered villages among the artisan classes and coal miners. They found it difficult to make headway in close-knit villages where they were opposed by an alliance of squire and clergyman. The old social system of tight dependency was beginning to dissolve in the light of the agricultural and industrial revolutions. Religion was a way of expressing some of the social tensions and revised social formations which were materialising.

Philosophically things were changing too. David Bebbington has persuasively argued that the 'evangelical version of Protestantism was created by the Enlightenment.'[15] The Enlightenment led people to believe that knowledge was based on what the senses experienced and that concepts of innate ideas were to be rejected. Evangelical religion was 'experimental religion'. The doctrine of assurance, which bound evangelicalism together, was certainly something to be experienced. Reason had its place and was not to be undervalued in favour of enthusiasm and feelings. Rational, scriptural evidence was given as a basis for faith. Religion and science were not in conflict with one another. Natural theology was an aid to belief.

Enlightenment assumptions regarding progress were also reflected by evangelicalism. The possibility of faith led to a rejection of fatalism. Providence smiled with favour and prospects for the future were bright. Postmillennial views were the theological expression consistent with Enlightenment optimism. Holiness naturally led to happiness and no one could know more pleasure than the Christian. In philanthropy and social action they were expressing the Enlightenment commitment to benevolence and liberty.

Opponents of the new evangelicalism, like William Gadsby and the Strict Baptists who rallied around him, were, in reality, often opposing the Enlightenment assumptions which lay behind them. They were children of an older age and its philosophical outlook. The Evangelical Revival had been brought about by God's Spirit and was a perfect vehicle for the proclamation of the gospel to a day of social upheaval and philosophical change. Evangelicalism showed itself perfectly adapted to the times.

The Early Nineteenth Century

The ripening fruit of early evangelicalism came to maturity in the early part of the nineteenth century. But then, in the 1830s, it took on an unexpected flavour.

THE CLAPHAM SECT

Anglican evangelicalism found its most mature expression in the Clapham Sect.[16] A number of laymen, who all occupied significant national positions, including William Wilberforce, Henry Thornton, Charles Grant, James Stephen, Zachary Macaulay and Lord Teignmouth, lived in Clapham and worshipped at the church where John Venn, son of Henry, was Vicar. They were known as 'the Saints'. They exhibited model evangelical lifestyles, characterized by self-discipline, integrity, reforming zeal and usefulness. Theirs was a practical religion.

Their best-known achievement was the abolition of the slave trade in 1807. It had taken them twenty years to achieve, against tremendous opposition from vested interests. They went on to see slavery itself abolished in 1833, through the vigorous campaign of Thomas Fulwell Buxton who took up their baton. But they had other achievements too. They were involved in the founding of the Church

Missionary Society, financed *The Christian Observer*, sponsored the reforming and tract-writing work of Hannah More in the Mendip Hills and founded societies for 'enforcing the King's Proclamation against Immorality and Profaneness' and for the relief of the poor and of prisoners. They were not concerned about changing the conditions which brought about social evils but, none the less, their evangelical faith led them to seek to change the world through energetic activism in a way in which others had not.

All this time, evangelicals were growing in strength numerically. 112 Members of Parliament were considered evangelical. It is estimated that between one-eighth and one-quarter of clergymen were evangelical. Three of their number became bishops: Henry Ryder at Gloucester in 1815, Charles Sumner at Llandaff in 1826 and John Sumner, his brother, at Chester in 1828. Charles Sumner, whose appointment was made for dubious reasons, went on to Winchester, and John became Archbishop of Canterbury in 1848.

THE INFLUENCE OF ROMANTICISM

The style of evangelicalism associated with Simeon and the Clapham Sect, based on Enlightenment optimism and confidence, was not to remain in vogue beyond their time. A change occurred around the 1830s which was partly due to continuing troubles in Europe and partly due to the emergence of Romanticism. It was to lead evangelicalism in unexpected directions.

At Oxford, Calvinism, with its sterner views of humankind, came back into prominence, through the ministry of Henry Bulteel. But the chief expressions of the change were found in the rise of Irvingism, the emergence of premillennialism and stricter views regarding the Bible. The common thread that wove these together with Romanticism was the place given to the supernatural.

Edward Irving,[17] a Church of Scotland minister who came to London in 1822, was striking both in appearance and speech. For a time he became the darling of the fashionable church-going population. But then he began to announce new prophetic views, to espouse a high concept of the sacraments and to encourage speaking in tongues. The latter had first appeared in Scotland and then, in 1831, in his own congregation in London. Tongues were considered an in-breaking of God's Spirit and evidence that the church were living in the last days.

Unfortunately, Irving was a somewhat erratic character. Already under suspicion because of his views regarding the humanity of Christ, he was removed from the Church of Scotland ministry in 1832. A split occurred within his church and led to the formation of a Catholic Apostolic Church. It was governed by an apostolic college of twelve; adopted a high view of liturgy, complete with vestments, incense and candles; and believed in apostles, prophets, evangelists and angels or messengers. The place of reason and scholarship was being downgraded in favour of taste, intuition and feeling.

Irving's prophetic views were shared by others. The normal evangelical view until this time had been that Christ would return after a period of prosperity (the millennium), following the spread of the Christian message and of improvements to civilisation. It reflected the belief the Enlightenment had in progress. Irving, and others, were now saying that Christ would return imminently, before the millennium occurred, and before improvements, through missionary endeavour, had taken place. Christ's return would be a personal, literal and cataclysmic coming.[18]

These views led to evangelicals turning their backs on the world and to much excitement and speculation about the times in which they lived. Much interest was shown in the Jews, who were expected to be restored to Palestine. When Napoleon's son died, one participant at a prophetic conference denied it could be so since, he said, that son was destined to be The Beast! Some ventured as far as to fix the date of the return. Daniel and Revelation became happy hunting grounds.

Henry Drummond called conferences to discuss the matter, annually between 1826 and 1830, at his estate in Albury Park, Surrey. Participants included Irving. It was influential in setting the direction and in getting premillennial views spread and accepted. A similar series of conferences were held in Dublin, at Powerscourt Castle, in the 1830s where a new version of premillennialism came to be expounded by John Nelson Darby, an Anglican clergyman who founded the Plymouth Brethren. Darby argued that there would, in fact, be two comings of Christ. The first would be when believers would be secretly 'raptured', taken up from the earth and removed for the period of the Great Tribulation. The second would be Christ's coming in judgement at the end of the Tribulation. These views, under the title of dispensationalism, became the most popular version of adventism and extremely significant for the subsequent history of evangelicalism.

At this time these views were novel to evangelicals. Simeon did not concern himself with them and the evangelical heavyweights, such as Samuel Waldegrave in his Bampton Lectures in 1854, contested them strongly. But the views caught on none the less, expressing as they did the more Romantic concerns with supernaturalism.

Another area to be affected was that of evangelical attitudes to the

Bible. Simeon went for plain, straight-forward interpretation and was
prepared to believe it contained 'inexact references to philosophic
and scientific matters.'[19] Others, admitting discrepancies, did not
regard it as all equally inspired and would not argue for verbal
inspiration. But if the Bible was to set out the course of future events
it had to be taken literally. Higher views of Scripture, therefore,
began to be accepted. Its divine authorship was exalted at the
expense of any human contribution and the idea that every word was
inspired, and therefore the whole was without any error, began to
gain currency in evangelicalism.

Romanticism led some evangelicals to take higher views of the
sacraments and liturgy than they had previously done. To begin
with, the Oxford Movement was unopposed by evangelicals. But
increasingly, as that Movement developed, evangelicalism came to
view itself in opposition to it.[20] In fact, evangelicalism defined itself
more and more in opposition to others and so brought its view of
evangelical orthodoxy into increasingly sharper focus. Anti-
ritualism, anti-Catholicism, and among Anglicans, anti-liberalism,
became the key. Moves towards Catholic emancipation led to the
formation of a Protestant Reformation Society in 1827 and the
subsequent mass immigration of Irish Catholics, due to famines, led
to increased anti-Catholicism.

Relations between Anglicans and Dissenters generally draw apart
during this period. Their political orientation was different. During
the Napoleonic Wars, Dissenters were suspected of having disloyal
political sympathies. Their disadvantaged state led them to plead for
civil rights, question the establishment of the Church and generally
to be radical in politics. Anglicans, more concerned for stability and
order, supported the establishment and were Tory in politics. The
repeal of the Test and Corporation Acts in 1828 and the Reform Act,
which enfranchised many Dissenters, in 1832, did nothing to create
harmony between them. Where they did co-operate, as in the
founding of the London City Mission (1835) or the Evangelical
Alliance (1846), their relationships were far from easy.

Romanticism had changed evangelicalism.

Mid- and late-Nineteenth Century Developments

For the rest of the century the two streams of evangelicalism
flowed on together, sometimes merging and sometimes separating.
The dominant stream remained that was substantially founded
on Enlightenment ideas. It produced a Christianity which was
devoted to moral reformation, seriousness and the task of

converting the nation. In reality, for all its worthiness, all was not well.

ANGLICAN EVANGELICALISM

Anglican evangelicalism entered the period with a false sense of confidence. Numbers were growing, though estimates vary. The majority of new clergy were either evangelicals or seriously influenced by them. Massive church growth took place, both through increased attendances and also by the building of many new churches. The growth, which affected all denominations, was particularly evident among evangelicals.[21] Evangelicals were represented in greater numbers on the bench of Bishops. With one of their number, as already mentioned, becoming Archbishop of Canterbury in 1848.

They had also won a significant legal victory in the case of the Bishop of Exeter *versus* Reverend Charles Gorham. The Bishop had refused to institute Mr Gorham to a new living in his diocese because the latter did not believe that a child was made regenerate in baptism unconditionally, as the High Church party did. The case went through endless trials, right up to the Privy Council, and in 1850 victory was granted to Mr Gorham. Evangelical views of infant baptism had been established to be authentically Anglican.

In spite of this, all was not well. Evangelicals lacked any ecclesiastical leader of stature. Sumner was a hard-working man but lacked leadership qualities. Their driving force was Anthony Ashley Cooper, the seventh Earl of Shaftesbury.[22] He epitomised mid-century Anglican evangelicalism and used his position, as Palmerston's step-son-in-law, to their advantage. He spent his life engaged in busy social reform and mission activity. From 1828 onwards he committed himself to the reform of lunatic asylums. From 1833 he worked on reforming conditions in factories, which led, in 1847, to an Act limiting child and female labour to ten hours a day. A Mines Act barred boys under ten from working in them and further acts provided women and children with greater protection in employment. Not until 1875 were children used as chimney sweeps granted legal protection. He also threw his energies into education, through the Ragged School Union.

He was equally involved in evangelical activity, especially through the British and Foreign Bible Society, the Church Missionary Society, the Religious Tract Society, the London Society for Promoting Christianity among the Jews and, as founder, the Church Pastoral-Aid Society.

Evangelical clergy devoted themselves to Herculean labours in their parishes. William Champneys, who inherited an empty church in Whitechapel in 1837, was typical. Through systematic visitation, with the help of CPAS, by 1851 he had 1,500 attending his morning services, 800 his afternoon ones and 1,600 his evening services. Equally typically a number of clubs and activities were also established in the church, including a mother's meeting, a Bank, a Coal Club, a Shoeblack Brigade and a Young Men's Institute.

Evangelicals were great founders of societies for reform, education and for home and overseas mission. Reform movements often took the form of protest movements. Evangelicals were against sin, especially those sins associated with vice and drunkenness, and stood against hindrances to people hearing the gospel. Education found its chief expression through the Sunday School movement which had its origins in 1770 and now became a powerful force in the land. Missionary societies spread rapidly and catered for every conceivable taste found among their supporters. At home many evangelistic endeavours drew cross-denominational support, such as City missions which expanded in number, as did other societies, to reach every section of the population by every conceivable means.

All this activity disguised the fact that all was not well. Three challenges faced evangelicals in the second half of the century for which they were not prepared. The first was the challenge of science which arose through the evolutionary teaching of Charles Darwin's *The Origin of Species*, published in 1859. Most evangelicals held to older scientific views based on Bacon and Newton and to a theory of design. They failed to see, though many others did, the time fuse which Darwin had lit which was to explode in a Victorian crisis of faith.

The second challenge came from the rise of biblical criticism. New views of Bible books and new approaches of the life of Jesus reduced both to a human level. For Anglicans, the challenge came to their doorstep in 1860 with the publication of *Essays and Reviews* by seven eminent churchmen. Although some attempt was made to engage in responsible reviewing of these new views, the chief immediate reaction was simply to repudiate them and to batten down the hatches in the hope of riding out the storm. The winds of modern criticism threatened evangelical views of the authority and inspiration of the Bible, which were, therefore, simply reaffirmed, with those who questioned them being marginalised. Further shocks were near to hand as views that stressed the humanity, as opposed to the deity, of Christ and others which stressed the incarnation, as opposed to his redemption, gained favour.

The third challenge came from the rise of ritualism. If evangelicals won legal cases in 1850, they were to lose them in 1890. High church views had been gaining in acceptability and Gothic architecture, quality music, vestments and ritual practices were becoming the order of the day. An Act of Parliament, passed in 1876, sought to suppress this, but it was widely disregarded. Evangelicals unwisely sought to use it to prosecute those who failed to observe it. Their Waterloo came when, in 1890, they tried to prosecute the ritualist Bishop of Lincoln and lost. Since Gorham, evangelicals had increasingly been in contention with others and had become seriously unpopular as a result. Ritualism was an issue to stir the temper. Anti-ritual riots were known to occur. But, even if the Act of Parliament was on their side, their argumentative manner gave them a reputation for being sanctimonious and arrogant and made them deeply unpopular.

So, at the end of the century, Anglican evangelicalism had failed to fulfil its promise and had become a narrow party in a broader church. It had reached a high point mid-century and entered the twentieth century in a much reduced state. It had achieved much, especially in the moral area, but it had not thought strategically enough. Its parish activism prevented it from seeing the need to engage intellectually and ideologically with the changing times.

THE NONCONFORMISTS

The Nonconformists can enter a worthy claim to be the religion of Victorian Britain. Their effect in the shaping of the nation socially, culturally and economically was enormous.[23] Today, a shadow of their former selves, their contribution is only faintly remembered in distant phrases, like 'the Nonconformist conscience'.

In many ways their story mirrors that of evangelical Anglicanism. More uniformly evangelical, it is the story of rapid growth and expansion, outstripping Anglicanism in London, with chapels also proving the religious backbone of cities like Bradford, Halifax, Nottingham and Stoke-on-Trent.[24] With Anglicanism, the growth disguised that they were actually declining, relative to the population, during the latter part of the century. With growth, and with the outworking of evangelical virtues, came prosperity, leading to a grander architecture, mightier organs, finer liturgy, a more educated ministry and more liberal theology.

Evangelical nonconformity was industrious. The number of clubs and activities attached to Whitechapel would have been found in many Nonconformist chapels. R. W. Dale, a leading Congregation-alist, commented, 'The evangelical saint of today is not a man who spends his nights and days in fasting and prayer but a man who is a zealous Sunday School teacher, holds mission services among the poor and attends innumerable committee meetings. Work has taken its place side by side with prayer . . .'[25] One reason for their growth must be their active evangelism which worked in harness with an active concern for mission overseas.

A case has recently been made out, by David Thompson[26] that there was also an evangelical social gospel during this time, thus questioning the consensus that the social gospel movement was a theologically liberal phenomenon. It was evident in the ministries of F. B. Meyer and R. W. Dale, among others, who specifically applied the gospel to society and campaigned for social righteousness from a theological platform. It meant an involvement in politics which some found dubious. But Dale countered by reminding people that the emancipation of slaves, which all acknowledged with admiration to be the result of evangelical activity, was a political act. The quest for social righteousness was one of the chief motivations behind the formation of the National Council of Evangelical Free Churches in 1896.

Nonconformity, too, faced the same challenges as the Church of England evangelicals from the mid-century onwards. Disputes arose as a result, two of which are celebrated. The Rivulet Controversy occurred in Congregationalism, in 1856, over the publication of a hymnbook entitled, *The Rivulet*. It contained a 'milder' theology than had hitherto been acceptable and was influenced by Romantic ideas concerning natural theology. Conservatives objected but did not win the day. Later, Charles Spurgeon, a redoubtable defender of evangelical orthodoxy who had contributed much to the growth of the Baptist denomination, had warned the Baptist Union about the slide to vaguer theological ideas, which reinterpreted the doctrine of the atonement. Matters came to a head in the Downgrade Controversy of 1887–8 and led to his separation from the Baptist Union but not to a great division.

Nonconformist churches differed from evangelical Anglicans in tending to absorb new ideas more easily and thus they became more diffuse theologically. They had a greater sense of freedom to enquire than their Anglican counterparts. With the changes in theology, so too, changes in lifestyle occurred. Old evangelical taboos became acceptable. Whereas, for example, at one stage football had been seen as a temptation of the devil now it was viewed as a positive asset for mission. Aston Villa had its origins in a Methodist church.

The major difference between evangelical Anglicans and the nonconformists lay in their civil and political position. Civil disabilities were not finally removed from nonconformists until after the middle of the century and consequently they were much pre-occupied with the quest for freedom. Many leading ministers were ardent protagonists for disestablishment, which was seen to go hand in hand with political equality. Liberalism came to express their views, and to express, too, the spirit of their times. Their chapels became schools for public speaking and organisation and gave people skills which were subsequently channelled in political, rather than religious, directions.

Nonconformity, then, ended the century with an illusory strength and without the theological homogeneity which had characterized it earlier. Early in the next century it was to undergo dramatic decline.

ROMANTIC INFLUENCES

The period saw the emergence of revivalism. Methodist groups, such as the Primitive Methodists, experienced a number of spontaneous revivals early in the century. These were periods marked by intense emotional fervour and a rapid ingathering of converts. But people were now learning that it was possible to 'arrange' a revival. Charles Finney's *Lectures on the Revivals of Religion* became available in Britain in 1839 and taught that certain techniques, such as the invitation to an anxious-seat, could be adopted to encourage conversions. His writings led to fresh evangelistic activities and were reinforced by a visit of James Caughey, an American, to Methodist churches in the 1840s.

In 1859–60 widespread revival broke out that J. Edwin Orr claimed, too grandly, to be 'the Second Evangelical Awakening'.[27] This revival, originating in the United States, had a great impact in Ulster, Scotland, where an impetus was given to it through a visit of Charles Finney, and Wales. It was characterized by prayer, physical prostrations, conviction of sin and multitudes of conversions. In England it had less impact; but everywhere it was seen as an incentive to redouble efforts at evangelism.

Revivalism became routinised and gave rise to evangelistic campaigns of a revivalist complexion. Most notable among these are the visits made to Britain by D. L. Moody[28] in 1873-1875. Though the visits had an unpromising beginning, since Moody was unknown and unmet, he enjoyed a major success in Scotland and this prepared the way for success in England. In a four-month campaign in London it is reckoned that he preached to more than two and a half million people. He was also successful in the surprising venue of Cambridge University. The impact was made as much by the music hall style singing of his colleague, Ira D. Sankey, as by his folksy but business-like preaching. Moody's visits had another important effect: they established a pattern of internominational campaigns which were to last throughout the next century.

The romantic stream was reflected most in the emergence of holiness movements and Keswick. Faced with threats to the evangelical faith from without, many evangelicals turned inwards, in a quest for holiness. The Keswick Convention, held first in 1875, was anticipated by a number of conventions, such as those at Mildmay and elsewhere. It was possible, too, because the leisured Christian classes took up attending conventions as a key mark of their evangelical culture. It became possible because the 1859 Revival had introduced interdenominational co-operation, and the acceptability of women's ministry. There were other connections with revivalism. Finney and his colleague, Asa Mahan, had a part to play in introducing the teaching. More important still was W. E. Broadman's *The Higher Christian Life*, published, aptly, in 1858. A further and still more important American influence stemmed from the visits of Phoebe Palmer and Robert and Hannah Persall Smith.

Keswick was Arminian in temper and drew from Methodist wells, although it led to a significant modification of Wesley's view on perfection and drew from other sources besides. So it was largely opposed by evangelicals with a reformed perspective on holiness, such as J. C. Ryle. It taught that sanctification was inherent in the believer's conversion and all that the believer had to do to experience unblemished communion with Christ was to receive what was already theirs. Holiness did not come, then, by struggling or battling, but by resting. The realisation of this implicit perfection might be associated with a second blessing experience.

Keswick was the perfect setting for a convention which taught the need to 'let go and let God have his wonderful way in your life.' Its messages, often laced with poetry, could be of a dreamy, sweet and sentimental kind, stressing purity, love and submission to the Master. Though preaching the need for activism in regard to certain things, such as overseas mission and temperance, it was largely a symbol of evangelicalism's contentment not to change the world but to withdraw from it. In its origin it was Romanticism in an evangelical guise. As such, it was paralleled by many other trends and movements, reacting in similar ways to the stresses of industrialism and the quest for peace.[29]

INTERDENOMINATIONAL EVANGELICALISM

The interdenominationalism seen at Keswick became common among evangelicals in the late century. Energies began to be channelled outside the churches into specialized groups, catering for the needs of particular segments of the population. Two significant ones, both concerned with evangelism, might be mentioned as illustrations.

In 1867 successful missions had been conducted for children, by Payson Hammond, an American. The idea was taken up at Mildmay, always a centre of evangelical initiative. It led to the founding of the Children's Special Service Mission, which provided special services for children on Sundays and special activities mid-week. They were successful among working class children. To complement that work, seaside services were begun for those children to be found at coastal places popular with the middle classes. Then, in 1879, a Children's Scripture Union was formed to encourage children to read the Bible from cover to cover, so augmenting the work done in missions and special services.

In the student world, too, evangelicals began work. Oxford started a Prayer Union in 1850. Evangelicals at Cambridge formed a Christian Union in 1877, which built on the prior Sunday School work undertaken by the 'Jesus Lane' lot in 1827 and daily prayer meetings started in 1862.[30] A significant slice of evangelical history was to be associated with the Cambridge Inter-Collegiate Christian Union. It was under D. L. Moody, at Cambridge in 1878, that C. T. Studd was converted. An England cricketer, he sailed for China in 1885 after arousing enthusiasm for missions with others of the Cambridge Seven. Studd was in many ways an evangelical ideal.

CICCU became a symbol of evangelical orthodoxy in splitting from the Student Christian Movement in 1910 because of its refusal to make the penal view of the atonement central. SCM had grown out of the Student Volunteer Movement, inspired by the Cambridge Seven. (SCM subsequently became a non-evangelical student movement running in parallel with the Inter-Varsity Fellowship, which was formed in 1927, with CICCU playing a major part in IVF's formation.)

The nineteenth century, then, saw evangelicalism's fortunes ebb and flow. It owed much to Enlightenment ideas but also drew on perspectives from Romanticism. The two tributaries account for something of the turbulent waters and diversity within evangelicalism. In the denominations the current began weak, grew strong and then became weak again, flowing into a side stream. Meanwhile, major outflows of energy poured into non-denominational activity which was not only to continue to run strong in the twentieth century but also spilled over into the creation of an evangelical subculture which was much dependent on the network of societies they had created.

The twentieth century

The story of evangelicalism in the twentieth century is one of growing strength, accompanied by growing fragmentation. Today, evangelicalism is probably stronger than ever. But it is a coalition of groups, rather than a united monolith. Of particular significance in the story is the emergence of another permutation of evangelicalism – the charismatic movement – due, in part, to fresh developments in culture.

Optimism was the dominant mood as the century opened but it was an optimism which was rapidly to dissolve in the face of the First World War. The darkness of the events gave impetus to those of a premillennial bent. Leadership, among Anglican evangelicals, was in the hands of the saintly Bishop of Durham, Handley Moule. A Bible scholar and prolific author, Moule was prominent in Keswick circles and it was Keswick, with its devotional, non-dogmatic use of the Bible, which was to be the binding agent that held evangelicals together for most of the century.

AFTER THE FIRST WORLD WAR

The war was hugely detrimental to the churches who, rather than seizing the opportunity of peace to engage in mission, became somewhat introverted and indifferent. Until this time evangelicals had a great commitment to social action but the rise of Christian socialism and of what became known as the social gospel movement caused them to react by withdrawing from social involvement. Some, like Campbell Morgan of Westminster Chapel, had no difficulty combining evangelism and social action. But many did. They were suspicious of the new movements because of their optimism about the future, which sat ill with premillennialism; because of their socialist interpretations of the Kingdom of God and their revolutionary tenor.

From about 1920 onwards, evangelicals tended to fight each other over the Bible rather than engaging in evangelism. Full-blown fundamentalism has never been a marked feature of British life but this period saw it rear its head. Theological views were loosening and in the face of these changes strict evangelical orthodoxy was asserted. Among the Methodists, a Wesley Bible Union was formed in 1913 in the wake of George Jackson's appointment to Didsbury College. Among the Baptists, a Baptist Bible Union was formed in 1922 in the wake of T. R. Glover's election to be Vice President of the Baptist Union. Keswick speakers fell under suspicion and some stalwarts, like Stuart Holden, were deposed. E. J. Poole-Conner formed what was to become the Fellowship of Independent

Evangelical Churches. The Anglicans focused their dispute on the Church Missionary Society, which was adjudged to be adopting broader views. It led to the formation of a more evangelical society, The Bible Churchmen's Missionary Society, in 1922.

Another fight to occupy the evangelical Anglicans during the period was that of the Prayer Book Revision, which took place against a background of Anglican-Catholic conversations. The law forbidding High Church practices was widely ignored. So it was proposed that a new Prayer Book should be authorised which would legitimate them and advocate rituals like the reservation of the sacrament and the adoration of the host as authentically Anglican. Some of the Bishops were the chief culprits but fierce opposition was mounted, from the evangelical side, by the evangelical Home Secretary, Sir William Joynson-Hicks. They were justifiably concerned about the doctrines which lay behind the practices. The Prayer Book was twice thrown out by the House of Commons. But it was published, none the less, in 1928 and allowed some limited use. Evangelicals did not come out well from the controversy. They had been less than united and once again their opposition to ritual practices caused resentment. Randle Manwaring describes the episode as 'through the waste lane'.[31]

Outside the main denominations new life was stirring. Missions had been led by Torrey and Alexander in 1903–1905 and Gipsy Smith was very active in evangelism. A revival had taken place in Wales in 1904, led by Evan Roberts, and was followed shortly by another at Azuza Street, Los Angeles, which was to have implications for Britain later. At Azuza Street many physical and ecstatic manifestations of the Spirit had been seen and in 1907, 'the fire of the Lord fell' at All Saint's, Sunderland. The revivals led to the founding of the Pentecostal Movement[32] in its various branches after the war: Elim in 1915, Apostolic in 1918, and Assemblies of God in 1924. Although for some time Pentecostals were held in suspicion on the fringe of the evangelical movement, because they added baptism in the Holy Spirit to the Bible and the gospel and had a distinctive culture of their own, they are now firmly part of the contemporary evangelical coalition.

The thirties began to see the dawning of fresh hope for evangelicalism. Michael Saward[33] puts it down to E. J. H. Nash's (nicknamed, Bash) decision to run élitist evangelical boys' camps, from which were to emerge a new generation of evangelical leaders like John Stott, Michael Green and Dick Lucas. He also points to the founding of the Biblical Research Committee by the IVF, in 1938, which led to a more constructive engagement by evangelicals with modern biblical scholarship. Others have pointed out the significance of Crusaders, a Bible Class movement for public school boys. The same decade saw expansion in the number of evangelical theological colleges. Foundations were being laid which were to lead to a reconstruction of evangelicalism immediately after the Second World War.

POST-WAR DEVELOPMENTS

John Stott became Rector of All Soul's Langham Place, London in 1950, having already served the church, as curate, for five years. Much of the revival of evangelicalism can be traced to his influence. The church became a model for others. Characterized by a ministry of biblical exposition, with an evangelistic heart and a social outreach, it became a centre for students and professionals who were to foster evangelicalism world-wide.

The fifties saw the re-emergence of evangelism. Tom Rees regularly filled the Albert Hall, London, for evangelistic meetings. Billy Graham mounted a twelve week crusade at Harringay in 1954 which was attended by over 2 million people and recorded 36,431 responses.[34] He returned again to Glasgow and Wembley Stadium the next year, as well as conducting a mission at Cambridge University. New evangelical initiatives resulted like the Filey Holiday Week and the founding of *Crusade* magazine. Subsequent visits in 1966, 1967, 1984, and 1991 may have had less media impact, and less sensational results, but saw Graham, and the evangelicalism he represented, becoming increasingly acceptable.

In the 1950s, Graham, and those like John Stott who associated with him, were held in some suspicion by the likes of Geoffrey Fisher, Archbishop of Canterbury, and Michael Ramsey, Bishop of Durham (later to move to Canterbury). A controversy was sparked in *The Times*, in 1955, raising the spectre that evangelicals were sectarian and anti-intellectual fundamentalists. Michael Ramsey was particularly trenchant in his criticisms, calling fundamentalism a menace and accusing it of stifling minds. John Stott (who engaged in a mission to Durham University during this period!) carefully wrote[35] in defence of conservative evangelicalism and distinguished it from anti-intellectual fundamentalism. He asserted the place of both mind and emotion in conversion, which could be both gradual and sudden. He affirmed the centrality of the cross, not a particular theory of interpretation about it, as the means of atonement. And he argued that the authors of the Bible were so inspired that their words were the words of the Holy Spirit, and distanced himself from theories of mechanical dictation or approaches which were closed to using contemporary scholarship to understand the Bible. A fuller defence was set out by J. I. Packer in *Fundamentalism and the Word of God.*[36]

The fifties, in fact, saw the rise of evangelical scholarship, with F. F. Bruce, Donald Guthrie and Donald Wiseman being worthy pioneers. The founding of London Bible College, in 1943, and of Tyndale House, Cambridge, in 1944, prepared the way for it.

The progress of Anglican evangelicalism is fairly easily marked. In 1955 the Eclectic Society was restarted for evangelical clergy under 40. Evangelicals in the Church Assembly became more organized in the 1950s. In 1960 the Church of England Evangelical Council was founded. Evangelicals in other denominations were to learn from some of this later. Then in 1967 a National Evangelical Anglican Congress was held at Keele, to be followed ten years later by another at Nottingham. Both congresses were marked by the growing confidence of evangelicals and by their commitment to the national church. Since the fifties, they have clearly worked to overcome Hensley Henson's jibe that they are 'semi-dissenters'. At Keele, they rediscovered the world and the need to engage with it once again. At Nottingham they discovered hermeneutics and the need to grapple seriously with issues of interpretation. All this has led to a growing place within the church, as witnessed by the number of bishoprics and other senior appointments now held by evangelicals, and, perhaps, by some withdrawal from interdenominational evangelicalism.

The growth of evangelical social awareness led to the founding of Tear Fund in 1968, to David Sheppard writing *Built as a City* in 1974, to the founding of the Shaftesbury Project and the London Institute of Contemporary Christianity, now combined under the name of Christian Impact. The maturing of evangelicalism was also demonstrated by the Lausanne Congress on World Evangelisation, held in 1974, where the questions of the cultural captivity of evangelicalism and the social implications of the gospel were put firmly back on the agenda.

Evangelicals in other mainline denominations have trodden a path similar to Anglican evangelicals. Among the Baptists, Mainstream was formed; among Methodists, Headway, and among the United Reformed Church, GEAR. In each, evangelicals have become more committed to their denominations.

A counter trend was seen in the growing interest expressed by some in the Puritan roots of evangelicalism. An Evangelical Movement in Wales was formed in 1955, the *Banner of Truth* magazine was launched the same year and the Trust was founded in 1959. In Scotland Reformed evangelicals, albeit with a great commitment to their denomination, gathered around William Still of Aberdeen. Some were fearful of a watering down of evangelical truth in the wider trends and in 1966 Dr Martyn Lloyd-Jones, at a

meeting of the Evangelical Alliance chaired by John Stott, issued a
clarion call to evangelicals to leave their historic, mixed
denominations and form a united pure church. John Stott graciously
begged to differ. But from that time on a division has occurred which
has led to some unhappiness between the more reformed and
separatist wings of evangelicalism and the rest.

THE CHARISMATIC MOVEMENT

A number of other trends emerged during the sixties. Theology
became radical, as it proposed the death of God, and was rebutted
by evangelicals. Ecumenism became serious and, although there was
evangelical involvement, many evangelicals were not at home with
it. But the most significant trend for evangelicals was the rise of the
charismatic movement.[37] Across denominations people were
encountering the Holy Spirit in fresh ways. It led them into a
rediscovery of gifts, like speaking in tongues, prophecy and healing;
to new forms of worship, including greater spontaneity, dance and
song with an emphasis on praise; to a new spirituality which was
life-affirming rather than world-denying; and to new relationships,
which were characterized by warmth, informality and networking.

Traditional evangelical churches found it hard to come to terms
with such developments at first, particularly as the emphasis of the
new movement was on experience rather than on the Word. Tensions
and divisions occurred. As the movement progressed many
expressed impatience with renewal groups working within
denominations, like Fountain Trust, and moved out of the old
inhibiting ecclesiastical structures to found new churches, like
Ichthus, Pioneer, Stream and New Frontiers. At first called 'house
churches', they were later known simply as new, community or
restorationist churches.[38] Many restorationist churches imbibed a
heady mix of charismatic experience with biblical literalism and
premillennial views about living in the last days. Other charismatics
stayed in mainline denominations to work for renewal from the
inside.

It changed the landscape of evangelicalism dramatically. Some
evangelicals retrenched. But the majority of denominational
evangelical churches have probably been touched by the effects of
the charismatic movement, at least in their style of worship, if not
in other ways. Strenuous efforts were made in the evangelical world
to ensure participants across the evangelical-charismatic spectrum
talked with one another and these seem to have borne fruit in a
growing *rapprochement*. On a formal level, conversations took place
in the Church of England leading to the publication of a statement
entitled, *Gospel and Spirit*. Many other conversations took place

under the auspices of the Evangelical Alliance. On an informal level, many evangelicals and charismatics have met together in constructive fellowship through Gear, Headway, Mainstream and, especially, at Spring Harvest.

The charismatic permutation of evangelicalism, like others before it, owes much to the influence of contemporary culture. Modernism, in the cultural sense as distinct from the theological sense, goes back to artistic and literary developments early in the century. But it worked through to mass culture only in the 1960s and accounts for the enormous social and cultural upheaval of that decade. Its chief characteristic is self-expression. In Germany it is known as 'expressionism'. Its participants were concerned to delve within, to see what was below the surface, in the unconscious, and then to express it frankly. The objective meaning of words was called into question and objective reality held suspect. It led to the challenging of existing structures, formalities, authorities and truths which had been taken for granted. Its orientation was towards the subjective rather than the objective, feeling and experience rather than mind and truth.

The parallels with the charismatic movement are hard to resist. That is not to say the charismatic movement was not also a work of the Holy Spirit. It is to say that the Spirit was reformulating evangelicalism, as had been done before, in a way which was congruent with its contemporary social and cultural setting.

Evangelicalism in Britain, then, has a history of fluctuating fortunes; weakness and strength giving way to each other. Revolving around the twin axes of Bible and gospel have been a constellation of diverse bodies: some churches, some societies; some enduring, some passing. Evangelicalism has been shaped and reshaped, by its history and its contemporary context. The heritage today is rich, and although people will find their own niche within the wider movement, there is no reason why they cannot be enriched by it all, as well as being humbled by its mistakes.

MINE EYES HAVE SEEN THE GLORY

The story of evangelicalism in the United States

According to William McLoughlin, it is as difficult to unscramble eggs as it is to separate evangelicals from nineteenth century American culture.[1] How did that come about and where did evangelicalism go from there?

Religion played a major part in the colonization of America. Puritan settlers led the way with the founding of colonies in Virginia and Massachusetts in the early seventeenth century. They carried with them the vision of a Christian state where they would be free. The Puritan soul became deeply embedded, and its way of life firmly stamped, on the New England colonies. Below them, in the middle colonies, subsequent waves of settlers brought pietistic religion with them from Continental Europe. Further south still, the religious scene was dominated by middle-of-the-road Anglicanism, which suited the slave-holding landowners of those parts. It was, of course, counterpoised by the development of powerfully creative negro religion.

The Great Awakening

From this soil blossomed a great awakening of religion in the 1740s, from which the origins of evangelicalism might more properly be traced. Stirrings of fresh religious faith occurred as early as 1720 among Dutch-speaking residents of New Jersey, through the preaching of the pietist Theodore Frelinghuysen. But its chief phase is associated with Jonathan Edwards and George Whitefield.

Jonathan Edwards,[2] a Congregational Minister in Northampton, Massachusetts, was a man saturated with a sense of the holiness of God, the sinfulness of men and women and their utter reliance on God for salvation. He became concerned about the spiritual state of the young people in his town and also about the growth of Arminian doctrines which led people to trust in themselves for salvation. The former he dealt with by visiting them all, individually, in their homes. The latter he addressed by preaching a series of sermons on justification by faith alone, in 1734. A radical change came over the community and a great sense of the presence of God swept Northampton. The revival rapidly faded but when Edwards published the account of it a few years later it stimulated others to thirst for a similar work of God.

They were not to wait long. In 1740 a great awakening broke out, in which George Whitefield played a prominent part. He had returned to America from Britain in 1739 and the dramatic nature of his preaching made him a sensation up and down the eastern sea board. In the Autumn of 1740 he devoted his energies to New England where he preached to 8,000 every day for a month. Thousands were converted to Christ, amidst much religious excitement. Whitefield's direct style of preaching reached people's hearts.

Whitefield continued to itinerate until his death in 1770. In the cause of the gospel he crossed over the Atlantic seven times. But because he lacked the organisational skills of John Wesley, the results of his work were not preserved in the way in which those of the Evangelical Revival in Britain had been.

Others played their part. Gilbert Tennant and Samuel Davies preached among the negro population. Tennant saw multitudes awakened. David Brainard, and his brother John, evangelised among the native Americans. Jonathan Edwards did not stray much from Northampton, but on a visit to Enfield, Connecticut, in 1741, he preached on 'Sinners in the hands of an angry God', a sermon which was to become the most famous of the Great Awakening. Edwards lent his brilliant mind to the theology associated with the Great Awakening. His many works dealt with the true meaning of religious affections, as opposed to mere religious emotion; the necessity of grace as the basis for morality; and the inability of people to please God except by an implanting of God's grace.

The fires of the Awakening did not last long, dying first in New England and then elsewhere by 1750. But they had spread far and had many remarkable effects. There had been a revival of experiential piety with thousands, maybe hundreds of thousands, converted. In the years immediately following church membership sharply increased. The Baptists benefited most, growing from 96 churches in 1740 to 457 by 1780.[3] In the South they became established as a genuine alternative to the Church of England. The Awakening had ensured that denominations which favoured revivalism made the running on the frontiers. Education received a fresh impetus. Styles of preaching had changed. New sources of authority had arisen, namely, the itinerant preacher, and the old source of religious authority, the institutional church, had had its position weakened.

Not surprisingly, the Awakening also caused division with those in the New England colonies splitting into New Lights (those who favoured the revival and its theology), 'old lights' (those who became liberal and rationalistic in theology, eventually often declining into Unitarianism) and those 'old Calvinists' who were in the middle. Edwards himself suffered from opposition and was dismissed by his congregation in 1750 for introducing strict regulation of the communion table.

The greatest effect was that English puritanism had given way to American evangelicalism,[4] with its greater emphasis on individualism. A number of explanations for the Awakening have been advanced, such as the economic circumstances of the time. Whether these can be justified or not, it must be admitted that by insisting on the need for personal response to the grace of God, rather than presuming on one's spiritual security as a member of the covenant, as the Puritans taught, the Awakening was in tune with the temper of its time. Evangelicalism has been marked by individualism and a stress on personal conversion ever since.

The consequences of the Great Awakening were long-lasting in shaping the style of American evangelicalism, even if they were not immediately apparent. In the short term they could only look forward to scattered minor revivals in the 1760s and 1770s. Otherwise energies were to be diverted into the War of Independence against Britain. The Awakening contributed to it indirectly by strengthening ideas of liberty and opposition to tyranny and by training a generation of men in public speaking and organisational skills. Christianity had become a voluntary faith and was no longer an inherited or imposed one. The voluntary principle in the church blended with the democratic principle in politics to produce a revolutionary cocktail. No denomination was to be established as the state church in the United States.

The Second Great Awakening

The end of the eighteenth century saw religion at a low ebb. The war had taken its toll and rationalism had caused an increase in scepticism. But some were urgently praying for revival. Whether what happened can be really dignified with the title of 'the second great evangelical awakening' is a moot point. But certainly there was a marked increase in fervent personal religion around the turn of the century, until 1810 or so.[5]

On the frontiers, where spiritual progress had been slow, revival came through camp meetings, like those called by James McGready and Barton W. Stone. The most famous took place at Cane Ridge in 1801 and lasted a week. It was attended by up to 25,000 people, from a mixture of denominations, and they responded to the simple folksy preaching with uninhibited emotion. From this awakening, camp meetings were bequeathed to future generations as a major means of producing conversions, revival and holiness.

The Great Revival altered the balance of churches in the south by greatly augmenting Methodist, Baptist and Presbyterian churches where they had previously been weak. These denominations appealed not only to whites but to many slaves who found, in the camp meetings, an emotional and expressive faith which helped both to make sense of their present circumstances and to promise redemption in the world to come.

In the conservative north-eastern states the revival may have taken on a more 'churchy' complexion but it was real none the less. One hundred and fifty churches experienced an outpouring of vital religion. One participant in New England was Timothy Dwight, a grandson of Jonathan Edwards, who was much concerned about the spiritual state of his students at Yale. In seeking their revival he was to become a significant figure in the next stage of evangelicalism's history.

In the early 1800s evangelicalism took another familiar direction in the USA by setting up numerous societies for home and overseas missions. These gave organisational shape to the Second Awakening and preserved its results in a way the First Evangelical Awakening had failed to do. In 1810 an American Board of Commissioners for Foreign Missions was established. One of their first missionaries was Adoniram Judson, who shortly afterwards was converted to Baptist views and set up a Baptist missionary society in 1814. He served in Burma for forty years. At home the early years saw the founding of the New England Tract Society (1814); the American Bible Society (1816); the American Colonization Society for liberated slaves (1817); the American Sunday School Union (1824); the American Tract Society (1825); the Society for the Promotion of Temperance (1826) and the like.

The Development of Revivalism

EARLY TENSIONS

The years that followed witnessed developments in revivalism and its canonization in evangelicalism. The developments were made possible by the changing theological outlook. Timothy Dwight had become President of Yale College in 1795. He was a conservative who opposed deist and infidel republicans, like Thomas Jefferson, and promoted the revival of religion among his students, albeit of a more restrained kind than that of the camp meetings. His students spread the revival message up and down the East Coast. But, more significantly, Dwight, in seeking faithfully to reinterpret his grandfather's theology for the new age, softened it. He was less philosophical in orientation than Edwards and more practical. He believed people were depraved in sin and needed conversion through God's grace. But that came through the use of more ordinary means, rather than by miraculous intervention. God addressed human beings as rational beings and induced voluntary obedience in them by operating on their minds.

Lyman Beecher, a Presbyterian student of Dwight's, led the transformation of revivalism into forms which were acceptable to the North East. He directed its energies into the societies mentioned earlier and encouraged a more romantic style in evangelistic preaching. The theological transition was advanced by Nathaniel Taylor, also a student of Dwight's, a Congregationalist, who struggled to reconcile Calvinist theology to revival methods which were proving effective. From Yale Divinity School, where he taught for thirty years from 1822, he outlined 'New Haven' theology and provided the foundations for a New School Theology. New School Theology relaxed stern Calvinism, which, through its emphasis on divine sovereignty, could sometimes paralyse revivalism. Sin was seen as the wrong-doing people did, rather than a disposition they inherited. People were no longer viewed as totally depraved and therefore unable to choose good and right. People became responsible moral agents with the power of choice.

The developments were not unopposed. Charles Hodge, an old school Presbyterian at Princeton, defended traditional Calvinism and pointed out how far from Scripture Taylor was moving. The distance Taylor was travelling became particularly evident when his view of the cross was published in 1859. Hodge argued that the old school stood on Scripture exactly where traditionalists had always stood. In fact, that was not entirely true for unconsciously Hodge and his like were affected, along with others, by the new scientific environment in which they lived.

All theologians of the period based their views, one way or another, on a phase of the Enlightenment known as 'Scottish common sense realism'. This philosophy taught that the human mind was capable of knowing the world in a straightforward way without needing to filter it through innate ideas. Based on Bacon's approach to science, it had many popular and practical applications and suggested that the plain man's interpretation was right. It featured in three great

American commitments at the time – the commitment to modern empirical science, to the justice of the American Revolution and to the production of rational and scientific evidence for believing the Bible. Princeton was affected no less than Yale. Hodge went for the plain interpretation of Scripture, but did not take into account its origin in a different culture and consequently used it to justify traditionalism. Dwight used the same philosophic basis to justify change.

CHARLES FINNEY

Traditionalists, however, could not stand in the way of the triumph of modified revivalism. Accompanying the New School in Theology were New Measures in revivalism. The chief, but by no means sole, exponent of the new measures was Charles Finney.[6] Finney, a former lawyer was converted in 1821 and ordained in 1824 by the Presbyterian church. They did so in spite of his admission that he had never read the Westminster Confession of Faith which was the theological foundation of the denomination. His lack of commitment to old school Presbyterianism soon became evident. He was called to account by church authorities in 1827 for his introduction of novelties, but successfully defended himself. He was, however, to break from traditional Presbyterianisms in the early 1830s.

Finney's career as a revivalist was, in fact, quite short. It stretched from 1825–32 and was chiefly confined to towns in New York State. He called it the 'burned-over district' on account of the number of revivals which had taken place there. His revivals usually resulted in hundreds being added to churches through his direct preaching and use of techniques to encourage conversions. But it was a revival in Rochester, in 1830–31, which saw some 60,000 added to the church, that shot him to prominence.

In 1835 he published his *Lectures on Revivals of Religion*, which revealed that revivals were no longer seen as remarkable events of God to be prayed down but organized events of men and women to be worked up. The adoption of techniques could lead to their success. Among Finney's innovations was the adoption of the Anxious Seat, a place where people could go at the end of the meeting to deal with their souls. He believed the use of protracted meetings, of three or four weeks duration, to be effective. Attention was given to music, the training of workers, prayer meetings, follow-up and organising co-operation between churches. Hindrances to revival were examined, including lack of expectation and ministers and churches who took the wrong stand in regard to any question involving human rights.

The book is a combative argument for change, which, he says, the churches always oppose. The apostles were great innovators. 'The present cry against new measures is highly ridiculous.'[7] It breathes a confident spirit. People do not have to sit and wait for God, they have the power in their own hands to accomplish things. God has given the means. God would not have told us to be filled with the Spirit unless we had the power to obey him.[8] 'Sinners ought to be made to feel that they have something to do, and that is to repent . . .'[9] 'The Scriptures ascribe the conversion of a sinner to four different agencies – to men, to God, to the truth and to the sinner himself.'[10]

Finney settled briefly as pastor of a church in New York before moving to Oberlin College, as a professor of theology, in 1837. Three other features of Finney's work are important for later evangelical history. First, as was evident in his *Lectures*, he became an ardent advocate of human rights and championed the cause of the abolition of slavery. Secondly, his theology was marked by belief in progress and its religious counterpart, postmillennialism. Like most evangelicals of the time, he had a vision of America as a Christian nation. Thirdly, he is associated with perfectionist views, believing it possible for believers to attain to a higher state of spiritual life as a permanent experience.

WIDER DEVELOPMENTS

Oberlin drew much on Wesleyan roots. Finney's new measures, which were much opposed by old school Presbyterians, were not all that novel in Methodism. And there is an argument that Finney's role has been over-played at the expense of others. Francis Asbury had been sent by Wesley to organize the American Methodist Church, which he did in 1784 at Baltimore, after a delay caused by the American War of Independence. He was a tireless evangelist, travelling some 300,000 miles on horseback to advocate Wesleyan doctrines of free grace and perfection, and to set up classes, circuits and conferences. From negligible beginnings there were 2,000 ministers and 200,000 Methodists in America at his death. Evangelicalism draws deeply, if often in an unacknowledged way, from the Methodist well.

Slave religion took divergent paths during this period. Many belonged to integrated churches. As those churches grew, white members often moved out to new buildings leaving negroes to use the old buildings as an adjunct church. Others belonged to independent churches. Fully participating in the life of congregations, as they did, gave them skills in speaking and organization and broadened the vision of their future place in society. Much mission work was conducted among slaves, especially as the Civil

War approached. Slave holders wanted to prove to the Northerners that they were not keeping their slaves in heathen darkness and so intensified evangelistic efforts, but thereby missed the point. Slave religion led negroes in different directions. It led some to accept their state. Compensation would be found later. It led others, like Nat Turner, in 1831, to rebellion. Some were content to integrate. Others struggled with the condescending attitudes of whites and eventually separated. Richard Allen, for example, in 1794, left St George's Methodist Episcopal Church, Philadelphia, where he was an energetic worker, in protest at the humiliating treatment of blacks, to form, with Asbury's support, a Methodist Church for blacks. Asbury ordained him in 1799 but further uneasy relations followed and in 1816 a separate American Methodist Episcopal Church was founded in Philadelphia. The orientation of slave religion was Bible-believing and stressed personal experience and so was thoroughly evangelical.

1858-60 was to see a further outbreak of revival. It did not touch the South (Finney thought because of slavery) but affected the great cities in the North. Finney played a part in it, but its character was different again from previous revivals. Sometimes called the Third Great Awakening, or the businessmen's revival, it was the result of prayer meetings sponsored by laymen rather than the preaching of evangelists.[11] Two thousand gathered for prayer at noon in Chicago's Metropolitan Theatre. Elsewhere, in New York, Philadelphia, Boston and so on, they gathered in their thousands. Public High Schools were affected with all but two boys professing conversion in the schools in Cleveland. The revival, which may well have had something to do with a troubling economic situation, is estimated by Edwin Orr[12] and others to have seen 1,000,000 converted.

Revivalism was firmly established as characteristic of American religion. Interdenominational in character; popular in style; vital and expressive in temper; liberating for women and blacks; periodic in occurrence; evangelical in its stress on Bible and gospel; it gave America a vision of itself as a Christian civilization in which conversion was a right of passage.

Mark Noll evaluates the status of evangelicalism in America's history from 1800-1865 in these words:

> Antebellum America was evangelical not because every feature of life in every region in the United States was thoroughly dominated by evangelical Protestants but because so much of the visible public activity, so great a proportion of the learned culture, and so many dynamic organisations were products of evangelical conviction. . . . The achievement of the evangelicals was remarkable: they managed to forge a

relatively cohesive religious culture out of disparate elements and make it effective throughout a sprawling, expanding land.[13]

The fading of a dream

Evangelical life appeared invincible. The denominations, where most of evangelical life was to be found, tripled in membership from 1860-1900. But, as in England, by the end of the century the appearance of evangelical prosperity was to prove deceptive. The same forces as in England were to undermine it - Darwinism, biblical criticism and urbanization. To these was added the special factor of immigration. Although Protestant churches tripled in the late nineteenth century, Roman Catholicism quadrupled due to the mass of industrial workers coming from abroad to work in the cities. Universities developed in size and wealth and, almost unnoticed, higher education was secularized in a generation. By the turn of the century American culture was not so much evangelical as secular.

Evangelical activity, however, continued apace and distinctive evangelical answers were mounted against the onslaught of these debilitating trends.

DWIGHT L. MOODY

The revivalist torch passed from Finney to Dwight L. Moody.[14] A shoe salesman from Chicago, Moody had been influenced by the 1858 revival in Chicago and was set to benefit in his own ministry from the framework of interdenominational activity it spawned. He gave up business in 1860 to work full-time in Sunday School and YMCA work. During the Civil War he worked among the troops. He teamed up with Ira D. Sankey and together they travelled, as unknown evangelists, to Britain from where, a couple of years later, they were to return as international sensations.

Moody's style was different from Finney's. There was a greater restraint about him; emotions were kept under careful control. The Anxious Seat was replaced by the enquirers' room. His preaching was built on sentiment rather than sensation.[15] The personal love of God, rather than his moral law, became his message. Liquor and laziness became the chief sins to be condemned. Never interested in doctrine, Moody would tell homely and concrete stories that provoked memories of a bygone age of the family. He could not argue the gospel, only alternately woo and browbeat people into the Kingdom. His message always related to the three R's of:

Ruined by sin
Redeemed by Christ
Regenerated by the Holy Spirit

Sankey's singing, which induced many a tear in his audience, was the perfect complement to his preaching.

'Charles Finney', comments William McLoughlin, 'made Revivalism a profession but D. L. Moody made it big business'.[16] Machinery was set up for his campaigns, involving meticulous preparation and plenty of committees. Secular halls were hired. Evangelical churches were requested to unite for a campaign. Businessmen were tapped for financial support. Sermon topics were announced in advance. Use was made of the media to advertise. Moody initiated the approach which was to be adopted by evangelistic preachers from his day to our own.

Moody set up institutions to exploit the benefits of his campaigns. Schools were started for girls (1879) and boys (1881). Bible conferences were established at Northfield. The Chicago Evangelisation Society, later to become the Moody Bible Institute was founded in 1886. The same year, the Student Volunteer Movement, which aimed at 'the evangelisation of the world in this generation,' was formed.

1890-1914 became the age of missions. Tremendous energy was poured into the Sunday School movement, Christian Endeavour, reform movements, such as the Temperance Movement. The evangelical infrastructure grew and with it the distinctive ways of an evangelical subculture.

NEW RESPONSES TO NEW CHALLENGES

The challenge of increasing secularization called forth new responses. Straight gospel preaching alone did not seem adequate to cope with the increasingly complex problems of a modern industrial society. Many adopted a solution which was eventually rejected by evangelicals. That was to turn the gospel into a social gospel. Although social concern was originally closely connected with evangelicalism, the social gospel movement became more identified with liberalism.[17] In America the idea of the social gospel is linked to the names of Washington Gladden, a Congregationalist, and later Walter Rauschenbusch, a Baptist. They advocated the need for structural reform, located evil in unredeemed social structures, saw the Kingdom of God in operation beyond the boundaries of the churches and argued that salvation was for society and not the individual. By comparison evangelicalism seemed a narrowing creed. In reaction to the social gospel, evangelicalism withdrew from social involvement and channelled its energies into other responses.

Evangelicals responded in three significant ways. They responded by the adoption of premillennialism, the embracing of holiness teaching and the rise of Pentecostalism. Moody was influential in the first two of these.

Premillennialist teaching[18] had been known earlier in the century. But its association with the eccentric movement led by William Miller, who taught that Christ would return in 1843, meant it had never been anything other than a minority evangelical view. Several factors now combined to cause evangelicals to adopt premillennialism. There was the breakdown of optimism associated with postmillennialism in the face of the Civil War and the problems of the cities. Postmillennial views of progress came to fit more easily with liberal ideas of a social gospel. Later views of premillennialism coming from Britain, and especially J. N. Darby, who travelled widely in America, commended themselves more easily than those associated with less stable personalities like Edward Irving. Premillennialism catered for a fascination with the future and an interest in the Jews.

But above all, premillennialism, in teaching that the world would not get better before the coming of Christ, explained the course history was taking. Furthermore it required a literal interpretation of the Bible which correlated with emerging views of evidence and facts, coming from the realm of science with Scottish Common Sense Realism, once more, underlaying it. Words had to mean exactly what they said. The Bible was a book of facts. It revealed the plan progressively. History, and the future could be divided and classified, as a scientist would do, into dispensations. Supernaturalism and science joined to make premillennialism popular.

All Moody's lieutenants, like Moody himself, became advocates of premillennialism. R. A. Torrey, his scholarly heir apparent; Cyrus Scofield, whose edition of the Bible was to become a chief means by which the views were propagated; A. C. Dixon, the editor of *The Fundamentals;* A. J. Gordon and others all taught it. It was enshrined in the teachings of the Moody Bible Institute and BIOLA, the Bible Institute of Los Angeles. Premillennialism became the new evangelical orthodoxy.

If the first evangelical response looked forward, the second looked inward. The holiness movement[19] had deep roots in Methodism where it found its chief outlet early in the century. It taught that in addition to conversion a secondary blessing, which came to be called baptism in the Holy Spirit, was needed to make one holy and deal with deeply inbred sin. Holiness came not through a continual struggle but simply by trusting. In the first half of the century the leading exponent of the teaching was Phoebe Palmer. Her influence was far from limited to the United States and extended to Britain, where her most significant achievement was to win William and Catherine Booth to holiness teaching. The Salvation Army was to become a major holiness sect later in the century both in Britain and the United States. When holiness fires dampened in Methodism, as they did in the 1840s and 1860s, attempts to revive them often led to tensions and division. Holiness was often promoted at camp meetings and in 1867 John Inskip founded the National Camp Meeting Association for the Promotion of Holiness which became the centre of an extensive network of camps, conferences, missions, publications and associations committed to holiness.

Holiness teaching was also to be found in the non-Methodist wing of the church, flowing particularly from Oberlin College where it was advocated by Charles Finney and the college's Principal, Asa Mahan, following their shared crisis in sanctification in 1836. Its concern for personal purity, if not the means of achieving it, was consistent with the rigorous piety of earlier Puritans.

But it was later in the century that the holiness movement became widespread and central among evangelicals. Hannah Pershall Smith's book *The Christian's Secret of a Happy Life* (1875) became the movement's classic, selling three million copies. The Keswick Higher Life movement crossed the Atlantic from the United Kingdom and numberless summer conferences spread the word.

Holiness teaching merged with premillennialism and became the evangelicals' preoccupation. Essentially a middle class movement, it was concerned about inner purity, temperance and philanthropy to the poor. But it had little wider social agenda. It spawned a host of new churches and organizations between 1880 and 1905 which gave it some institutional form. Among them was the Christian and Missionary Alliance, founded by A. B. Simpson in 1881; the Church of God, founded in Anderson, Indiana, in 1881, and the Church of the Nazarene, founded in Los Angeles in 1895. It is thought that 100,000 spilled out of the mainline denominations into holiness circles during these years.

The third response looked upwards. It was Pentecostalism[20] Not unconnected with the holiness movement, which had shades of faith healing about it, Pentecostalism was pioneered by Charles Fox Parham. Parham served in Methodist pastorates before leaving that church to become independent in 1895. Following a deep investigation of the holiness movement he returned to Topeka, Kansas, in 1900, to set up a Bible school and prepare students for the outpouring of the Holy Spirit which he anticipated as part of the latter days. He taught that the experience of the Acts of the Apostles were for his day and not just for the early church. So, to the established evangelical beliefs in conversion, sanctification, premillennialism, and, even, healing, he added an emphasis on the outpouring of the Holy Spirit as a sign of the last days and as demonstrated in the receipt of the gift of tongues. On 1st January 1901, one of his students spoke in tongues and shortly afterwards Parham himself and half his students followed suit.

In the next six years Parham's fortunes oscillated between revivals and failure, leading to his alienation from the movement from 1907 onwards. But the Apostolic Faith Movement had been founded. One of those who attended Parham's relaunched Bible school in 1905 was a black evangelist called William J. Seymour. Seymour went to Los Angeles where rumours of revival, built on the back of the Welsh Revival, were spreading. But it was his preaching to a small company when the Spirit fell and they began to speak in tongues which led to the Azusa Street Revival[21] that put Pentecostalism on the map.

THE BIBLE AND SCIENCE

While these developments were taking place another issue, which was to prove of the utmost importance for the later course of evangelicalism, was beginning to be addressed. That was the status of the Bible. Darwinism and biblical criticism were raising questions about the integrity of the Bible and, 'it would be difficult to overstate the critical importance of the absolute integrity of the Bible to the nineteenth-century American evangelical's whole way of thinking.'[22]

Scientific and historical advances called into question whether the Bible was without error. The new views met with a great deal of acceptance and attempts to integrate them with the Bible became common. But that opened the door to a more relaxed view of the truthfulness of the Bible and some began to speak of errors and contradictions in the Bible. The champions of the old orthodox position were once again found at Princeton. A. A. Hodge and Benjamin Warfield rallied to the defence of the position that the Bible was without error, or, inerrant. Warfield,[23] the more significant of the two, did so at the same time as believing that there was nothing in Genesis 1 and 2 which needed to oppose evolution.

Between 1878 and 1906 nearly all major denominations had to face the issue and numerous heresy trials took place. The Presbyterian, Charles Briggs of Union Theological Seminary, for example, was tried for his views and deemed guilty with the result that he left the denomination. But for all the victories of the conservative evangelicals the drift to more liberal views of the Bible was rapid and most Seminaries in the North were teaching broader views of the

Bible and theology early in the new century.

The most significant result of the battle is that it crystallized the opposing positions. The Bible's flawless authority had been taken for granted until then. Now it was being defined more closely and what had been assumed was being turned into a test of orthodoxy. The lines were being formed for the next phase of the story of evangelicalism.

Fundamentalism versus Modernism

Between 1910 and 1915 a series of twelve paperbacks appeared called *The Fundamentals*. Written by a range of conservative scholars they reaffirmed traditional Christian beliefs but did not advocate any particular stance on questions of the millennium, separation from mixed denominations, holiness, or even, evolution. They did not attract any particular attention at the time but the name became important as a symbol of the next phase of evangelicalism. It was to be a militant phase with evangelicals aggressively opposed to the twin evils of modernism and evolution.[24]

The term 'fundamentalism' was coined in 1920 by Curtis Lee Laws, the editor of a Baptist periodical, who used it to speak of those ready 'to do battle royal for the Fundamentals'. Besides militancy, Fundamentalists were a coalition of evangelical Protestants bound together by revivalism, premillennialism, inerrancy, Victorian morality and Scottish Common Sense philosophy. It derived its energy from the crisis facing civilisation which had found its sharpest focus in the First World War. Its mindset was an anti-mindset. It was anti-modernism, anti-evolution, anti-socialism and anti-Catholic. Fundamentalists were opposed to modernism which sought to adjust the outward forms of Christianity to the contemporary world. Modernists stressed religious experience, rather than truth and the immanence of God rather than his transcendence. They made use of modern science, biblical criticism and social sciences. And they were optimistic in their view of history. A particular symbol of such liberal trends was to be found in their acceptance of evolution.

W. B. Riley called together a World's Christian Fundamentals Association in 1919 and, the next year, fundamentalists in the Northern Baptist Convention called a conference to oppose liberal trends within that denomination. It was the first of many conflicts which arose within northern denominations, leading to splits and the adoption, by fundamentalists, of separatism as a distinctive mark. H. E. Fosdick, America's most famous preacher at the time, appealed for tolerance in a sermon, preached in 1922, entitled, 'Shall the Fundamentalists win?' But the conflicts went on. The most prominent Northern spokesman for the fundamentalists was the Presbyterian, J. Gresham Machen, of Princeton, who waded into the debate with a book called *Christianity and Liberalism* (1923). In it he argued that liberals denied the basic truths of Christianity and therefore could not claim the title 'Christian'. As a matter of integrity, therefore, they should leave the church to found their own religion. It was, however, Machen who was to move, not the liberals. He left Princeton in 1929 to found Westminster Seminary.

The chief evangelist of the time was Billy Sunday. Sensational in style, black and white in preaching, strong in his denunciation of sin and concerned about reform of a limited kind, he became fundamentalism's representative revivalist.[25] Raised in poor rural surroundings, Sunday struggled from insecurity all his life. He was a converted baseball star who served with the YMCA in Chicago and then underwent an apprenticeship as an evangelist with J. Wilbur Chapman before striking out on his own in 1896. After 1908 he rose to become a great urban evangelist and friend of the rich and famous. It is estimated that a million people 'hit the trail' during his campaigns. (The use of the phrase 'hitting the sawdust trail' to describe those who came forward to shake his hand as a sign of their desire to follow Christ was doubly apt. The floors of the tabernacles Sunday used for his mission were covered in sawdust. But the phrase also referred to the practice of lumberjacks who, on entering a dense forest, would lay a sawdust trail in order that they might find their way to the light once again. Thus it provided a potent picture of the meaning of conversion.) After 1921 fame and fortune took its toll on Billy Sunday who not only declined in spiritual effectiveness but suffered from family tragedy and the embarrassment of his sons' behaviour.

Fundamentalism was more at home in the South where conservatism dominated, and it was there that it eventually settled. In that region it did not take the form of denominational divisions but instead channelled its energies into opposing evolution and all that it stood for. The conflict came to its peak in 1925 in the famous Scopes' Trial, held in Dayton, Tennessee. John Scopes was a young teacher brought to trial for teaching biological evolution, despite state laws forbidding him to do so. The trial became the most celebrated event in the fundamentalist–modernist controversy because Scopes was defended by Clarence Darrow, a flamboyant trial lawyer and agnostic, and prosecuted by William Jennings Bryan, a populist Democrat and three-times Presidential candidate. Bryan saw evolution as a threat to the ethical foundation of the United

States, as well as undermining the Bible and argued that it had given rise to militarism in Germany.

At the climax of the trial Darrow put Bryan in the witness stand to question him as an expert witness on the Bible. Bryan was made to look ridiculous and fundamentalism revealed as narrow, ignorant, bigoted and simply unequal to the modern world. The hoped-for victory against Scopes turned into a rout for fundamentalism.

Fundamentalism's last major onslaught was to mount opposition to Al Smith, a Catholic, who stood as a Presidential Candidate for the Democrats in 1928. But it was a spent force.

In the 1930s the willingness of fundamentalists to remain in denominations which embraced modernists was considered tantamount to promoting modernism. So the call for separation arose. In the north the General Association of Regular Baptists was formed and the Orthodox Presbyterian and Bible Presbyterian churches were formed. In the south a more solid platform was given to fundamentalism by the Southern Baptists and the Lutheran Missouri-Synod which were already separatist in perspective. From then on fundamentalism went quiet for a little while, only to re-emerge in different guises later.

Fundamentalism was essentially an American phenomenon. England was not amenable to it. England, a more compact nation, had no experience of the values and place of settled inhabitants being threatened by successive waves of immigration. It was this displacement which Marsden believes gave rise to fundamentalism.[26] English society was based on Christendom of a broad and tolerant kind. Its established church was inclusivist. Revivalism had never triumphed in the UK in the way it did in America, and was not, therefore, under threat as in America. The UK had a gradually developing constitution whereas in the USA constitutional changes had been radical, dramatic and recent. The sharp polarities accepted by fundamentalists, therefore, did not have the same appeal to the British mind.

Evangelicalism: realignment and resurgence

NEW EVANGELICALISM

The word 'evangelicalism' was not much used during the 1930s. But all the time great energies were being poured into the construction of a network which was going to lead to its realignment and eventual resurgence. It was the way the fundamentalists coped with the defeat which had been inflicted on them by the Scopes trial. They channelled their dynamism into the establishment of Bible churches, schools and evangelistic agencies. They largely side-tracked the main denominations, of which they were suspicious, and built their own institutions. Around the institutions grew a sub-culture which taught its own ethical norms, provided comprehensive social life, encouraged busy activism, and trusted in the Bible.

The signs of this life could be seen in the establishment of radio programmes. By 1931, the *Sunday School Times* listed 100 programmes and 70 broadcasters. Moody Bible Institute's broadcasts received 20,000 letters in response daily.[27] Fundamentalists were not always against the modern world. They were quite capable of using it, especially its technology, when it suited their ends. Head and shoulders above others stood Charles Fuller, who started broad-casting in southern California in 1931 and was nationally networked from 1938. It propelled him into stardom as a revivalist and led to major meetings in Boston in 1941. Confidence began to grow and the old insular and defensive fundamentalism began to give way to a greater sense of openness and a keen sense of expectation.

The 1940s saw a number of crucial developments. In 1942 a National Association of Evangelicals was formed 'to promote evangelism' and to overcome divisions. Led by Harold J. Ockenga, of Park Street Congregational Church, Boston, and other non-separatist followers of Gresham Machen, it was formed in the face of the more fundamentalist and negative-orientated group, The American Council of Christian Churches, founded by Carl MacIntyre the previous year. The Southern Baptists never joined the NAE, viewing the word 'evangelical' as Yankee terminology. Even so, it became a major meeting place for evangelicals.

Youth for Christ was born in 1945 and met with a phenomenal success. It grew from 300 centres to 900, with a matching increase in the number of young people being reached from 300,000 to one million, in its first year. Among its earliest staff members was a young evangelist called Billy Graham. Turning international in 1946, within two years it was established in forty-nine nations. Its work received the imprimatur of William Randolph Hearst whose decision to 'puff YFC' in his newspapers greatly aided it.

In 1947 two significant things happened. Carl Henry, destined to become the theologian of the new evangelicalism, published *The Uneasy Conscience of Modern Fundamentalism*. It symbolized the rediscovery of the world and a fresh engagement with culture and society by evangelicals. Rigid fundamentalism and premillennialism was proving unsuitable for the task of reconstruction in post World War America.

Charles Fuller also established Fuller Theological Seminary that year, whose subsequent history was to be closely intertwined with developments in evangelicalism and to capture them in microcosm. Fuller himself desired to stay in the background of the new school and defer to Harold Ockenga's leadership. Ockenga, the school's President, wanted the school to be a 'force for renewal and broadening of fundamentalism and evangelicalism.'[28] Broader in sympathies than Charles Fuller, Ockenga shunned a separatist line and had a desire to see evangelicalism becoming an influential voice within the denominations once more as well as a respected voice in the world of academia.

Tensions between old-style separatist fundamentalism and new-style conservative evangelicalism, which was neither separatist nor closed to the world, were manifold. Fuller experienced the full force of them throughout its early years which were marked by many painful episodes. The seminary occupied an uncomfortable position. Suspected by fundamentalists for deviating from the faith, it was equally suspected by the denominations for being divisive. But, in spite of the problems, 'the new evangelicalism,' as it came to be called, was getting a grip both there and elsewhere.

Billy Graham was to play a crucial role in it becoming established. Throughout the forties and fifties he had been rising in status as an evangelist. He was very much in the tradition of older revivalists but was free from the eccentricities which marked some of his predecessors, like Billy Sunday, for example. He cultivated political contacts and business support and, in 1956, was instrumental in the launching of *Christianity Today* which was to prove a key organ for the dissemination of new evangelical views. He was also on record as saying that the feuds and divisions of fundamentalism were the reason for the lack of revival.

In preparation for the New York Crusade, to be held in 1957, Billy Graham decided to aim for ecumenical co-operation. It meant that enquirers would be sent back to their own churches, whatever their theological complexion, and not referred only to fundamentalist or evangelical churches. Fundamentalism rallied its waning strength in protest. The decision caused a parting of the ways. Evangelicalism and fundamentalism separated.

New evangelicalism had no clear identity and for many years adolescent tensions over the boundary markings existed. Many who wanted to identify with it still had a fundamentalist mentality with opposition to communism, with adoption of certain economic views and suspicion of scholarship. Carl Henry, for example, was too progressive for some and did not remain as Editor of *Christianity Today* because his views over Vietnam were not sufficiently militant. On the other hand his successor and former colleague at Fuller, Harold Lindsell, launched a blistering attack on the path taken away from inerrancy by seminaries, like Fuller, in his *Battle for the Bible*, published in 1976. It was a battle soon to spread to the Southern Baptists and affect their life for a decade or more.

RECENT DEVELOPMENTS

For all its success, which was great, evangelicalism during the 1970s experienced a growing fragmentation. Some became more serious about a commitment to the world and adopted radical forms of discipleship. The best known is the Sojourners Community in Washington, led by Jim Wallis, which engaged in a major critique of American society and of theological positions which were politically conservative. Others, like the 'orthodox evangelicals' who met and issued the Chicago Declaration in 1977, rediscovered their lost roots in catholicity, the creeds, church authority, sacraments and ecumenism. They called for these things to be put back high on the evangelical agenda together with a commitment to develop a holistic approach to salvation.[29]

The late seventies saw the mirror-opposite of Sojourners springing into prominence once more. The rise of the New Christian Right,[30] under the leadership of Jerry Falwell and Pat Robertson, was really a version of old fundamentalism on the march again. Essentially a Southern movement, it sought to preserve values which were fast disappearing and claimed to have a vision of a Christian America. But its vision was truncated and it sought to defeat the reigning philosophy of 'secular humanism', as the New Christian Right termed it, on a narrow platform of family issues, school prayer, anti-homosexuality, anti-communism and anti-abortion. Although not a broadly-based evangelical movement, it gained much support from the evangelical constituency and spoke a similar language. Its identification with televangelists further served to cause many to confuse the two.

Most evangelicals did what they had always done. They poured their energies into mission. Campus Crusade for Christ was formed in 1951 by Bill Bright, an erstwhile student of Fuller who did not stay to complete the course because souls needed saving. It absorbed the talents and energies of thousands of evangelicals in the sixties and seventies, as did evangelistic missions, revival campaigns, foreign missions and, latterly, aid and development agencies.

The charismatic movement[31] came to birth in 1960 in St Mark's Episcopal Church, Van Nuys, California, where its rector, Dennis Bennett, and many of its communicants were baptised in the Holy Spirit. It spread quickly, partly because of having several articulate advocates, partly because of its fit with contemporary culture. In spite of opposition from some authorities it rapidly entered mainstream Christianity and embraced most denominations, including the Roman Catholics, although it was resisted by the Southern Baptists and Lutheran-Church, Missouri Synod. It manifested itself in many different forms. Some laid stress on authority and shepherding in order to encourage the growth of discipleship. Others dissociated themselves from such ideas. A particular development, from 1983 onwards, which has had widespread implications, is the so-called, 'third wave', associated with John Wimber of Vineyard Fellowship, and Peter Wagner of Fuller's Church Growth School. The 'third wave' derives its name from being the third wave of the movement of the Holy Spirit in the twentieth century after Pentecostalism (the first wave) and the charismatic movement (the second wave).

Evangelicals have been much affected by the charismatic movement in its various forms but have not always embraced it easily. The involvement of the Roman Catholics, the apparent devaluing of doctrine in favour of experience and the preference for the present word of God, as in prophecy or words of knowledge, as opposed to the written word of God, as in Scripture, have made many evangelicals cautious. Even so, the evangelical subculture has been far from insulated from the charismatic movement and its ideas have become popular through its books, cassettes, conferences and TV programmes. The 'third wave' has had a special appeal to evangelicals since it originated in the scholarly environment of Fuller Seminary and made evangelism and church growth its central concern.

Evangelicalism has inevitably been affected by other changes in its environment. The careful researches of James Davison Hunter[32] show how flexible and adaptable a movement evangelicalism is, whatever its public rhetoric might say. Although evangelicalism is to be found in those sections of society which are most distant from the forces of modernity, nevertheless, it has accommodated to the pressures of modernity. Evangelicalism has learned to market its message in a way which is appropriate to contemporary society. The message has been codified into sound bites; conversion has been systematized into easy steps; discipleship has been reduced to simple laws and formulae and its spreading of the gospel has become highly organized and technological. Its message has toned down and become more civil with its most offensive elements being qualified. People may still be told that they are sinners on the way to hell, but they will be told in a friendly manner and with a warm smile. It is a far cry from Edwards's famous sermon in 1841.

Perhaps the most significant change has been the way in which evangelicalism has become subjectivized. The bookstores are full of shelves on how to discover oneself, to find happiness, to fulfil one's potential, to achieve emotional balance, to overcome depression (in three easy steps), to release inner healing, to acquire psychological health, and so on. A recent offering by Pat Robertson, for example, is entitled, *The Secret Kingdom: Your Path to Peace, Love and Financial Security.* Books on doctrine are hard to find! Books on mission and service are not so common. It's a long way from the old pietist and puritan spirituality in which evangelicalism was born. Premillennial works are still popular. Hal Lindsay's, *Late Great Planet Earth*, the best-selling paperback of the 70s, is evidence of that. But it underlines the fact that evangelical faith is privately engaging but publicly irrelevant.

Hunter followed up his initial study with an investigation into the views of the coming generation of evangelicals who were to be found in evangelical colleges and seminaries.[33] It revealed further elements of accommodation to modernity. Theology was emerging from its ghetto and students were becoming less demanding in what they expected of the Bible. Its objective authority was being replaced by subjective perspectives. The traditional view of the family, much paraded by popular evangelical speakers and authors, actually gained little support from the students.

The traditional commitment to the Protestant work ethic, with its overtones of self-discipline and success, was also under threat. Quality of life, leisure, relations and family were all seen as more important, with a consequent shift towards the values of self-expression and self-fulfilment. Politically, the views of the Moral Majority did not receive widespread support because they were considered to have breached the rules of the civil society by demonstrating intolerance and refusing to accept a limited place for religion in a modern democratic state. Wither the vision of a Christian nation?

Higher education seems to have a major impact in eroding traditional evangelical views and since higher education is set to continue growing it is likely that the trend towards accommodation to modernity will also continue. Such a trend will not go unopposed, as it has never been unopposed in the past. Consequently, many to whom Hunter spoke envisaged that evangelicalism would suffer a division once again into separatist and moderate camps. History would repeat itself. Hunter's pessimistic conclusion was:

> Whether or not there is a split, American evangelicalism seems to face an uncertain future, a future as ambivalent as its own present nature. It is hardly imaginable that conservative Protestantism will disappear, but what it will look like and the degree of resemblance it will have to what previous generations have taken as the true heritage of Christianity and how large it will become demographically are all unknown. While no one can predict with any certainty, the prospects are not bright.[34]

There have been periods when American evangelicalism saw the glory, not only of the coming King, but of the coming of His kingdom on earth. Though the strength and buoyancy of the evangelical subculture is beyond question it is also true that the evangelical vision is now fragmented with the myriad parties of evangelicals seeing their own partial vision through their own chosen spectacles. Whether modernity is a lens that will bring the vision into sharper focus, or blur it, is an open question yet to be determined.

PART TWO

DOCTRINES

5

THE BIBLE TELLS ME SO

Evangelicals and the Bible

The most characteristic feature of evangelicalism is the place it gives to the Bible. Its supreme symbol mid-century was Billy Graham, preaching to thousands, declaring, 'The Bible says . . .' The backbone of the evangelical world is the multitudinous Bible Schools and Colleges. The quintessence of evangelical leisure is attendance at a Bible Conference. The lifeblood of evangelical publishing is the Bible itself, or Bible commentaries. And much internal energy is consumed on debates about the Bible.

Evangelicals see the Bible as the supreme authority for all matters concerning life and faith; what they are to believe and how they are to behave. For them, 'It is the Bible, the whole Bible and nothing but the Bible.'[1]

Their concentration on the Bible, however, is often misunderstood and misrepresented. The mistaken impression arises partly because evangelicalism and fundamentalism are lumped together without distinction and partly because popular evangelical use of the Bible sometimes invites it. There have been times when evangelical preachers have been able to score high points with their audiences by pouring scorn on modern scholars and asserting, 'The Bible says it, so I believe it.' Naive proof-texting is not unknown!

For all the bravado about taking the Bible at face value, not even the most narrow evangelical is a literalist. None, to my knowledge, would want to defend the three-decker view of the universe with the solar system revolving around planet earth. None are incapable of appreciating the use of metaphor and simile in the Psalms, or, that the human terms used to describe God are not intended literally. What really characterizes evangelicalism is not that they are literalists but that they seek to go for the plain, natural interpretation of the Bible. So, there is no difficulty in understanding parables as stories, but other narratives which give the impression of being fact, rather than fiction, are read as historical events. The most celebrated illustration of this is the resurrection of Jesus Christ. There is not the slightest indication that it was a story invented to keep his memory and ideals alive. On the contrary the accounts breathe the atmosphere, both in general and in detail, that here was something which happened. So, evangelicals believe it to be an actual event, even if it is one on a different level than others.

Evangelicals are further misrepresented as believing in the dictation theory of inspiration; that is, that God dictated the Bible to its various authors as we might dictate to a dictaphone or put words into a word processor. This theory guarantees the accuracy of the Bible as divine revelation but denies any real place to its human authors. If this view ever was propounded, it is certainly not current amongst today's evangelicals. The view that the Bible is inerrant, that is, without any error on any issue, however, does command support among evangelicals but not universally. It is a much debated issue as we shall see.

What, then, do evangelicals believe about the Bible? What does their history suggest is an evangelical position on the Bible? Where are they united and where are they in debate with one another?

Early foundations

Evangelical attitudes to the Bible are built on the foundations laid by Martin Luther in the Reformation. The principle of *sola scriptura*, which he asserted, made the Bible the supreme authority in the church and the determining norm by which the traditions of the church or the decrees of Popes and councils should be tested. Luther found in the Bible the resolution to his own spiritual struggle and so used it as an effective weapon when on trial. Consequently, he devoted his life to careful study of Scripture. He believed it to be inspired, to have a divine origin and to be free from error. It was the Bible that set people free from the illegitimate and oppressive powers of church and tradition.

This attitude to the Bible entered the bloodstream of evangelicalism. John Wesley, for example, wanted to be known as 'a man of one book'. The Bible was, for him, 'the only standard of truth', 'the Christian rule of right and wrong' and 'the touchstone by which Christians examine all, real or supposed, revelations'. He believed it to be the 'Word of the living God', inspired in the fullest sense. They were words taught by the Holy Spirit. 'How high a regard ought we, then, to retain for them?' He could do no other than 'declare just what I find in the book.'[2]

Another significant voice in the formation of the evangelical attitude to the Bible was that of Charles Simeon of Cambridge.[3] He had a high view of Scripture and its inspiration, but not a naive one. Whilst the Bible was for him, the 'Oracles of God' or the 'Word of

God', none the less, he was not what we today would call an inerrantist, for he wrote, 'No error in doctrine or other important matter is allowed; yet there are inexactnesses in reference to philosophical and scientific matters, because of its popular style . . .' There were things which he could not reconcile and issues where not all questions would be resolved. There were also passages where the language was stretched and not to be taken literally. None of this gives us any ground for questioning Simeon's evangelical integrity. Rather, we must note, that inerrancy was not a test of the faith in Simeon's day.

We owe to Simeon the style of biblical exposition which has become characteristic of evangelicalism. He shunned 'systems', such as Calvinism or Arminianism, which wanted to impose certain interpretations on a passage of Scripture and place it in a strait-jacket. He wrote, 'My endeavour is to bring out of Scripture what is there and not to thrust in what I think might be there.' He explained, 'My mode of interpreting Scripture is this. I bring to it no predilections whatever . . . I never wish to find any particular truth in any particular passage. I am willing that every part of God's blessed word should speak exactly what it was intended to speak, without adding any single iota to it, or taking from it the smallest particle of its legitimate import.' So he took each passage and expounded it as it stood. If one passage suggested a Calvinist perspective and another an Arminian, so be it. Apparent contradictions, like the parts of a watch that appeared to be working against one another, would, he believed, be found actually to be working to a common purpose.

Luther, Wesley and Simeon lived in the days before modern biblical scholarship raised questions which led to divergences appearing among evangelicals in their approach to the Bible and to the hardening of attitudes which has marred contemporary evangelicalism. But they laid the foundations. Evangelicals have a high view of Scripture as the supreme rule for life and faith. They believe it to be inspired and free from any error regarding doctrine and faith. They argue that it should be interpreted plainly and above all, that it should be obeyed.

Inspiration and authority

What is meant when the Bible is said to be 'inspired'? Why is it that the Bible is granted such authority? The two questions are inextricably linked.

The authority of the Bible lies in its inspiration by God. The word 'inspiration' here is used in a particular sense. It is not used in the popular sense in which a painting or piece of music might be said to be 'inspired', but to mean, 'a supernatural, providential influence of God's Holy Spirit upon the authors (of the Bible) which caused them to write what He wished to be written for the communication of revealed truth to others.'[4] The Bible, therefore, is a unique revelation of God and consequently is often called 'the Word of God'.

THE ARGUMENT FOR INSPIRATION

Inspiration cannot be proved. Ultimately it is a matter of faith. But the Bible claims it for itself and the case can be set out.

In the Old Testament, the prophets confidently claimed to be speaking the words of God. Jeremiah, for example, says of his call, 'Then the Lord reached out His hand and touched my mouth and said to me, "Now, I have put My words in your mouth" ' (Jeremiah 1:9). Amos and others constantly used the phrase 'This is what the Lord says' (1:1,3,6,9,11,13; 2:1, etc.) of their own words without any embarrassment. The Jews subsequently affirmed their words were indeed the words of God and enshrined them in the canon of Scripture.

Jesus, Himself, granted authority to the Old Testament. He used it extensively in His own life, as for example in resisting the temptations, in His teaching and in explaining His own ministry. He asserted that 'the Scripture cannot be broken' (John 10:35) and was acutely aware that they would be accurately fulfilled (Matthew 26:54). Its words were the words of God (Matthew 19:5). Throughout, Jesus demonstrates a loyalty to the Old Testament. He goes beyond it but never against it. Consequently, in John Stott's words, 'Submission to Scripture is for us evangelicals a sign of our submission to Christ, a test of our loyalty to Him. We find it extremely impressive that our incarnate Lord, whose own authority amazed His contemporaries, should have subordinated Himself to the authority of the Old Testament Scriptures as He did, regarding them as His Father's written word.'[5]

Some seek to argue that Christians should look to Jesus as their authority and not to the Bible; to the living word, not the written word. But this is to drive a false wedge between Jesus and the Bible as His own attitude to the Old Testament makes clear. To grant Him authority is to grant the Scripture authority. Even so, the warning has merit. Bernard Ramm cautions, 'The temptation of biblicism is that it can speak of the inspiration of the Scriptures apart from the Lord they enshrine ... There can be no formal doctrine of inspiration; there can only be a Christ-centred doctrine of inspiration.'[6]

In the rest of the New Testament further support is found for granting the Bible inspiration and authority. The early preachers, for example, attributed the sayings of people in the Old Testament to God (Acts 4:2; 28:25; Hebrews 1:5-8,10 and 13). Added to this are the direct claims of inspiration to be found in 2 Timothy 3:16 and 2 Peter 1:21, which stress not so much the resulting truth of the Scripture but its adequacy to achieve God's intended purpose.

All this is very well, but, of course, it only applies to the Old Testament. But the same factors are found in the New Testament. The words of Jesus were granted authority by the early Christians (1 Corinthians 9:14; 11:23-25) and would obviously not be accorded a lesser authority than those of the Old Testament.

The apostles were no less conscious of writing or speaking the words of God than the Old Testament prophets (1 Corinthians 7:10,12,40; 2 Corinthians 13:3; Ephesians 2:20). When their message was received they rejoiced, as at Thessalonica, that people 'accepted it not as the word of men, but as it actually is, the word of God . . .' (1 Thessalonians 2:13). They reveal evidence, too, that their own writings were being put on the same level as the Old Testament Scriptures (2 Peter 3:16).

The church later confirmed their understanding by collecting the books and letters which we now have as the New Testament and placing them in the canon, alongside the Old.

THE METHOD OF INSPIRATION

So the claim to inspiration is clear, but what of the method? The question which so fascinates us is one on which the Bible itself is silent. It is easy to understand why the question should be asked since it relates to how much of the Bible can be granted authority and how accurate it is.

The simplest solution is to say that God must have dictated the Bible using the human authors as his transcribers, putting their own mental activity into suspension while the process happened. But that clearly is doubtful. The variety of style in the books of the Bible is, alone, sufficient to say that the writer's contribution cannot be limited to being a mere scribe. The books are stamped with differences which clearly arise from the varying personalities and creative gifts of the people who lie behind them. Add to this contemporary views that many books, as they have come down to us, are the end product of an editorial process and the dictation theory is all but sunk. But, as J. I. Packer has written, the theory 'is a man of straw. It is safe to say that no Protestant theologian from the Reformation till now, has ever held it; and certainly modern evangelicals do not hold it.'[7]

If that view is rejected, the fear is that God must, therefore, have in some way accommodated the revelation of his truth to the limits and sinfulness of human authors with the result that his words must have suffered in their transmission and so not be wholly trustworthy. But it is not necessary to let the pendulum swing from shallow dictation theories to despairing accommodation theories. There are other suggestions.

One suggestion is that inspiration takes the form of 'concursive action'.[8] In this view, human action and the working of the Holy Spirit coincide. It is a form of the doctrine of providence. We often explain things from two complementary viewpoints without finding it necessary to choose between them. Creation can be explained both as God's handiwork and from a scientific perspective. Sanctification is both the work of the Holy Spirit in us and a result of our own wills and actions. We affirm both the fully divine and fully human natures of Christ. So, too, Scripture can be both divinely inspired and humanly authored. God worked in and through human writers to cause his revelation to be recorded faithfully, capitalizing on, rather than overriding, their setting, skills and personalities, which were God-given, in any case.

No explanation is free from problems. Other evangelical writers have approached the subject differently. William Abraham,[9] for example, argues that the clue lies in our normal use of the word 'inspired'. So, just as a great teacher inspires a pupil to produce work that would have been impossible without his or her creative guidance, so God inspired the authors and compilers of Scripture. Since God, who initiated the process, is omniscient and infallible it follows that writings themselves will partake of that same character. But to record just one criticism of this view, it builds its case on the English meaning of 'inspiration' rather than its original biblical meaning of the word, that of 'God-breathed', which is more potent.

The issue of how Scripture was inspired is unlikely to be resolved to everyone's satisfaction. That it was inspired is the important point, rather than how. Evangelicals hold to the Bible both as a fully divine book and a fully human book. God has spoken and revealed himself in it to his world. At the same time human authors have written and compiled it, people who have left their stamp on it, in the reflection of their own personalities, writing skills and cultural contexts.

Infallibility and inerrancy

Two words much associated with evangelical views of the Bible are 'infallibility' and 'inerrancy'. Infallibility means that it is utterly reliable and trustworthy, and free from misleading or inaccurate contents. Inerrancy sharpens the focus of infallibility and means that it is without error in every detail and is entirely trustworthy in all its assertions, not just its teaching regarding faith, but in statements of history, geography, philosophy and other matters as well. Sometimes the phrase 'plenary verbal inspiration' is used, meaning that all its actual words are fully inspired and consequently the very words of God.

Infallibility and inerrancy are both logical deductions from inspiration. If the Bible is inspired by a God who is incapable of lying, altogether trustworthy and true, then his revelation must partake of the same character.

At first glance it would seem that that was the position adopted by older evangelicals. John Wesley said, 'If there be any mistakes in the Bible, there may well be a thousand. If one falsehood is in that book, it did not come from the God of truth.'[10] Henry Venn spoke, in 1763, of the Bible as 'the infallible world of God' and Edward Bickersteth wrote, 'The Bible is altogether TRUE.'[11] Apparently they believed the Bible to be utterly true not only in matters of faith and doctrine but on every issue and in every detail. But not all evangelicals shared that view. Simeon, for example, as we have seen, was quite prepared to grant that there were errors in the Bible without jeopardizing his belief in its full inspiration. The errors, such as they were, were only incidental. No matter of doctrine or substance depended on them. Henry Martyn believed the sense of Scripture to be inspired but not necessarily its words. But this did not prevent him from spending a life-time translating it into Persian.

It was only later that the issue was brought into sharper focus because of the changing direction both of thought and of opposition to the gospel. Bebbington[12] attributes the origin of more defined views of inerrancy to Robert Haldane who resisted the Romantic influences of his day, with their woollier views of inspiration and, in his book *The Evidence and Authority of Divine Revelation* (1816), wrote that the Bible made 'a claim to infallibility and inspiration'. This viewpoint was immediately put to the test in a controversy with the fledgling British and Foreign Bible Society who included the Apocrypha in some of their editions. To Haldane, this was to adulterate the pure word of God. A split occurred, ensuring that the matter of the infallibility of Scripture was placed higher on the evangelicals' agenda.

Throughout the nineteenth century the doctrine of the infallibility and the verbal inspiration gathered momentum. It was a common sense view of the Bible, based on the scientific outlook of Bacon and Newton. It fortified faith in the Bible against Enlightenment attacks and Romantic devaluations. It was aided by

an association with premillennialism which depended on being able
to see the Bible as an encyclopedia of facts in order to say what was
to happen next. By the end of the century C. H. Spurgeon was
asserting that, 'the plenary verbal inspiration of the Holy Scripture
is a fact and not a hypothesis.' The position was championed at
Princeton Seminary and was set out in elaborate and painstaking
detail by one of their most eminent scholars, B. B. Warfield.

THE PROBLEM OF INERRANCY

Whilst evangelicals have always been united about the fullest
inspiration of scripture and in the assertion that the Bible is without
error in all that it affirms and teaches, they have never been united
about the word 'inerrancy'. F. B. Meyer and J. C. Ryle, redoubtable
evangelical champions who believed in the verbal inspiration of
Scripture, stopped short of asserting its inerrancy. Other British
evangelical leaders, like, W. H. Griffith Thomas, G. T. Manley and
T. C. Hammond, from earlier this century, also refused to assent to
it, finding it hard to admit to no errors in the biblical text.[13] The
Doctrinal Basis of UCCF, formerly Inter-Varsity Fellowship, which
is often considered the touchstone of evangelical orthodoxy, chooses
the word 'infallibility' but not 'inerrancy'.

The theory of inerrancy is regularly advocated with vigour. Edward
Young wrote *Thy Word is Truth*, in 1957. Harold Lindsell wrote *The
Battle for the Bible*, in 1976, and the *Chicago Statement on Biblical
Inerrancy* was published in 1978 and gave rise to a number of
volumes of exposition and defence. Lindsell proposed that only
those who believed in inerrancy were entitled to claim to be
evangelicals. But the evidence would dispute such a narrow
definition. The claim seems only to have been made in recent
decades and even those, like Carl Henry, who believe in inerrancy,
reject such a conclusion. Evangelicals have not tended to rally
around inerrancy. Indeed, the rallying points have often been those
where the practical use of the Bible has been uppermost, like
Keswick, rather than where its precise status has been under
scrutiny.

Why have many been unhappy with inerrancy, in spite of it
seeming to be a simple logical deduction from a high view of
inspiration? There are many reasons. Stott,[14] who in the end accepts
the word, dislikes it because it is a negative, or more precisely, a
double-negative, word. He would prefer the use of a positive word like
'trustworthy' or 'true'. Others argue that 'inerrancy' is too flat a word
to be useful. Howard Marshall[15] says that such a word correctly
applies to factual statements but that the Bible is composed of far
more than factual statements and straight propositions. It includes,

for example, a great variety of forms of language, opinions voiced by human beings, truth that applies at different times and in different ways. God communicates in a variety of verbal ways, not simply through propositions.

Still others struggle with alleged discrepancies or mistakes in the Bible. This has led some to argue for limited inerrancy: that is, they concede that the Bible may not be without error in matters of history, literature, philosophy or science whilst maintaining it is inerrant in matters of faith. Full-blown inerrantists, however, have a different way of handling such problems. Inerrancy applies not to the text as we have it but to the original autographed manuscripts. They allow that some errors may have crept in during the process of transmission. They spend a good deal of time harmonizing the alleged discrepancies and believe that further research may well eradicate the problems, as past research has often done.

Perhaps the major problem with the word 'inerrancy' is that it suggests we are trying to impose on Scripture a standard of precisions which, whilst fully understood and accepted in our day, would not have made sense in the Bible's own day. It is an anachronistic idea arising out of a particular stage of intellectual history, with its penchant for historical accuracy and scientific exactness.

The Bible used to be the standard around which evangelicals united. The pity of the inerrancy debate is that the Bible has now become the battlefield where evangelicals have become divided. Energies have been sapped and vigorous efforts which should have channelled into proclaiming the message of the Bible have been siphoned off into defending positions on the evangelical spectrum of orthodoxy.

Biblical Criticism

A related area, and one which drove some evangelicals into the arms of inerrancy, is that of biblical criticism, as the modern scholarly approach to the Bible is called. Older evangelicals were capable of holding to firm but imprecise statements about the authority and truthfulness of the Bible because they did not face the questions imposed by this modern development.

In the second half of the nineteenth century people began to study the Bible in a new way. Applying techniques they might use on other literature, and therefore seeming to degrade the unique status of the Bible, they began to work on the numerous manuscripts to establish the original wording; to investigate the sources which lay behind the biblical books; to question received wisdom about their date and authorship and to look more closely at some of its historical claims and discrepancies. Allied, as the movement was, to rationalistic philosophy which was sceptical about supernaturalism, the conclusions reached were often devastating to the traditional view of the Bible and undermined its teaching.

Early publications by biblical critics displayed a low view of inspiration. They drove a wedge between the Jesus of the Gospel, who was portrayed in very human terms, and the religion of Paul. The Pentateuch, far from being written by Moses, was a patchwork quilt of different sources, all of which had their own concerns, woven together at a much later date and containing a good deal of myth. Later the issues under scrutiny became extensive and included questions about the historicity of Jonah, the date of Daniel and whether Isaiah was written by more than one author. The storm centres tended to be in the Old Testament, although some viewed the supernatural elements of the New Testament with scepticism from the beginning. Subsequent generations began to raise questions about how much of Jesus's words in the gospels actually came from him and questioned the authenticity of the authorship of several New Testament letters. The Bible seemed full of holes.

The reaction to biblical criticism was varied from the outrightly hostile to the cautiously accepting. Many evangelicals would have adopted D. L. Moody's pragmatic approach. He thought it was a waste of time and asked the biblical scholar George Adam Smith, 'Why talk of two Isaiahs when most people don't know of one?'[16] Others showed a more serious engagement with it.

THE BRITISH RESPONSE

The reaction to biblical criticism differed somewhat on either side of the Atlantic. Initially, evangelicals in Britain showed a negative reaction to views that appeared to undermine the Bible's inspiration. *Essays and Reviews* (1860) introduced some of the modern German views and was received negatively. W. Robertson Smith, of the Church of Scotland, was dismissed from his post as a Professor of Hebrew and Old Testament in 1881 for espousing modern views. C. H. Spurgeon weighed in to the attack and never accepted the validity of a critical approach to the Bible. Many Baptists followed his lead.

But on the whole there was soon a much more open approach than in the USA.[17] Henry Wace, for example, expressed a guarded optimism about biblical criticism in 1903. The majority of British contributors to *The Fundamentals* spoke of biblical criticism as legitimate and necessary, although Sir Robert Anderson thought it was a clear choice between Christ and criticism. In 1925, a number of Anglican Evangelicals published a book called *Evangelicalism* which included contributions from G. T. Manley and T. C. Hammond, which spoke of the value of the new movement. If the results of Biblical criticism were not always persuasive, evangelicals did not always feel threatened by them either.

How was it that British evangelical views were so amenable? Chief among the reasons was that British criticism was far more moderate than its American counterpart. New Testament scholars like J. B. Lightfoot, F. J. A. Hort and B. F. Wescott were using criticism to defend the trustworthiness of the Bible's account of the early church and to vindicate it against the charges coming from Germany. Evangelicals could therefore see it as a useful tool.[18] Unbelieving scepticism was not a necessary component of rigorous biblical investigation. The instrument could be wielded without leading to destructive results. But there were a number of other factors as well. Evangelicals in Britain did not have a flat view of revelation and were already speaking of revelation in progressive terms. It enabled them to vindicate the unity of the Bible and overcome some of its apparent conflicts. With that was a much more accepting attitude towards evolution than in the USA. It was never the evangelical bogey that it became there. Evangelicals belonged to mixed denominations where 'pragmatic tolerance' was encouraged. And they saw the enemy, not as criticism so much as Deism and rationalism.

During the inter-war years little impact was made by evangelicals whose achievements in scholarship were modest. But in 1938 IVF established the Theological Students' Fellowship and, the next year, a Biblical Research Committee was set up, leading to the establishment of Tyndale House in 1943. The IVF encouraged scholars and scholarly evangelical publications, with *The New Bible Commentary* (1953) and the *Tyndale Commentaries* heading the list. A further reason for the more open approach to scholarship in Britain became evident in the post-war years. Most work was being done by people like F. F. Bruce, W. J. Martin, R. V. G. Tasker and others in university settings, and not in evangelical ghettos. The universities in Britain, although secularised, had not been subject to such rapid and advanced secularisation as those in the United States. With classical education as a background such scholars had particular approaches to questions of history and textual criticism and these often led to conservative, rather than radical, interpretations of the Bible. They were more free from the philosophical flights of fancy seen elsewhere.

THE AMERICAN RESPONSE

Mark Noll[19] has outlined evangelical attitudes to biblical criticism in the United States in the following terms. Between 1880 and 1900, evangelicals were equal partners with others in the academic market place. From 1900 to 1935, they retreated into a fortress of faith. It was the period when fundamentalism rose. The universities had been rapidly secularised, evolutionary teaching was rampant and evangelicals withdrew into their own separatist institutions. Little scholarship was undertaken, except at Princeton.

From 1935 to 1950 they slowly emerged from the ghetto and saw the value of a wider participation in the academic world. Some evangelicals undertook graduate programmes at secular universities and the Evangelical Theological Society (1949) was formed. From 1940 until 1975 they were finding strategies to put themselves back into the picture. Scholars of the stature of George Eldon Ladd and Bruce Metzger and E. Earl Ellis began to publish, and credible seminaries, like Fuller, were formed. A new engagement with the wider scholarly world and professional associations was underway.

THE CURRENT SCENE

From 1960 onwards evangelicals on both sides of the Atlantic were confronting the dilemmas which resulted from their success. Exposure to the wider scholarly world had led the next generation of scholars to challenge some traditional evangelical viewpoints, whilst asserting their faithfulness to the inspiration of scripture. Robert Gundry caused a stir in his commentary on Matthew when he attributed sections of the book to Matthew himself, albeit a divinely-inspired Matthew, rather than directly to Jesus. The same year, 1982, James Dunn raised serious questions about infallibility and inerrancy in *The Churchman* which jeopardized his membership of the Tyndale Fellowship. Bernard Ramm, who had done much to secure the post-war evangelical revival, pleaded that the full humanity of Scripture be accepted, including some errors. The *Word Bible Commentary*, a massive undertaking to express contemporary evangelical scholarship, which began publication in the early 1980s, contains many views on dating and authorship, literary form and editorial process which previous generations of evangelicals would have found objectionable.

It would seem that David Wright's plea, in reviewing James Barr's *Fundamentalism*, has become even more pressing. He wrote, 'One of the most urgent unfinished tasks is the elaboration of a satisfactory doctrine of Scripture for an era of biblical criticism . . . In particular . . . we have to work out what it means to be faithful at one and the same time both to the doctrinal approach to Scripture as the Word of God and to the historical treatment of Scripture as the words of men'.[20]

But whatever the disagreements among evangelicals, they are

bound together, as R. T. France has pointed out,[21] by three common statements:

1 Special revelation is necessary for a true knowledge of God
2 The Bible is the supreme and only sufficient locus of such revelation
3 The Bible is the inspired Word of God

These not only bind evangelicals together but at the same time they separate evangelicals by a great distance from many other scholars handling the Bible.

Interpretation

In practice, the sacred cows of evangelical loyalty to the Bible do not occupy today's evangelical scholars much. The goal posts have been moved and the current concern is with the interpretation of the Bible, rather than matters of 'introduction', that is, questions of authorship and date. Twenty years ago, Michael Green admitted that not too many evangelicals would worry about the authorship of the gospels and Hebrews or if John's Gospel and Revelation were said to be written by two different people, since these things were not claimed, at least unequivocally, in the text. Even that would have been giving away a lot for some. But he went on to comment that where a letter claims to be by Paul or Peter and scholarship was questioning that claim 'the question of truth was involved'. 'It does not', he wrote, 'seem likely that God should have used false claims in these documents as vehicles of his truth'. The arguments would have to be weighed carefully and, if deemed conclusive, would cause evangelicals to rethink. Either the documents should be excluded from the canon of Scripture, or, evangelicals would have to come to terms with the fact that God, odd as it may seem, used the practice of someone writing under a pseudonym to convey truth.[22]

Today, the pseudonymous nature or 2 Peter is accepted by many, and leading evangelical scholars argue that whether Peter actually wrote 2 Peter or not does not have a bearing on the authority of the message of 2 Peter. It is said that it would have been perfectly acceptable in the ancient world for someone to have attributed the letter to Peter, believing that they were being faithful to him, without in any sense being deceptive. (Practices have changed!) Free from secondary questions of introduction, which often put the evangelical scholar in a defensive position, he or she can now devote energies to unlocking the message of the Bible.[23]

But the question is, 'How?' Evangelicals have traditionally

affirmed a number of principles of interpretation:

1 The natural meaning of the words, in their historical,
   literary and cultural context is crucial to our understanding
   of the text;
2 The author's purpose in writing is determinative of its
   meaning;
3 Scripture must be used to interpret scripture, with obscure
   passages being illuminated by more straight-forward ones;
4 Scripture, for all its diversity, is a unity and finds its
   coherence in Christ;
5 We are dependent on the Holy Spirit for our understanding;
6 We must ask what application the text has for today;
7 We must make a response to it: it is a word addressed to us
   by God to be believed and obeyed.

All seemed simple. But then, in 1977, at the National Evangelical
Anglican Congress at Nottingham, evangelicals were introduced to
the discussion of hermeneutics which was taking place in the wider
intellectual world. Hermeneutics is the technical word for
interpretation.[24] The insight, new for many, was the idea that we do
not come to interpret the text in a neutral way. We are members of
a particular culture and that shapes the way we think and the
questions we are likely to ask. They may be very different from the
way the writers of the Bible thought or the questions they were
answering. So we must be careful to enter fully into the world of the
Bible and distance ourselves from it before we try to relate it to our
own world. Failure to do so will mean we always read the Bible
through our own spectacles, the spectacles we acquired in our
culture, denomination or group where we were nurtured as
Christians, and may fail to see its meaning or message at all.

  The issue touches a raw nerve for evangelicals who have always
thought that they were going for the obvious and natural
interpretation of Scripture. Some resist the idea as a red herring.
Others, however, have begun to engage with it seriously and none
more so than John Stott who, writing of our own cultural captivity
and the Bible's cultural conditioning, has said, 'The first step towards
the recovery of our own Christian integrity will be the humble
recognition that our own culture blinds, deafens and dopes us. We
neither see what we ought to see in Scripture, nor hear God's Word
as we should . . .'[25]

  The recognition of our own cultural conditioning raises immense
questions for scholars and ordinary evangelicals alike. How is one
to distinguish between the competing interpretations of Scripture

which are to be found in evangelical, feminist or liberation sections of the church? Does it not render all interpretations of scripture relative? How can one determine what parts of scripture were merely culturally conditioned or interpreted and what parts stand for all time, irrespective of culture? In fact, the path need not lead to a relativistic cul-de-sac and distinctions between what is culture-bound and what is truth for all cultures can be made. But it does lead to a search for more evangelical scholars who will engage with the Bible and contemporary culture in depth.

The wider hermeneutical discussion, in fact, is very relevant to evangelicals. It should renew the commitment, expressed by Charles Simeon, not to read anything into Scripture but rather to let it speak for itself. It should explain, at least in part, why evangelical interpretations of the Bible, over issues like the Second Coming, had differed down the years and enable us to look at those differences with fresh eyes. It should also warn us against some popular uses of the Bible which too readily impose a Christian interpretation on the Old Testament, before the Old Testament passage has been allowed to speak in its own context, or, which too readily impose a particular evangelical interpretation on the Bible before we have let the text speak for itself.

It is to the popular evangelical use of the Bible we now turn.

Popular evangelicalism and the Bible

Most evangelicals do not encounter the Bible in the world of the scholars and the finer points of debates about inspiration and inerrancy often pass them by. That does not mean that they are unaffected by them, nor that they refrain from asserting their strongly held opinions on the matter! Their encounter with the Bible is often through sermons, attendance at Bible conventions and through regular devotional reading. Here, too, a number of issues are raised.

BIBLIOLATRY
Evangelicals are often charged with bibliolatry, that is, idolising the Bible. Until the advent of the charismatic movement, it was sometimes said that the evangelical trinity was composed of the Father, the Son and the Holy Bible. Paul Holmer argues that in evangelicalism, 'instead of getting to know God, one tends to get to know the Bible.' And he complains, 'There is too much said about the Bible, almost as if the Bible cannot speak for itself and show one the Saviour without sundry helps.'[26]

There would seem to be plenty of evidence for the prosecution in devotional habits which lead many to read the Bible daily, to carry it around not only to meetings but to work, to resort to it frequently to settle matters in dispute by the deft quoting of a text and in the way that evangelicals spring eagerly to its defence when it, or their interpretation of it, is attacked.

It is true that care needs to be exercised, for loyalty to the Bible can easily become a substitute for loyalty to Christ. Evangelicals can become scribes who defend a text or lawyers who quibble over it, rather than disciples who imitate the Master. Unloving and un-Christlike attitudes are now unknown among those who revel in the Bible. Evangelicals must constantly remember the stricture of Jesus on the Pharisees, 'You diligently study the Scriptures because you think that by them you possess eternal life. These are the Scriptures that testify about me, yet you refuse to come to me to have life' (John 4:39–40).

But that is not the evangelical ideal, nor the reality as practised by millions. The Bible is a means (not an end in itself) to getting to know God. Of itself, it is not magic. It must be read with faith. With knowledge must go obedience. Its purpose must be to lead us to Christ. John Stott has helpfully explained it this way:

> To suppose that salvation lies in a book is as foolish as supposing that health lies in a prescription. When we are ill and the doctor prescribes some medicine for us, does he intend that we should go home with the prescription, read it, study it and learn it by heart? Or that we should frame it and hang it on our bedroom wall? Or that we tear it into fragments and eat pieces three times a day after meals? The absurdity of these possibilities is obvious. The prescription itself will not cure us. The whole purpose of a prescription is to get us to go to the chemist, obtain the medicine prescribed and drink it. Now the Bible contains the divine prescription for sin-sick souls. It specifies the only medicine which can save us from perishing. In brief, it tells us of Jesus Christ who died for us and rose again. But we do not worship the Bible as if it could save us; we go to Christ. For the overriding purpose of the Bible is to send us to Christ and persuade us to drink the water of life which He offers. [27]

CONSISTENCY

A second question concerning the ordinary evangelical's use of the Bible is whether or not he or she is consistent in doing so. Many would wish stoutly to defend its accuracy and assert its infallibility. Some would argue for its inerrancy. In pursuit of their loyalty to a high view of Scripture, they have often been dismissive and uncharitable about scholarly attempts to translate the Bible. The RSV which commended itself widely, none the less drew the fire of some for failing to pass muster at a few points where evangelical interpretations were at stake. Ire was expressed towards its non-evangelical translators.

Yet, ironically, the same evangelicals have no hesitation in using the *Living Bible* which is a free paraphrase and from a scholarly viewpoint seriously flawed in places. Indeed, they turned it into a best seller.[28] Former generations did the same with J. B. Phillips' paraphrase of the New Testament. Why the inconsistency? Perhaps it betrays that the commitment to inerrancy is not so deep after all? Perhaps comprehension is uppermost in the evangelical mind.

ACCURACY
A related question asks whether evangelicals are really concerned to listen to what the Bible says, or whether they have already made up their mind and read their own interpretations into it. The question has been posed most sharply by James Barr but is voiced by many others too. Barr says that fundamentalism (his word for conservative evangelicalism) 'is not basically concerned with the Bible and what it says, but with the achievement of dominance for the evangelical tradition of religion and way of life.'[29] And in his conclusion he writes, 'Contrary to all that might be expected from polemic documents, conservatives often ignore the literal sense of the Bible, often minimize miracles and the supernatural, often postulate substantial corruptions in the text, and so on.'[30]

These are grave charges against a movement which protests that it takes the Bible more seriously than anyone else. But the evidence from popular evangelicalism sometimes lies in Barr's favour. How can those who claim to take the Bible seriously have so little to say, and more importantly to do, with the poor, when the Bible raises their place in society on some 200 occasions? How can it dismiss issues of social justice as unimportant while Amos and Micah are still in the canon? How can it support right-wing tyrannical governments while the book of Revelation remains in the New Testament? How did it ever lend support to racism and apartheid? How can it preach a prosperity gospel when the New Testament so clearly teaches and demonstrates that the way of Jesus Christ is the way of the cross? How can it be so individualistic and concerned with spiritual self-indulgence in the light of the Bible's concern with community and self-giving?

There are a number of reasons why evangelicalism often does not live up to its ideal of letting the Bible speak. First, the Bible is often read through particular lenses, those of Calvinism, Arminianism, Premillennialism or more recent systems. These impose an interpretative framework on the Bible which force verses to be read in certain ways, often like forcing a foot into an ill-fitting shoe.

Second, there is an over-defensiveness in guarding certain doctrines, especially those to do with the virgin birth of Christ and substitutionary atonement. Again, certain verses are made to conform to these doctrines, whether the evidence justifies it or not. Third, the evangelical subculture leads to Scripture being read a certain way, in order that its concerns and lifestyle may be shored up by the Bible. Fourth, in reality, evangelicals are often more concerned about their own experience than about the Bible.

A recent manifestation of that, but by no means the only one, is to be found in the charismatic movement. For a time experience was exalted over doctrine and feeling over truth. Healthy correctives which bring the two into a much more wholesome balance now appear to be in progress.[31] But the charismatic movement also raises another question in regard to the evangelicals' use of scripture.

SUFFICIENCY

With the emergence of prophecy some have been led to question whether evangelicals believe the Bible to be sufficient any longer.[32] 'Prophecy' is used in the sense of God speaking to his people through a living human voice today - a gift of the Spirit widely practised in renewed churches. If, it is argued, it is necessary for God to speak in this way there must be something lacking in the original revelation given in Scripture. Otherwise, all that would be necessary is for his people to explore and expound the word already given. The use of prophecy has sometimes threatened or marginalised the place of the sermon, the hallowed evangelical symbol of the importance placed on the preaching of the word, but it has probably done so no more than testimony-giving did at various times of revival.

But, to my knowledge, no one in the contemporary renewal movement claims that these words of prophecy are adding to revelation or to Scripture. They are often simply words of encouragement, or caution, direction or upbuilding, akin to those mentioned in 1 Corinthians 14:3-4. There seems no necessary problem here. Even so the warning is useful. If evangelicals believe what 2 Timothy 3:16-17 says, then the Bible will be sufficient for all our needs.

The practice of popular evangelicalism does indeed raise questions as to whether evangelicals are as true to their stated position on the Bible as they would claim.

Summary

Bishop J. C. Ryle began his work on evangelicalism by saying, 'The first leading feature in evangelical religion is the absolute supremacy it assigns to Holy Scripture, as the only rule of faith and practice, the only test of truth and the only judge of controversy.'[33] There can be no doubt that this is where evangelicalism still stands, at least in a formal sense. The divine inspiration of the Bible marks it off from other books and puts it in a unique position as a revelation of God and an authority above all others. The desire of the evangelical is to hear its message and obey.

Differences exist over whether the Bible is best described as inerrant or not. But the current debate about inerrancy is a rather recent one and the issue is one over which evangelicals have never been wholly agreed. It is inaccurate to define the evangelical view of the Bible in terms of inerrancy. Evangelicals would want to argue that the Bible is entirely trustworthy and true. But even here they may differ as to whether that claim extends to every detail of history, geography, science and philosophy or whether it was an absolute claim in relation to God and matters of faith and practice, whilst being substantially true in regard to incidental details.

Similarly, attitudes to biblical criticism and scholarship have varied. In Britain they have generally been much more open than the popular image leads one to believe. In the United States positive attitudes were late in developing but are now firmly established. There is no evidence that involvement in biblical scholarship necessarily erodes evangelical beliefs in the Bible. Many are fully engaged in the task whilst remaining committed to high views of inspiration and authority. The questions now being faced by biblical scholars relate to matters of interpretation rather than older questions of history and authorship.

Popular evangelicalism is in no position to look too suspiciously at evangelical biblical scholars, for its rhetoric about the Bible often outruns reality. Firmly committed to the Bible it often does not listen to it with adequate care, read it without prejudice or obey it in sufficient measure.

6

THE WONDROUS CROSS

Evangelicals and the atonement

John Bright complained about the evangelicals, 'The atonement, always the atonement! Have they nothing else to say?'[1] In voicing his exasperation he rightly identified the central core of evangelical belief and preaching. Evangelicals make redemption the pivot of their faith. Where others place the doctrines of creation or of incarnation evangelicals place the atonement. It is quite simply the heart of evangelicalism.

The centrality of the cross

It is not that other doctrines are unimportant. They are. But this one colours the evangelical understanding of those other doctrines. Creation, though good in its original state, is now fallen and in need of redemption. Even before creation God's plan of redemption was in place (Ephesians 1:2-7). The new creation is inescapably tied to that plan of redemption. The incarnation does not stand on its own. From the beginning, it is clear that the purpose of Christ's becoming a human being was to die for our salvation. Redemption is the key to the interpretation of all Christian truth.

Expressed in a few words, 'Evangelical Christians believe that in and through Christ crucified God substituted Himself for us and bore our sins, dying in our place the death we deserved to die, in order that we might be restored to His favour and adopted into His family.'[2]

It was this message which was at the heart of preaching in the Evangelical Revival, the period from which evangelicalism properly takes its origins. It is said of John Wesley that, 'With the apostle Paul, he was prepared to strip his message of all that was peripheral, and to know nothing among his hearers except Jesus Christ and him crucified.'[3] Nothing was of greater consequence to him than the atonement. He wrote, 'The substance of all is, "Jesus Christ came into the world to save sinners." ' More precisely, he taught, 'It is the blood of Christ alone, whereby any sinner can be reconciled to God; there being no other propitiation for our sins, no other fountain for sin and uncleanness.'[4] He thought that scripture plainly taught that Christ died as the penal substitute for people's sin. It was this message which led to many turning to Christ in conversion and experiencing forgiveness for their sin.

An early Anglican evangelical Bible commentator, Thomas Scott, similarly wrote of the central evangelical discovery, 'Christ indeed bore the sins of all who should ever believe, in all their guilt, condemnation and deserved punishment, in his own body on the tree.'[5]

The atonement, understood as a gracious action of God in which Christ substituted himself for us to bear the penalty of our sin, has been at the heart of evangelicalism ever since. Where those who on other grounds, such as their looser attitude to the biblical text, may not have been fully evangelical have expounded the atonement in these robust terms, they have been welcomed by evangelicals. This is particularly true of three great writers of various periods, namely, R. W. Dale, author of *The Atonement* (1875), James Denney, author of *The Death of Christ* (1902) and P. T. Forsyth, author of *The Cruciality of the Cross* (1909). Each of these, for example, played a part in leading Dr Martyn Lloyd-Jones, who was already preaching of the helplessness of people in sin and their need for rebirth, to discover his need to make the cross central to his preaching and so to preach the evangelical message in all its fullness.[6]

Conversely, where people have declined to make the cross central, or weakened their views of the atonement, evangelicals have parted company, leading to David Bebbington's conclusion that, 'To make any theme other than the cross the fulcrum of a theological system was to take a step away from evangelicalism.'[7] The evidence for this can be seen at a number of points in evangelical history. Spurgeon, for example, had long expressed unease at the weakening emphasis on the atonement before the dispute between him and fellow Baptists culminated in the Downgrade controversy of 1887. In 1881 he had protested, 'If you leave out the atonement, what Christianity have you got to preach?'[8]

In 1910 the parting of the ways between the Cambridge Inter-Collegiate Christian Union and the Student Christian Movement revolved around the question of the atonement. When overtures were made by SCM in 1918 to CICCU, Norman Grubb, then Secretary of CICCU, asked the secretary of SCM, 'Does the SCM put the atoning blood of Jesus Christ central?' When the hesitant reply was received, 'Well, we acknowledge it, but not necessarily central,' the matter was settled. CICCU did not reaffiliate to SCM.[9]

Similarly, the place of the atonement was crucial in the parting of the ways with 'liberal evangelicalism'. In 1920, Canon E. W. Barnes, later Bishop of Birmingham, preached a sermon discounting the fall as an historical event and explaining it, instead, merely as a parable about the origin of sin. Liberal evangelicals welcomed his progressive ideas but mainstream evangelicalism vigorously rejected them as the thin end of the wedge which would lead to the undermining of the doctrine of the atonement.[10] Liberal evangelicals tried to hold on to basic evangelical principles whilst embracing modern ideas; holding to a much looser view of Scripture whilst regarding the traditional evangelical idea of substitutionary atonement to be 'crude'. A parting of the ways took place between conservative and liberal evangelicals with the latter eventually fading from the scene.

Why is it so important?

Why is it that evangelicals make the death of Christ so central whilst others are prepared to find a different centre for their theological systems? Two answers are constantly advanced: the gravity of sin and the holiness of God.

THE GRAVITY OF SIN

Sin may be a light matter to modern people but the evangelical takes the Bible's teaching about it seriously. Human beings were created by God with such potential but now, through the introduction of sin, they are marred masterpieces. Sin is the cause of all our difficulties and a predicament for which a solution must be found. It runs deep. Sin is not only the wrong acts which we do, or fail to do, but an inherent predisposition in our natures. It is ingrained; we are born to it. It is a fatal flaw in our character. Therefore, no superficial solution will work.

The Bible's description of sin is multi-faceted. It is to violate God's law, to transgress over a boundary set by God or to trespass into territory forbidden by God. It is to be unrighteous or wicked. It is to be corrupted, polluted, defiled and unclean. The most commonly used word for sin is one which speaks of human beings 'missing the mark' or failing to be what God intended them to be. It is, therefore, to be ungodly, to be self-centred and to live in a broken relationship to God. At its root, as Genesis 3 suggests, is the desire to live independently of God. Less harsh images of sin are included in the kaleidoscopic description the Bible provides, such as, to be lost or sick. But these neither lessen the gravity of sin nor minimize our human responsibility for it.

The consequences of sin are catastrophic. Primarily it leads to our alienation from God and a disruption in our relationship with our

Maker. Rather than being a loving Father to us, He appears as a stranger or even an enemy. Sin places us under God's judgement and makes us subject to His wrath. It results in our living in darkness and ignorance. We are in a state of spiritual death now, of which the physical death to come is a symptom. Life now is inevitably less than God intended it to be and life to come is denied, unless a solution can be found. Being 'out of sync' with God leads to our being out of sync with ourselves, with others and with our world. It leads to distortions and destruction.

The Bible's view of sin is based on the twin foundation of God's moral law and our human responsibility. God has expressed His character and will in a moral law, which we break, both because we are spiritual descendants of the first Adam, who broke God's law, and inheritors of his fatal legacy, and also because of our own actions. Sin is, therefore, an offence against Him. It is right that we should be held accountable for doing so since we have been created as morally responsible beings. If we were not, it would not be our fault. Although it is popular today to place the blame elsewhere - placing it in everything from our genes to society - it is responsibility which makes us human. Responsibility may be diminished but not erased. Without it we would be indistinguishable from the rest of animal creation.

These twin premises lead us to the conclusion that we are guilty before God. True guilt is to be distinguished from the false guilt and psychological guilt-feelings which enthusiastic preachers sometimes try to induce and from which many sadly and unnecessarily suffer. But moral guilt before God is real.

THE HOLINESS OF GOD

Contemporary pictures of God, where He is believed in at all, stress His accommodating nature, toleration and love. They admit surprise when the holiness of God is mentioned. But in doing so they betray that their origin lies more in our tolerant and indulgent age than in Christ's revelation of God or the Bible's unveiling of Him.

Long ago, P. T. Forsyth pointed out that it is much more accurate to speak of the 'holy love' of God, rather than, merely, His 'love'. Both holiness and love belong to God and are the inseparable essence of His character. The Bible speaks of God as 'the Holy One', who is 'high and lifted up', dwelling in majesty and unapproachable glory, whose name (that is, being) must be honoured. When people encounter Him, they fall on their faces in unworthiness. He is a 'consuming fire' whose purity compels a burning anger against sin. Sin is simply incompatible with His holiness. In Habakkuk's words, 'Your eyes are too pure to look on evil; you cannot tolerate wrong' (1:13).

God's holiness results in his wrath against sin, a quality which has been much debated in recent theology and which fits ill-at-ease with contemporary society. It is taught in the Bible none the less, as logically it must, if God is holy. God's wrath is a frequent theme in the Old Testament. It is asserted categorically, spoken of metaphorically and illustrated frequently. Thus, God warns the children of Israel that if they do not listen to him, 'then in my anger I will be hostile towards you and I myself will punish you' (Leviticus 26:28). The Lord's anger, we read, burned against Moses (Exodus 4:14), Uzzah (2 Samuel 6:7) and Amaziah (2 Chronicles 25:15) because the first argued with him, the second failed to keep a respectful distance from the Ark of the Covenant and the third committed spiritual adultery. God is jealous for his people's holiness and acts in a manner consistent with preserving or re-establishing it. Further, strong language is used in which God speaks of arranging for the land to spew out (literally, 'vomit') his people in rejection if they fail to live according to his law (Leviticus 18:25-28; 20:22-23). The anger of God is equally asserted in the New Testament with direct references being found in John 3:36; Romans 1:18; 2:5,8; 5:9; Ephesians 2:3; 5:6 and in many other places too.

One can understand the hesitancy which has been expressed in recent days in talking of the wrath of God. C. H. Dodd is among those who have tried to soften its apparently shocking nature by arguing that God's wrath is not personal but the inevitable outworking of the impersonal consequences of our sin. But the Bible writers clearly thought of it as a personal expression of God's displeasure at sin and those who practised it. The mistake is to think that because God is spoken of in anthropomorphic language, that is, language which we apply to human beings, God suffers from the same limitations and deficiencies as human beings. But, when applied to God, the words do not imply loss of temper, petulance, sinfulness or unrighteousness as they might if applied to us. Though personal, God is not a human person and does not share our finite and sinful human natures. The characteristic, therefore, may be applied to God without reservation. As P. T. Forsyth wrote, 'Without a holy God there would be no problem of atonement. It is the holiness of God's love that necessitates the atoning cross ...'[11]

John Owen summed up these twin concerns of the gravity of sin and the holiness of God in saying, 'He who has slight thoughts of sin, had never great thoughts of God.'[12] Equally the reverse is true. He who had slight thoughts of God, had never great thoughts of sin. If sin is not grave, God would not be offended. If God is not holy, sin would not matter.

Understanding the Cross

Offence against this holy God needs a remedy. The evangelical believes that the remedy has been fully provided for in the cross of Christ. But, how? Evangelicals have struggled down the centuries to understand what happened through the cross and have asserted that one interpretation of it, whilst not the sole legitimate interpretation, is 'the heart of the gospel.'[13]

It is readily understood that there are other ways in which Christians have striven to make sense of the Cross. It is also understood that many find the evangelical view unpalatable today. To aid our understanding, first, we shall look at some of the major interpretations of the cross down the centuries. Second, we will look at the evangelical view and, third, we will then consider objections which are raised against it.

ALTERNATIVE VIEWS

Though the Bible asserts with utmost clarity that the cross is the means of our redemption it does not provide a ready-made theory as to how it did so. Its approach is to make frequent resort to word pictures which portray its meaning. So, the cross is an act of redemption or ransom, a price paid to liberate a person, or property, and restore them, or it, to freedom or to their proper use. Or, drawing on the rich teaching of the Old Testament, it is seen as a sacrifice. Again, using other images, Jesus, through the cross, bore our curse, cancelled our debt, brought about our justification and our reconciliation to God. But Christians have often sought to piece these pictures together in such a way as to provide a coherent explanation of what they mean and how they were achieved.

One early explanation was that on the cross God offered Christ to Satan as a ransom in exchange for the release of sinners he held in his power. Although it contains an element of truth, this view did not commend itself for long. The problems with it are several. It credits the devil with more power than he really has and presents God as subordinate to him. It makes the cross to be a payment to the devil of his due. And it only works if one accepts that God brought about our salvation by deception. It relies on Satan being tricked into thinking that Christ had been given over to him whilst, in fact, on the third day Christ was to break loose from his bondage through the resurrection. Though rejected in its crude form, a modified version has more recently been put forward by Gustav Aulen who argues that the central meaning of the atonement is to be found in Christ's victory over sin, death and Satan. It builds on verses like Colossians 2:15 and emphasises that the dominant note to be heard ringing from Calvary is a note of victory.

A second explanation speaks of God satisfying, not the devil, but his own honour through the cross. The theory was set out by Anselm, Archbishop of Canterbury from 1093 onwards, and owes much to the world-view of the Middle Ages. Anselm viewed God as a medieval king whose honour had been breached by his subjects' sin and in whose debt, therefore, humankind stands. How is the debt to be repaid and satisfaction rendered? Human beings are incapable of paying it themselves. God alone can do so, but he must do so as a human being, or else human beings have still not made satisfaction to God. Hence, it was necessary that one who was God-man should make it. The theory has much to commend it but belongs to a different world than our own and was in danger of imposing medieval views of lordship on God. Whilst it is good in stressing the gravity of sin, the holiness of God and the worthiness of Christ, it goes beyond the biblical picture in its assumptions of a rigidly stratified moral order where honour has to be satisfied and causes of dishonour punished.

A third explanation was put forward by Peter Abelard, a younger contemporary of Anselm, who objected that Anselm's view was unjust. It was both cruel and wicked that an innocent person should suffer in the way Anselm proposed and even more disagreeable that God should have connived at this in the death of his son. What God was satisfying on the cross was neither the devil, nor justice, but the demands of his own love. So, he suggested, the key to understanding the cross was that it was a great demonstration of love and a voluntary act of self-sacrifice on the part of the cross which, in turn, draws forth from us a response of love. It is this love which delivers us from bondage and sets us free to be the true children of God. Luke 7:47 and 1 John 4:19 provide something of a basis for his view, which cannot be rejected completely. But it is far from doing justice to the full teaching of the Bible about the atonement.

Abelard's approach is known as a subjective view of the atonement because it stresses the effect the cross has on us rather than the work God does through the cross. Evangelical interpretations of the cross are objective. But subjective theories are much more widely accepted now than once they were, being more in tune with the tenor of our times.[14]

The reformers picked up another strand of interpretation, that had been current in earlier centuries, which involved a further idea about satisfaction. This time the need for satisfaction arose, not from the devil, nor due to the violation of honour, but from the breaking of the law. This view states that the moral law is fixed and cannot be broken without penalty. The essence of the atonement is that on the cross Christ stood in our place and took the penalty of our law-breaking upon himself. Since the punishment has been borne by Christ, it no longer has to be borne by us.

It is from this view that evangelicals derive their understanding of the atonement. Even so, it is not without its problems. To cite just one, just as the idea that the cross was a payment to the devil put Satan in a position superior to God so this view, crudely stated, can make the law independent of, and superior to, God. But the law is nothing other than an expression of the character of God himself and is never outside or independent of him. In R. W. Dale's words, 'In God the law is *alive*; it reigns on his throne, sways his sceptre, is crowned with his glory.'[15] Further objections will be considered later.

Recent views of the cross, as has been mentioned, have tended to stress the subjective elements of the atonement. Modern theologians are coy about suggesting that the cross changed anything in God, that is, turning His anger into love, but they are keen to suggest that the cross changed us. By its example we are moved to respond to God and to change our way of living. As our representative Christ showed us the way. A further theme which has proved very popular in recent times has been that the cross demonstrates God's solidarity with His suffering creation. Jurgen Moltmann is a leading exponent of this position.[16] It takes seriously the suffering of the world, especially in the light of events like Auschwitz, and argues that through the cross God suffers too. The focus of such theologies is particularly on Jesus' cry of dereliction which shows God entering into the godforsakenness of our world.

All these theories have much to commend them. But, to the evangelical they do not get to the heart of the matter. It is to the evangelical view we now turn.

THE EVANGELICAL VIEW

A cluster of words indicate what evangelicals believe about the cross. They speak of it as a 'propitiation', a 'penal substitution' and a means of 'justification'. Taking their cue from the reformers, evangelicals basically hold to a view that explains the cross in terms of it being the means of satisfying a holy God whose person has been alienated and whose law has been broken by sinners.

As we have seen, satisfaction is an idea which needs to be approached with care. It is too easy to make the object of satisfaction something other than God Himself and so to make God subordinate to something independent and outside of Himself. But, in this view, it is God Himself who is to be satisfied; the God who is a God of holiness and purity and whose law is an expression of the perfection of His character.

God is true to His own character. He cannot, therefore, simply 'wink' at sin, writing it off as an unfortunate mistake which does not matter. It does matter. He cannot simply say, 'Forget it. I love you and that is all that matters.' That would be sentimental love, whereas His is a holy love. Forgiveness is not simply forgetting. It cannot be that cheap. Forgiveness is costly. But who is to pay the cost and satisfy the demands of holiness, as well as of justice?

As law-breakers, human beings are incapable of satisfying God themselves. Their sinful nature means they can never repay the debt they owe and do not have it within them to overcome the penalty of their wrong-doing, which is judgment and death. So, if satisfaction is to be made, it must be made by God Himself.

In the cross, holiness and love meet. For there God Himself provided the means by which His own holiness could be satisfied and His unreasonable love made available to sinful men and women. He did so by providing His own Son to be the substitute for us and to bear the penalty for our sin. That is the plain meaning of the words 'Christ died *for* us' which frequently occur in one form or another. 'For' means in our place, on our behalf.

> Bearing shame and scoffing rude,
> In my place condemned he stood;
> Sealed my pardon with his blood:
> Hallelujah! what a Saviour!
>
> Guilty, vile and helpless, we:
> Spotless Lamb of God was He:
> 'Full atonement!' – can it be?
> Hallelujah! what a Saviour!
>
> *Philipp Bliss*

His death, then, was not a natural death but a penal death, a death which paid the penalty for sin. It was not the death of a martyr to a cause, but of a sacrifice to make atonement. It was not the exemplary death of a teacher for his disciples but the effective death of a saviour for guilty sinners.

Evangelicals believe that it is only when this becomes the core interpretation of the atonement that full justice is done to the Bible's many-sided teaching about the cross. Lying behind so much of the New Testament's understanding of the cross is the Old Testament's idea of sacrifice. Echoes of it can be heard in Galatians 1:4; Ephesians 5:2; 1 Peter 3:18, and elsewhere, in addition to it being the main interpretation of the work of Christ given in the Letter to the Hebrews. Sacrifices were of various kinds and for various purposes but the sin offering involved the idea of the blood of the sacrificial animal becoming a substitute for the blood of the sinner (Leviticus 17:11). The life of the sacrifice was given in exchange for the life of the guilty party.

Further references to Old Testament imagery endorse this view. Christ is 'our Passover Lamb' (1 Corinthians 5:7) who, like the Passover lamb of old (Exodus 12), sacrificed His life to enable others to keep their's. Christ is the suffering servant (Mark 10:45, 1 Peter 2:21-25) of Isaiah 53 who, innocent himself, 'was pierced for our transgressions (and) was crushed for our iniquities' (Isaiah 53:5) and who had the sin of others laid on him in order to bring those for whom he substituted forgiveness, peace and healing.

As John Stott, in his majesterial work on *The Cross of Christ*, puts it,

> It is clear from the Old Testament usage that to 'bear sin' means neither to sympathise with sinners, nor to identify with their pain, nor to express their penitence, nor to be persecuted on account of their human sinfulness . . . nor even to suffer the consequences of sin in personal or social terms, but specifically to endure its penal consequences, to undergo its penalty.[17]

A careful examination of the words of the New Testament supports this conclusion. Take, for example, the major debate which has occurred over whether the New Testament teaches that Christ's death was a 'propitiation' or only an 'expiation' for sin. These words need some explanation. To propitiate means to appease one who has been offended. To expiate means to make amends for wrong. As J. I. Packer has incisively put it, 'The difference is that expiation only means half what propitiation means.'[18]

In a number of places the New Testament speaks of Christ's work as a 'propitiation' (Romans 3:25; Hebrews 2:17; 1 John 2:2; 4:10) although the word has been lost in most modern translations because it is archaic. The clear reference would seem to be to Christ's death turning away the anger of a holy God. And so it was usually taken to be until C. H. Dodd, in his *Commentary on Romans*, began to argue that the words really meant 'expiation' rather than 'propitiation'. He argued both on linguistic grounds and also from the standpoint that to talk of God as angry was increasingly outmoded and considered unworthy of the Christian view of God. His arguments were subjected to careful linguistic analysis by Leon Morris who begged to differ on both counts. Expiation was involved but that was not the full meaning of New Testament teaching about the death of Christ. The depths could only be plummed by understanding it as propitiation. To speak merely of expiation was to lessen God's horror at sin and to compromise his holiness. 'It is,' Morris concluded, 'the combination of God's deep love for the sinner with His uncompromising reaction against sin which brings about what the Bible calls propitiation.'[19]

A further set of words has to do with the righteousness of God and to our being made righteous by Christ, which is the running theme of the Letter to the Romans. It is a picture which comes from the law courts. In view of their sinful lives and their sinful status, how can people be put right with God? One thing is clear, it does not lie within the grasp of human beings to justify themselves. There are no grounds for self-justification. The guilt is obvious, but we are powerless to do anything about it (Romans 3:10,23). But, through the cross, God's love is unreasonably made known to us. God freely justifies us, making over His own righteousness to us. He takes the initiative in doing what we could not do for ourselves and graciously gives us the gift of salvation (Romans 3:24; 6:23; 8:33). So the sinner is acquitted, set free and no longer under any condemnation (Romans 8:1).

That God justifies us is an act of grace on His part accomplished through the death of Jesus and the shedding of His blood (Romans 4:25; 5:6-10; 6:10). It took a sacrifice to bring it about (Romans 3:25). It is, then, not simply an amnesty but a costly forgiveness. Christ paid the wages for our sin (Romans 6:23), so discharging the demands of justice. In this way grace and justice have both been perfectly satisfied by the cross. The benefits of the cross become available to us through faith in Christ (Romans 1:17; 3:28; 5:2). It is the trusting of ourselves to God in Christ, in the most fundamental way, that enables us to receive the free gift of His grace.

This, then, in outline, is the heart of the evangelical view of the atonement. Christ died as the sinner's substitute, bearing the punishment for sin, to satisfy a holy God and appease His wrath. In the same cross we see the love of God made available for He provides, out of grace, the atonement we could not make for ourselves. Through that cross He acquits guilty sinners who believe and restores them to a relationship with himself.

OBJECTIONS TO THE EVANGELICAL VIEW
The evangelical view of the cross is not above criticism and the easy way in which it is sometimes preached, as if it offered cheap grace, amply merits criticism on occasions. The objections are in fact serious but here we must deal with them but briefly.[20]

The first objection is that the evangelical view tends to drive a wedge between an angry God and a suffering Son. It can seem to divide God into two and set them over against one another. It almost seems as if an angry God has to be reluctantly persuaded to forgive sinners by a Son who is willing to substitute Himself for them, or, alternatively, that a loving God has to persuade a reluctant Son to be the victim for others' sins, while He remains untouched in heaven. But these are caricatures. God is One and care must be taken to avoid division. On the cross it was nothing less than God, in Christ, who was suffering. God Himself entered into the darkness, pain and death of Calvary. As John Stott has put it, divine self-satisfaction was obtained by divine self-substitution.[21]

Second, it can cause the work of Christ to degenerate into something like a mere legal fiction. The penalty having been paid, the transaction done, the sinner goes free, regardless of how he or she then lives. Opponents of the view say it is too easy and omits the deep relational dimension which must be involved where there is true forgiveness. But, again this is a caricature. It ought to be remembered more, as Paul Fiddes has pointed out, that the legal background against which Paul was writing was not that of Roman law but of Jewish law. Roman law was criminal law but Jewish law was civil law. The whole question of being in the right, therefore, inextricably binds relationships and justice together.[22] Furthermore, any understanding of what evangelicals mean by faith, and the repentance which must accompany it, must lead to an acknowledgement that justification will result in a radical reorientation of one's life and to an introduction into the community of God's people. It is not a mere transaction where no further commitment is required. Whilst wishing to affirm that salvation is a matter of unqualified grace, by which a sinner is acquitted once and for all, recognition is also given to salvation as an unfolding present experience of discipleship which is not to be fully realized until completed in death or at the second coming of Christ.

Third, it is questioned how it is possible to transfer sin, guilt and its penalty from one person to another. Our own world does not find the idea of substitution so easy. Some find the whole idea immoral. But far from being a strange idea, the concept of substitution is one which lies deep within human nature, especially where a family is involved. It is not uncommon for parents to offer themselves in exchange for their children when a siege takes place and hostages are taken. Why should it be thought so strange that God in Christ would do the same? But the question goes deeper, since it is about the transference of sin and guilt to Christ, is such transference possible? Again, the objection has weight. But the clue lies in Christ's identification with us through the incarnation. Transference was possible because he too was a human being; one like us in every respect, but without sin. Because he entered into solidarity with our humanity and voluntarily bore our burden, the idea of substitution is, indeed, possible.

A fourth objection is that this forensic view of sin and salvation does not as readily fit the temper of our times which lays greater stress on the personal than the legal. To present the cross as concerned with legalistic niceties and in a legalistic manner is, indeed, to trivialise it. But behind the objection lies the two different approaches to the atonement which have been mentioned. Contemporary views stress the subjective nature of the atonement, speaking of it as a present experience and a process, and looking to the response it calls forth from us. The evangelical view stresses the objective aspects of the atonement, speaking of it as a past, once for all and completed event and looks to the effect it has on God as well as on us. Whilst much of what subjective views of the cross have to say is of benefit, it would be erroneous to reject the objective perspective. To do so would be to imperil any idea of what is right and to lessen any thought of God's holiness.

DEEPER EVANGELICAL PERSPECTIVES ON THE ATONEMENT

Whilst the centre of the evangelical view of the atonement lies in the idea of penal substitution, that does not define its circumference. Evangelicals know the cross to be a many-sided thing, the meaning of which can never be exhausted. D. L. Moody, for example, stood more in the tradition of moral influence theories of the atonement.[23] But this did not prevent him from being respected as the greatest evangelist of his day. Equally today, ideas of reconciliation[24] and of the other New Testament words about the cross abound among evangelicals.

An interesting and recent example of this can be found in a little book by Leon Morris, a New Testament scholar who had championed not only the defence of the word 'propitiation' as biblical, but had expounded in careful detail other words which lay at the root of the evangelical view of the atonement.[25] In his Gheens Lectures, given in Louisville, Kentucky, in 1988, he spoke of some of the other ways of looking at the cross. These were not views to be held instead of the traditional evangelical view but aspects of the cross which could be held to supplement it.

So, building on a number of New Testament passages he developed the themes of the cross as an answer to futility, to ignorance, to loneliness, to sickness and death and to selfishness. Each of these themes addresses questions posed by the age in which we live and finds their answer in the atonement. The work demonstrates an ability to embrace alternative views of the atonement, like Moltmann's emphasis on Christ's cry of dereliction, even subjective ones, although not uncritically. Often Morris brings these other views into contact with the traditional evangelical viewpoint and shows how by doing so they may be deepened even further.[26] He notes that there is ample evidence of the truth of Paul's words that 'the creation was subjected to frustration,' or futility (Romans 8:20) in today's world. The frustration is seen in creation, naturally so since it 'has been disturbed and thrown out of kilter by the coming of sin' (compare Genesis 1:31 with Genesis 3:17). In the non-material realm (the world of our thoughts and personal living) there is much futility as well. Paul addressed this issue in speaking of the Gentiles as walking 'in the futility of their thinking. They are darkened in their understanding, and separated from the life of God because of the ignorance that is in them due to the hardening of their hearts . . .' (Ephesians 4:17-18). But Peter asserted that the cross redeemed us from futility (1 Peter 1:18). How did it do this? Redemption is the payment of a price for the release of prisoners and their restoration to their rightful owner. So it is with futility. People live in futility because they are slaves to masters and principles which have usurped God's rightful place in their lives. The cross sets people free from these idols and restores them to living for God.

There is, of course, much more to Morris' argument than that. He notes that the creation was subjected to frustration 'in hope' and develops the theme of the expectation we have that Christ will one day reconcile all things in himself (Colossians 1:20). He notes the importance of Paul's teaching that our faith is based on the fact of Christ's death and resurrection and not on a religious fiction. If it were not so we would still be living in futility (1 Corinthians 15:14-17). But enough has been said to illustrate his approach.

Overall, he concludes:

> In all this we discover that the atonement is vaster and deeper than any of the traditional theories affirms. I am not suggesting we jettison any of them. I gladly affirm what they affirm. But I want to go on from there to say that Scripture gives us grounds for affirming that there are other things that the atonement effects, some of which are very important for twentieth-century citizens. It is well if we enlarge our horizons to embrace them.[27]

So, although evangelicalism may be clear as to the central meaning of the cross it is keen to explore the cross from every angle in order that the wonder of it may be heightened, calling forth yet more gratitude from our lives for the One who died for us.

Charismatic Renewal and Evangelical Views of the Cross

Charismatic renewal has had a three-fold implication for evangelical views about the cross. First, for a time it appeared to dislodge the atonement from its central place in Christian experience and replace it with a new centre, that of the baptism of the Spirit. Pentecost was replacing Calvary. A theology of glory, with its emphasis on resurrection, life and power, was supplanting a theology of the cross. The songs of the movement were particularly noted as having changed the emphasis but it was true of the writing and preaching too.

Even some of the advocates of charismatic renewal were worried that it was so. Michael Harper, writing in the early days of charismatic renewal, warned of the danger of 'thinking of Pentecost and the Baptism in the Holy Spirit as the answer to everything. The death of Christ is then removed from its central position which it should hold in the thought and experience of the believer. Without a clear understanding of this the church which opens its doors to the Holy Spirit in the new way will be in for a hard time.'[28] He went on to caution about the selfishness of power-seeking, as seen in the church at Corinth.

Renewal movements often over-stress that which has been long neglected and under-stress that which has been constantly stated. So it was with Pentecost and Calvary. There is evidence that the pendulum is swinging back to find its true centre. Tom Smail, a respected statesman of the charismatic movement, for example, has recently argued that a theology which has its centre in the experience of Pentecost but which does not connect it closely to the experience of the cross will be inadequate on the two grounds of the Bible and experience.

Biblically, the Pentecost model of Luke and Acts needs to be joined to the Paschal model of John and Paul. In them the giving of the Spirit flows from the cross. 'According to the Pascal model of Christian renewal,' he writes, 'the cross and the resurrection of Jesus are the saving centre of all God's dealings with us, and all that He does in us by His Spirit will proceed from His passion and rising and be conformed to them.'[29] The power of Jesus is none other than the power manifest in the cross. Experientially, 'The Pentecost model can offer us a theology of healing and triumph, but it cannot provide the basis for a theology of suffering and failure, which we need just as much.'[30] But both the power to heal and the failure to heal can be explained by the cross. 'What heals is not esoteric techniques, or even special supernatural endowment as such; what heals is Calvary love.'[31] Failure and weakness are accommodated too, at the cross, as Paul discovered through his thorn in the flesh. For it is there that 'grace is made perfect in weakness'.

The second implication arises out of the first. Even if the cross is being put back centre-stage, what interpretation of it is dominant? The view of Christ as victor over the powers has some natural attractions for charismatics, rather than the traditional evangelical view of penal substitution. Gustav Aulen's idea that Christ is *Christus Victor*, the one who victoriously fights against and triumphs over the evil powers of the world and the tyrants which keep human beings in bondage has appeal for those who have made power a central theme of Christian experience, who believe in the present-day activity of demons, who see the drama of salvation as a conflict between the Kingdom of God and the Kingdom of Satan and who speak much about spiritual warfare.

Indeed, the attraction is confirmed by Nigel Wright but not without qualification. Although he describes Aulen's theory as 'accurate' and 'basically sound', and welcomes it as an explanation of the work of Christ in relation to the powers of evil, he only does so having firmly laid the stress first on Christ's death as an atonement for sin: a propitiation of the wrath of God and an expiation of the sins of humankind.[32]

In any case, the victory of Christ over the powers is a true aspect of the atonement which, perhaps, had been too long neglected by evangelicals. Its rediscovery is to be welcomed provided it stands alongside and does not usurp the central truth that 'Christ died for our sins'.

In the third place, charismatic renewal has posed the question of the scope of the work of the cross. Does it only deal with sin and defeat demons or is it effective, in the here and now, in healing sickness and curing psychological problems? How comprehensive is its scope? A cursory reading of Matthew 8:16–17, where Matthew quotes from Isaiah 53 and connects the work of the suffering servant with the healing of the sick and the driving out of demons, suggests its scope should be wide. Peter, too, speaks of his wounds healing us (1 Peter 2:24). Should we not, then, expect physical benefits from the cross in the here and now?

Evangelicals have generally taught that the concern of the cross is with our sin and any further healing is a bonus of God's grace, not inherent, for the moment, in the atonement. The typical evangelical position has been voiced by John Stott. 'We sinners still, of course have to suffer some of the personal, psychological and social consequences of our sins, but the penal consequence, the deserved penalty of our alienation from God, has been borne by Another in our place, so that we may be spared it.'[33] But is not that to manifest a depressingly low and an unnecessarily restricted expectation of the benefits of the cross, as some charismatics would claim? An understanding of the context both in Isaiah and Peter indicates that the 'healing' they had in mind was the healing of our sin, transgressions and iniquities. In the ministry of the Messiah this healing was signified by the healing of body and mind, as on occasions it will be today. But these are exceptional and are signs of the healing of our relationship with God. If healing of body and mind was meant to flow from the cross one would expect Scripture to make it much plainer than it is in the references given, to be referred to more frequently than it is, and not to acknowledge the presence of sickness and suffering, as it does (Philippians 2:27; 2 Corinthians 12:7-10; 2 Timothy 4:20) without further comment. The clear connection is between the cross and our sin.

In fact, there has been much more convergence between evangelicals and charismatics than the stark statement of the positions suggests. Experience has muted the claims of some charismatics that physical or mental healing automatically flows from the cross for those who have faith. Evangelicals have learned that God indeed does work in the body and mind through the power of the cross and that the atonement can bring substantial healing in all the dimensions of a person's life, physical, mental and social, as well as spiritual.[34]

Summary: is the cross still central?

Whilst the fact that 'Christ died for us' is clearly central in the New Testament, evangelicals agree that how the death of Christ works is never explained in precise terms. With others, down the years, they have sought to understand it and have concluded that seeing it as an act of penal substitution for our sin makes the most sense of the Bible's teaching. It gives weight to the gravity of our sin, the holiness of our God, the need for propitiation, whilst, as an act of self-substitution, it gives weight, too, to the love of God. Grace is at the heart of the cross.

Since the Bible, itself, is not confined to this view of the atonement, neither can evangelicals be so confined. Whilst maintaining it to be the heart of the gospel, they welcome and embrace other views and are constantly striving to find new ways to express the meaning of the cross for the contemporary world.

At the end of the day, people will always find the cross an unreasonable, foolish and even offensive message (1 Corinthians 1:18-25). It stands the world's values and strategies on their head. So there will always be the temptation to shy away from it and to preach or live by something more comfortable. Evangelicalism's present emphasis on power and success, on signs and wonders, on growth and management,[35] suggests they may be falling into that temptation. The question which must be faced is whether present-day evangelicalism is true to its heritage and still takes its stand on Paul's boast, 'we preach Christ crucified' (1 Corinthians 1:23). Is it really true that evangelicals today have 'decided to know nothing . . . except Jesus Christ and him crucified' (1 Corinthians 2:2)? Is the cross still the heart of their message? Would a contemporary observer of evangelicalism complain, as John Bright did, 'The atonement, always the atonement!'?

O HAPPY DAY

Evangelicals and conversion

When the Cornish vicar, the Revd William Haslam preached on the Pharisees one day he realized that he was no better than they and felt a change coming over his soul. The joyful cry went up among his parishioners, 'The parson is converted'. When the American gangland wiretapper, Jim Vaus, attended a Billy Graham campaign in Los Angeles in 1949, he came face to face with his conscience and got converted. The press wires soon flashed the news 'Wiretapper Vaus hits the sawdust trail!' They were two very different people, with different backgrounds and from different times, but they shared the common experience of conversion.

Nothing has been more characteristic of evangelicalism than the preaching of conversion and nothing has been more subject to suspicion, contempt and even hostility than that message. From Jonathan Edwards to Billy Graham and beyond, the new birth has been like a thread on which the other beads of evangelical doctrine and experience have been hung. Yet, even here, evangelical preaching and understanding has undergone, albeit minor, modification.

It was the experience of evangelical conversion for George Whitefield, John Wesley and Jonathan Edwards that changed formal religion into dynamic faith and which lay at the roots of the rise of evangelicalism. Finney, Moody, Sunday and Graham, the great evangelists all experienced decisive conversions which became the launching pads for their own evangelistic ministries. Their stories, to one degree or another, can be duplicated by millions of others who have entered into the 'born again' experience.

Jonathan Edwards was converted in the spring of 1721. He spoke of how, as he read the words of 1 Timothy 1:17, 'There came into my soul, and was as it were diffused through it, a sense of the glory of the Divine Being; a new sense, quite different from anything I ever experienced before.'[1] Later he wrote:

> They who are truly converted are new men, new creatures; new, not only within but without; they are sanctified throughout, in spirit, soul and body; old things are passed away, all things are become new; they have

new hearts, new eyes, new ears, new tongues, new hands, new feet; i.e., a new conversation and practice; they walk in newness of life, and continue to do so to the end of life.[2]

Billy Graham 'went forward' to 'make his decision for Christ' in 1934 in response to the preaching of Mordecai Ham. He, too, immediately looked for the signs of change in his life which he found in modest improvements, more attention to Bible study and prayer and 'a resolve to manifest the distinctive marks of the Evangelical Christian, bearing witness to the good news.'[3] Throughout his evangelistic ministry he has preached the new birth as a radical change. Insisting that it is more than moral reformation, in which an unchanged person is bound to fail, he compares the change to that of a caterpillar being transformed into a butterfly. Graham quotes Wilbur Smith, saying, that to be born again means:

> Something tremendously radical. What we are by nature we are because we were born . . . To be born again at least implies an absolutely new beginning, not a reformation of life, not a turning over of a new leaf, not the addition of some new attribute or aspect of capacity, but something so radical that by it we are going to be something altogether different from what we have been . . .[4]

The theology of conversion

The word 'conversion' literally means 'to turn', 'to change direction'. In a spiritual sense it is to turn away from sin and to turn to God. In the Old Testament the prophets continuously invite the children of Israel to turn back to God. But the invitation is by no means limited to them. 'Turn to me and be saved, all the ends of the earth: for I am God and there is not other' (Isaiah 45:22). Only by turning their backs on an idolatrous or godless way of life and by seeking forgiveness, reconciliation and by being committed to walk in God's ways can the safety and salvation of the nations be secured.

Jesus spoke of the need for conversion: 'I tell you the truth, unless you change (literally, turn or be converted) and become like a little child you will never enter the kingdom of heaven' (Matthew 18:3). The preaching of the apostles was characterized by the invitation to turn to God (Acts 3:19; 14:15) and 'turning' became a regular way of describing those who had become disciples of Jesus Christ (Acts 9:35; 11:21; 1 Thessalonians 1:9-10).

REPENTANCE, FAITH AND BELIEF

Turning to God involves a turning away from sin in repentance and a turning to God through faith in Jesus Christ. Repentance is not 'a cringing self-contempt', nor even a feeling of sorrow, on its own, but a change of mind about sin that leads the penitent to recognize that sin is wrong, to change his or her mind about the rightness of living in it, and to adopt a new feeling for the holiness of God and a new determination to live free from wrongdoing. Over the years a change has taken place in evangelicalism at this point. Gone is the prolonged agony over sin which characterized former generations, especially those influenced by puritanism. In those days people were encouraged to tarry until feeling great conviction of sin and a desperate sense of unworthiness before hastening on to exercise faith in Jesus Christ. Today, repentance has become a more perfunctory matter and the journey between repentance and faith shorter. Billy Graham argues that how much inner conflict, or conviction, a person experiences in the initial stage of conversion will depend on their temperament or their environment.[5] But, whatever the feeling, repentance must be genuine.

Faith is the exercise of personal trust in Jesus Christ as Saviour. What or who you have faith in is the crucial issue. In conversion people put their faith in Jesus Christ as the only means of their salvation. Another word for faith is 'belief' but this can sometimes be misunderstood to imply that all that is required is mental assent to certain doctrines. But that is not what faith or belief means. Faith is a whole-hearted commitment and total personal trust in Jesus. In Leighton Ford's words, 'Faith is not belief without evidence but commitment without reservation.'[6]

THE HUMAN ELEMENT

Conversion is the human side of Christian experience. It is the human decision to turn to God, the act of the will to follow Christ and the determination to become his disciple. It cannot take place unless God is at work in a person's life. Conversion goes hand in hand with regeneration; that is, the giving of spiritual life by the Holy Spirit, his making a person new from within. Hence the ideas of conversion and regeneration are closely connected and sometimes, wrongly, confused. In a strict sense, the favourite text used in preaching about conversion, when Jesus says to Nicodemas, 'You must be born again' (John 3:7) applies not to conversion but to regeneration.

Another change in evangelicalism since its inception is the increasing emphasis on the human side of conversion. The stress now lies on 'deciding for Christ', on 'receiving Christ' and on 'accepting Jesus as your Saviour' rather than on the sovereign work of God in giving new life, which issues in conversion. The change can be seen, again, in the characteristic shift between Jonathan Edwards and Billy Graham. For Edwards, 'Conversion is a great and glorious work of God's power, at once changing the heart, and infusing life into dead souls.'[7] For Billy Graham, who would not dissent from that, the emphasis is different. It is the exercise of the prerogative of a free moral agent, an act of acceptance and commitment.[8]

The twin movement of conversion and regeneration brings into being an entirely new creature (2 Corinthians 5:17). It is the firm evangelical belief that the thief, the sexual pervert, the alcoholic, the materialist, the busy-body and the terrorist, to name but a few, can be transformed by conversion and, through the consequent reception of new God-given abilities to overcome sin, they can adopt new standards, values, and attitudes in life and live in an entirely new way, with a desire to be godly; in other words, become a new person.

Not surprisingly evangelicals sing:

> O happy day, that fixed my choice
> On thee, my Saviour and my God!
> Well may this glowing heart rejoice,
> And tell its raptures all abroad.
>
> *Philip Doddridge*

The conversion experience

Evangelical theology affirms that there is no one archetype conversion experience. The rhetoric of the evangelists, backed-up by the testimonies of converted entertainers, sportspersons or other evangelical superstars,[9] sometimes implies there is. But honest examination of the evidence leads to the conclusion that there is no typical conversion event. Popular evangelicalism runs into trouble when it tries to impose one on people.

The heart of the problem revolves around whether conversion is gradual or instantaneous, a process or a crisis. The great discovery of the early evangelicals was that what the Puritans had taught to take months, if not years, could happen in a moment. Subsequently, Finney and the later revivalists employed strategies and means to facilitate conversions and these had the effect of reducing the conversion experience into a systematised form of mass production.

A superficial reading of Acts suggests that if the man from

Ethiopia, Paul, Cornelius, and the Philippian gaoler are typical then conversion is to be an instant and very conscious event. But a closer reading of the stories, together with a look at some other passages, suggests that neither the Ethiopian nor Cornelius were instantaneous conversions. They had been thinking about the faith for some time. Paul, too, had been deeply enmeshed in issues to do with Christ. Furthermore, in spite of the similarities, there were major differences between them. For Paul, conversion was the swing of a pendulum. For others, like the Ethiopian or Cornelius, it was a development of and a new departure in their thinking. For still others, like many of the Jews who had been looking for the Messiah, it was a reinterpretation of their past and a coming to fulfilment of what they had believed.[10] The variety increases still further as other conversion experiences are examined in Acts. So no one pattern of conversion is to be found in Scripture.

Evangelical history has always been divided on the issue. Whereas evangelical nonconformists stressed instantaneous conversion, evangelical Anglicans tended towards gradual conversion. Moody said, 'One minute a slave, the next a free man. That is instantaneous isn't it?'[11] But Simeon said, 'We require nothing sudden.'[12] It was only after Finney, with the growth of mass evangelism as a technique, that conversion came to be mass-produced and so moulded into hundreds of identical crisis experiences.

Contemporary evidence also shows that most people do not get converted in a crisis event but through a gradual process. *Finding Faith Today*, the most recent research available as to how people become Christians, shows that in evangelical churches only 37 per cent of people experienced sudden conversion, with the figure declining to 20 per cent for churches of any complexion. On average, only 31 per cent said their conversion was a dateable experience.[13] It took, on average, four years from the start of a spiritual journey to a public confession of faith in Christ.

The fact that many gradually grow in faith explains why many evangelicals are looking with interest at theories of faith development rather than working for sudden conversions. These theories, put forward for example by John Westerhoff and James Fowler, suggest that children develop in faith, just as they develop physically and intellectually. They identify a number of stages through which faith develops. Westerhoff,[14] the most straightforward, speaks of:

- Experienced faith (the basic trust of the young child)
- Affiliative faith (the sharing in the faith of the family and others by the growing child)

- Searching faith (the questioning of the adolescent as self-identity emerges)
- Owned faith (where a person comes to own what they believe)

Each may often take the form of a conversion experience.

These psychological theories are complemented by a new interest in the practice of the early church whereby people made a journey towards faith through instruction prior to baptism.[15] People under instruction were called catechumens. Given the widespread ignorance of the basic elements of the Christian faith in our secular society, the approach has much to commend it.

If this is so, why is the myth of conversion as typically a crisis so hard to overcome? It is not only that this is its most visible face, seen again and again in mass evangelism, but it is also probably because evangelicals want to hold on to conversion as a real experience. They distinguish it from a mere religious upbringing or training. Religious socialisation does not guarantee a personal relationship with God, but many mistake the one for the other. Billy Graham makes the point in an arresting manner in declaring that, 'In one recent crusade sixteen clergymen came forward to receive Jesus Christ as Saviour.'[16] Along with others he denies that conversion has to be an instant dateable experience, but he wants to safeguard it as a real experience and therefore stresses that it must be a conscious experience. 'Whether they can remember the time or not, there was a moment when they crossed over the line from death to life. You cannot tell the exact moment when night becomes day, but you know when it is daylight.'[17] Such talk, paradoxically, leads the convert to think it is preferable to have an experience which you can date since it is easier to derive assurance from an event you can put in your diary than from a gradual change that, almost imperceptibly, has come upon you.

The crucial issue has been pinpointed by James Packer. He pleads that evangelicals should correct the habit of questioning the authenticity of someone's Christian faith by checking up on their conversion experience. Instead, he writes, 'the only proof of past conversion is present convertedness.'[18] He is right. An evangelicalism which is true to its heritage will preach and work for conversions but will never gauge someone's Christian credentials by whether some past event, like going forward in response to an appeal, occurred but only by whether that person displays the signs of holiness now. For conversion is an initiation into a new life which is marked by obedience to Jesus Christ and which bears the fruits of holiness.

The means of conversion

PREACHING

By tradition, evangelicals have exalted two means of conversion as primary: preaching and personal work. The evangelical devotion to preaching as an evangelistic means takes its cue from Romans 10:17, '. . . faith comes from hearing the message, and the message is heard through the word of Christ', from the many other references to 'the word' being preached, growing or spreading elsewhere in the New Testament and from 1 Corinthians 1:21. The stress on 'the word' is not only consistent with the word-oriented character of Enlightenment evangelicalism but also with its commitment to truth. The gospel is not an opinion, nor an impression, but truth to be communicated. Charles Spurgeon laboured the point in *The Soul Winner* (1897):

> To listen to some preachers, you would imagine that the gospel is a pinch of sacred snuff to make them wake up, or a bottle of ardent spirits to excite their brains. It is nothing of the kind; it is news, there is information in it, there is instruction in it concerning matters which men need to know, and statement in it calculated to bless those who hear it. It is not a magical incantation or charm, . . . it is a revelation of facts and truths which require knowledge and belief. The gospel is a reasonable system and it appeals to men's understanding; it is a matter for thought and consideration and it appeals to the conscience and the reflecting powers. Hence, if we do not teach men something, we may shout 'Believe! Believe!' but what are they to believe?[19]

In saying this, Spurgeon was representative of much evangelical thinking of his day. It led to conversion being closely tied to the understanding of a scheme of salvation and, therefore, to demanding an ability to engage in abstract thought, instead of it being about a living relationship with the Lord. It led, too, to a negativism about attempts to communicate other than with words. These debates have not gone away but, rather, have intensified with the passing of time. Even as he spoke, evangelicals were being influenced by Romanticism and, subsequently by Modernism, so the primacy of the word, with its consequent endorsement of preaching as the means of evangelism, has been questioned. Existentialism led evangelicals to talk of conversion much more in terms of 'a personal encounter with Jesus Christ' than the overcoming of ignorance or the acquiring of truth. As visual, dramatic and musical means of communication have increased, all of which, as contemporary modes of communication, are to be welcomed, the primacy of preaching has declined. The 'third wave' has further placed the question of power evangelism on the agenda, that is whether the most effective means of communicating the gospel does not lie through signs and wonders, rather than through words (e.g., 1 Corinthians 4:20).[20]

The issues raised are still hotly debated back and forth the evangelical spectrum but, for all the diversity, the central belief, which is reflected still in the practice of most evangelical churches, is in preaching as a primary means of conversion. Whatever other methods of communication are employed, most evangelicals would agree that, at some stage, there must be a verbal explanation of the gospel for people to respond to it.

PERSONAL EVANGELISM

Personal work, as it was called, was always regarded as the essential accompaniment to preaching. William Wilberforce used to prepare 'launchers' for use at dinner parties and social occasions so that the conversation might be steered in the direction of the gospel. Wilberforce was a master at such conversation, especially among the Royal family and aristocracy. Invited to dine with the Prince Regent, to whom he had been trying to witness, he was warned not to raise matters which might cause the Prince offence.[21] No opportunity was to be missed. Visitors to the Great Exhibition of 1851 and the crowds who lined the streets for Queen Victoria's funeral procession were among the many who met with Christians seeking to distribute tracts and to engage in conversation about spiritual matters. Similar initiatives are taken in our own day for the importance of individual witnessing has not diminished.

It became popular to write manuals and provide instruction courses on these matters. Charles Finney included it in his *Lectures on the Revival of Religion*. Christians were to testify to ten particular aspects of the Bible:

- the immortality of the soul
- the vanity and unsatisfying nature of earthly good
- the satisfying nature of religion
- the guilt and dangerous position of sinners
- the reality of hell
- the love of Christ
- the necessity of a holy life
- of self-denial
- of meekness and integrity
- the necessity of an entire renovation of character and life for all who would enter heaven.

Winning souls required wisdom. The right time had to be selected. Members of the family were to be spoken to individually. Conversation had to be kind, respectful and addressed to the conscience. Their particular sins had to be pointed out, but briefly. Patience had to be shown. Their side was never to be taken against God. Pray with them, for 'if you converse with them and leave them without praying, you leave your work undone.'[22]

C. H. Spurgeon's *The Soul Winner* declared that it was 'a joy worth words to win souls' and it ought always to be the Christian's aim, though he, himself, confessed to finding personal witnessing far from easy. To him, individual conversations were only secondary in importance to preaching. People were to be spoken to after sermons; acquaintances and relatives buttonholed; letters were to be written and visits made in the interests of the gospel. If a Christian could do little else they could take someone along to hear a sermon. There was a dark side to the gospel which emphasised the law of God, the death of man and the damnation of the impenitent. The gospel should be taught as truth. So important was it that people should be converted, rather than merely influenced, that abruptness was even countenanced – a desperate case requires a desperate remedy. The motivation for personal evangelism was three-fold. A lack of conversions brought dishonour to God. Only by conversions would society be transformed and its social evils swept away. Then, there was the terrible future of those who were unconverted.[23]

Numerous other personal evangelism manuals were produced stretching into our own day. Among the most popular were those by R. A. Torrey, *How to Win Men for Christ*; Lorne Sanny's *The Art of Personal Witnessing* which was much used in connection with earlier Billy Graham crusades; Paul Little's *How to Give Away your Faith*, popular in the student world, and James Kennedy's *Evangelism Explosion* which tied personal conversations into a church visiting programme. It is interesting to observe the elements in these which do not change, such as the goal of conversion and the use of Scripture. But there are also elements which do change, with increasing space being given to human technique and apologetic method and less stress being placed on the spiritual qualifications of the witness and on sin.

Finding Faith Today has recently confirmed the importance of personal relationships in bringing people to faith.[24] The friendship of Christians is shown to be the main avenue by which people travel towards faith. This may not be quite the same as the old evangelical strategy of personally speaking about the Saviour, for the evidence indicates that it is the attractiveness of a Christian's life and the drawing of an unbeliever into a circle of Christian friendship, rather than what Christians say, that is more significant in bringing people to conversion. But it vindicates the traditional evangelical emphasis on the personal as a chief means of conversion, none the less.

The growth of the evangelistic empire

It is from its emphasis on conversion that evangelicalism chiefly gains its activist character. Evangelicals have been unable to sit by while others do not share the blessings of the gospel. Efforts must be made to convert them. Because of that simple truth evangelicalism has been like a volcano, erupting in explosive missionary energy and showering down evangelistic societies and strategies in a million fragments on an unsuspecting world.

ROUTINE CHURCH WORK

The routine work of the regular church should not be underestimated as a means of bringing people to faith in Christ. Attention is often directed exclusively to the special missions, revivals and mission societies at the expense of the regular church. But David Bebbington has rightly pointed out that:

> Most of the nineteenth-century impact of evangelicalism, however, was achieved not through revivals but through regular methods of mission. Ordinary Sunday services were fundamental. At the evening service, normally the second or third of the day, the pattern of worship and the style of preaching were adapted to the supreme task of implanting the gospel in the hearers, who, by that hour, would include domestic servants and (in the countryside) agricultural labourers. In the less inhibited denominations, evening service would be followed by a prayer meeting or after-meeting where a significant proportion of conversions would take place.[25]

Denominations undertook the organisation of home missions. The Baptist churches took initiatives in itinerancy from the late eighteenth century onwards and throughout the nineteenth century. They demonstrated an untidy and sporadic patchwork of ventures at local, associational and at national level, resulting in fits and starts in evangelism. Among Independents, a Home Missionary Society was formed in 1819 which joined with the Congregational Union in 1840. The Methodist Contingent Fund was formed in 1815 to give temporary assistance to pioneer causes but lapsed into being a means of permanent assistance for churches until revamped in 1855 to become the Home Missionary and Contingent Fund. Among

Anglicans perhaps the most significant initiatives were the founding of the Church Pastoral Aid Society in 1836 to assist in parochial evangelism, and the Church Army, founded in 1882, in conscious imitation of the Salvation Army. The Salvation Army itself, founded in 1865, was essentially an evangelistic mission. The Brethren, who had always had a number of 'gentlemen' evangelists, started Counties Evangelistic Work in 1899.

SPECIALIZED AGENCIES

Interdenominational mission work started at an early date. The *Societas Evangelica*, founded in 1776 'to extend the Gospel in Great Britain by itinerant preaching' depended on the principle of churches of different persuasions associating together to accomplish its aims. Another early interdenominational society was the British and Foreign Bible Society, formed in 1804. In the nineteenth century interdenominational societies gradually gave way to nondenominational societies. These grew in number and drew away enormous evangelistic energies from the churches and channelled them into agencies catering for specific forms of evangelism or for particular sections of the population. Among the most notable societies are: Religious Tract Society (1799); British Sailors' Society (1818); Soldiers and Airmens Scripture Readers Association (1838); Shaftesbury Society (1844); Open Air Mission (1853); The Evangelisation Society (1864); Bethnal Green Medical Mission (1866); Scripture Union (1867); Christian Colportage Association (1874); Railway Mission (1881); Evangelical Tract Society (1882); The Boys' Brigade (1883); The Faith Mission (1886); Scripture Gift Mission (1888); Student Christian Movement (1889) which was originally evangelical.

The publication of tracts and other good Christian literature was a primary means of securing conversions. Hannah More noted that the appetite for reading among the lower classes was increasing and wrote to friends to say, 'I propose printing striking conversions, holy lives, happy deaths, providential deliverances, judgements on the breakers of commandments, etc.'[26] She had an eye to what people would read and so consciously varied the form of her tracts. Sermons alone would not have achieved the objective. So in 1795 she started to publish her *Cheap Repository Tracts* at a rate of three a month. Others followed suit. On the fiftieth anniversary of the Religious Tract Society in 1849 they claimed to have circulated over 500 million copies of 5,000 separate titles. Short tracts were supplemented by evangelistic books, the most used of which was Leigh Richmond's, *The Dairyman's Daughter* which sold over four million copies and was cited by many as being influential in their conversions.[27]

A prominent feature of evangelism in the Victorian era was the attempt to win the cities for Christ through the establishment of city missions. David Naismith was the catalyst for city missions. His work led to the founding of those in Glasgow (1826), Dublin (1828) and London (1835), among others. In 1830 he visited America and Canada and, on that single trip, established sixteen city missions. Most great cities, like Liverpool, Leeds, Manchester and Birmingham, founded city missions during the early nineteenth century. The London City Mission had a less than promising beginning. Naismith wanted to secure the co-operation of Anglicans and Nonconformists in its work but met with much opposition, especially from the Bishop of London. Its attempt to ensure that its workers avoided trespassing on the work of the churches only served to underline the fact, to some, that it was, as John Campbell put it, an artificial institution and a 'promiscuous body' which owed allegiance to no one. Regardless of the opposition and the turbulent internal relations between Naismith and others, the work became established and is recognised today as a major city institution commanding widespread admiration.

The object of the London City Mission was 'to extend the knowledge of the gospel irrespective of peculiar tenets in regard to church government ... by domicilary visits for religious conversation and reading the Scriptures, by meetings for prayer and Christian instruction, by promoting the circulation of the Scriptures and religious tracts, by stimulating a regular attendance on the preaching of the gospel' and by using other such means as might be appropriate.

To achieve its objective, LCM divided the city into districts and employed agents to engage in systematic visitation. They were required to spend not less than thirty-eight hours in weekly visiting and the holding of meetings. They were to pay one hundred visits weekly, with five visits less being allowed for each meeting held. They were closely supervised and had to report regularly. Shaftesbury noted that a key to the success of the city missions lay in the type of man they employed as agents, for, 'the classes from which the missionaries are selected are akin to those they are appointed to visit.'[28]

No serious research has yet been done to estimate the effectiveness of the city missions in securing conversions, though the stories of conversions abound in the reports and magazines, as they must if continuing support from evangelicals was to be maintained. But a tribute in the *Edinburgh Review* of 1853, which was usually critical of evangelicals, is high praise. The *Review* commented, 'They have not hesitated to preach in filthy courts and alleys, the haunts of vice and infamy to audiences which could not be tempted to listen under any other roof but the sky.' It concluded that it was largely due to them that 'the profound darkness in which the English peasantry were enveloped at the beginning of the century has been gradually dissipated.'[29]

VISITING EVANGELISTS

All this activity took place alongside the periodic visits of the revivalists from the United States. The Methodist James Caughey visited the United Kingdom from 1841 to 1847, much to the chagrin of the Methodist Conference who regarded him as irregular and eventually expelled him from their number in 1846. But in Liverpool his preaching led to decline being interrupted and in six years the churches there experienced 20,000 converts. He visited Sheffield in 1844, a city already described as 'a crucible of revival'. When he left, 5,000 converts were claimed in all, 20 per cent of whom came from within the church.

Charles Finney visited Britain from 1849 to 1851, meeting with only modest success in the Midlands but more success in London. There he made an impression on establishment and poor alike and dealt with thousands of enquirers, resulting in about 200 new members joining Moorfields Tabernacle, where he was based, alone.[30] He returned in 1859 and helped to stimulate the revival of that time. But the next major visit of an American Revivalist was that of D. L. Moody, on his third visit to Britain, in 1873. Estimates vary as to how many people heard him during that time between one and a half million and two and a half million.[31]

The nineteenth century set the style of evangelical efforts at conversion which were to continue into the twentieth century. Regular churches and national denominations continued to engage in routine evangelism. In 1948, the Church of England published a report, entitled *Towards the Conversion of England*, but not too much seems to have resulted from it. Meanwhile much energy was channelled by evangelicals into specialist societies and into mass evangelism. The number of societies has continued to grow unabated. The early twentieth century saw some excitement in evangelism and the work of Gipsy Smith and the visits of R. A. Torrey, Charles M. Alexander and J. Wilbur Chapman should not go unnoticed. But from the 1920s to the Second World War little happened. After the Second World War a new tempo rose in British mass evangelism with a British evangelist, Tom Rees, holding regular meetings in the packed Royal Albert Hall. These meetings were a worthy precedent for the visits of Billy Graham, which were to start on a large scale from 1954 onwards. The most recent phase has seen a reluctance to rely on mass evangelism and a concern that evangelism should be the responsibility of local churches and its organisation devolved to church bodies.

A similar story could be told regarding the history of evangelism in the United States, if space permitted. That country saw the same interweaving of sporadic revivalism (a much greater tradition there than in the United Kingdom), regular church outreach and specialist societies (like the YMCA and City Missions), with the addition of missions to native Indians.

OVERSEAS MISSIONS

In neither the United Kingdom nor the United States of America was concern for conversions limited to their own land. The modern missionary movement 'was in its origins an exclusively evangelical phenomenon.'[32] The trigger for it was William Carey's *Enquiry into the obligations of Christians, to use means for the conversion of the heathens* (1792). But his very scientific enquiry, which surveyed the world scene and produced detailed statistics of world population and their religious state, was built on the back of a prayer movement seeking a visitation of the Holy Spirit. That movement was fed by the vision of Jonathan Edwards who believed that the Great Awakening of 1740 heralded the last days which would see the universal spread of the gospel.

As with home missions, overseas missions quickly spawned a multitude of societies. The Baptist Missionary Society was formed to support Carey's work in India in 1792. It was followed by the London Missionary Society in 1795. The LMS set out to unite Anglicans and dissenters and to be a mission for all evangelicals. The Church Missionary Society was formed in 1799, with the active involvement of the Clapham Sect. The Methodists entered the field in 1818.

Later in the nineteenth century, often as a result of the revivalistic emphasis within evangelicalism, new interdenominational societies were formed. Following the 1859 Revival, Dr Henry Grattan Guiness was involved in the founding of the Regions Beyond Missionary Union and the North Africa Mission and establishing a training college for overseas missionaries. He trained more than 1,300 volunteers for missionary service who went to serve under thirty denominations in forty missionary societies. Such was the extent of the evangelical empire.[33]

The best-known missionary society to arise at this time was the China Inland Mission, now known as the Overseas Missionary Fellowship. Founded by J. Hudson Taylor in 1865, when no other missionary society would employ him to return to the newly-opened China, it became the advanced guard of Protestant missions in that country. It established itself on the faith principle of not appealing for money, but trusting in God to supply resources. In this it set the pattern for many future evangelical missionary societies. In other respects, too, it was influential in laying down principles which were to become commonplace later. Taylor insisted on close identification with the people he sought to convert and so, for example, wore native costume. He also insisted that the missionary operation be directed from the field rather than the home base.[34]

CIM was also to have a close link with the Keswick movement which was increasingly to support overseas missions. A missionary vocation came to be seen as the ideal of a life of total consecration in evangelical circles. That ideal has declined somewhat in the late twentieth century, with fewer and fewer candidates offering themselves for overseas service, for a number of reasons. Partly, there have been changes in evangelical spirituality with the deeper life movement no longer having the hold that once it did. Partly, there has been an opening up of the world so that there are many more opportunities for people to work overseas, in capacities other than strictly missionary ones. Partly, it is due to the growing emphasis on relief work as distinct from mission work among evangelicals, which suggests that evangelicalism is not immune from secularising influences which led to this-worldly concerns eclipsing other-worldly ones. Partly, it is due to the success of the missionary movement evidenced by the growth, both in numbers and confidence, of indigenous churches world-wide.

The centrality of conversion in evangelicalism, then, led to the generation of a huge industry of missionary endeavour, at home and around the globe. It is this which largely accounts for its activist character. Missionary endeavour has been so characteristic that some believe it is only that which gives the movement coherence. But that is to overstate the case. Certainly, the missionary commitment of evangelicalism is a major feature of the movement and it does contribute significantly to forming the lifestyle and values of its subculture. But truth about fundamental issues also matter, whatever doctrinal disagreements there may be, and the desire to convert does not explain the whole of evangelicalism.

Challenges to conversion

RELATIONSHIP TO BAPTISM AND THE CHURCH

Down the years the evangelical view of conversion has been subject to a number of challenges. Historically, one of the important challenges arose over its relation to baptism. Was regeneration conferred through the act of baptism or not? If not, what was the significance of baptism? This question landed the Revd Charles Goreham in trouble with the Bishop of Exeter in 1846.[35] Goreham did not believe in baptismal regeneration, whereas the bishop did. The dispute between them dragged on and went right up to the Privy Council for arbitration in 1850. They judged in Goreham's favour and he was permitted to remain a priest. But the issue would not go away.

C. H. Spurgeon[36] caused offence to many Anglican evangelicals in 1864 by preaching a sermon on the subject, based on Mark 16:15-16. Baptismal regeneration was, he said, an 'error which is growing in England in direct opposition to the text.' Belief was the sole requirement of salvation and the idea that a child was made regenerate through baptism was erroneous. He accused his evangelical Anglican friends of hypocrisy and encouraged them to resign their livings. His sermon provoked a storm of controversy and a pamphlet war broke out. Spurgeon, himself, resigned from the Evangelical Alliance over the incident since he was deemed by many of its supporters to have broken the spirit of unity for which the Alliance stood. But still the issue persisted.

J. C. Ryle set out his position in *Knots Untied* (1877). 'The principle of the Prayer-book,' he explained, 'is to suppose all members of the church to be in *reality* what they are in *profession* – to be true believers in Christ, to be sanctified by the Holy Ghost . . . the minister addresses those who assemble together for public worship as believers.'[37] It would be absurd, he said, to have a liturgy for unconverted persons and invidious if another service had to be substituted by the vicar if unbelievers were involved. Charity must be allowed and the principle of Luke 10:5,6 practised. Baptism, 'when rightly and worthily received', is a means of inward and spiritual grace. The matter came to the fore again around 1928, at the time of the Prayer-book controversy. It still recurs today, causing a crisis of conscience for some evangelical clergy who are asked to baptise the children of those in their parishes who are manifestly unconverted.

The issue of conversion's relation to baptism also opens the door on a related issue. Granted that no evangelicals would say that regeneration is conveyed through baptism, what of the related issue of initiation into the church? Should conversion automatically lead to baptism, or to joining the church, of which baptism is a rite of entry? Evangelists like Billy Graham have always instructed their enquirers to join a church but today, when denominations are considered unimportant, there is the danger of making conversion the supreme act of individualism, a private act in response to proclamation, rather than an act of initiation into the body of Christ.

Some evangelicals, working independently of the church, have encouraged that misconception. For example, it is said by his biographer, that Moody had no doctrine of the church. In its place he substituted work, by which he meant supremely activity to christianize the nation. Where previously living as a member of a kingdom community and growing within, as seen in Wesley, it had been seen to be the fruit of conversion, now, the engagement in busy evangelism took its place.[38] In so far as this is so, evangelicals have a less than full understanding of the Bible, whose authority they champion and a faulty view of the early church's evangelism which they claim to imitate. With good reason, William Abraham,[39] as mentioned, has argued that the early history of the church viewed evangelism much more as a process of initiation into the kingdom community and life-style, and conversion as an integral part of it, rather than an act that stands on its own.

THE RELATIONSHIP TO SOCIAL CHANGE

On the relationship between conversion and social action evangelicals are nearly unanimous. Social action is to be the fruit of the new creature in Christ. Writing in 1965, before the renewed emphasis on social concern generated by the Lausanne Congress, Billy Graham stressed the point. God was interested in 'the great social issues of our day, such as immorality, destitution, racial problems and crime. The Apostle James said: 'Faith without works is dead (James 2:20)'.[40] In *World Aflame* he devotes a whole chapter to the social involvement of the new Christian and the need to stand for justice. Similarly John Stott quotes the Bangkok Assembly of the World Council of Churches approvingly as saying, 'personal conversion always leads to social action'.[41]

But on another issue there is division. How is society to be changed? The older evangelical view was that society would be changed by changing individuals, as in Spurgeon's statement above. The priority had, therefore, to be evangelism. The *Life of Faith* summed it up, '. . . when once the human heart gets right with God, everything else falls into line'.[42] The view seems largely to have been emphasized as a reaction to the social gospel movement which seemed to regard conversion as irrelevant and proclaimed that society would be changed, not by spiritual regeneration, but by social and economic transformation.

Contemporary evangelical views are more realistic. Recognizing that conversion does not always bring about long-term or wide-scale social transformation, and that sin is located in our fallen world not just in sinful individuals, they now generally believe there are two tasks to be accomplished, that of evangelism and social action. John

Stott, in answering the question, 'Isn't it impossible to expect social change unless people are converted?' answers with an emphatic, 'No'. Whilst longing for people to be converted there is something else to be done, which is a legitimate Christian activity in its own right. 'Legislation can secure social improvement, even though it does not convert people or make them good.'[43]

THE NATURE OF REPENTANCE

Jim Wallis would regard the evangelical view that conversion should lead to social action as too complacent by far. In *The Call to Conversion* (1981) he looks back to his own conversion and speaks of it as being a spiritual abstraction, unrelated to any real historical situation. By contrast, he sees that:

> Conversion in the Bible is always grounded in history, it is always addressed to the actual situation in which people find themselves . . . that turning is always deeply personal, but it is never private. It is never an abstract or theoretical concern; conversion is always a practical issue. Any idea of conversion that is removed from the social and political realities of the day is not biblical.[44]

Conversion means a change of lords. In making the change there are no neutral zones; nothing is left untouched. If it is genuine conversion, therefore, it must affect a person's concrete historical situation causing repentance for past oppressive social actions and leading to a determination to bring the kingdom of God into the world 'with explosive force'. 'The connection between conversion and the kingdom cannot be emphasised enough.'[45] Conversion means to make Jesus King.

Zacchaeus is seen as a paradigm for the conversion of rich Christians in today's world. His conversion led to immediate giving away of his wealth and in doing so he showed the concrete evidence of repentance. The church today, however, acts differently. Contemporary evangelicalism has made the gospel more palatable and by an alliance with the media and politics it has effectively betrayed the gospel. If evangelicals were to turn again to Jesus they would rediscover the social meaning of sin and salvation, for His teaching was shot through with it, as the Sermon on the Mount testifies. Issues of wealth and poverty, violence and the bomb, are not optional extras for the Christian who has graduated beyond the basic stages of conversion, but rather integral to the nature of repentance and conversion itself. Wallis calls for the church to become a genuine community of Jesus, of love and of sharing, believing that, if they do, they will become a community of resistance to the culture in which they live. He concludes, 'May God convert us to such foolishness'.

PLURALISM

The notion of conversion is also under attack because of pluralism. Among the great sociological changes of the last few decades have been that people in the western world now find themselves living alongside those of other faiths and that the media has shrunk our world to a global village. This has not happened without a resulting alteration to people's perceptions so that the varying cultures of the world, together with the religions associated with them, are now perceived to be more relative than once they were. This relativization has deeply affected the church at large, the ecumenical movement in particular and the modern missionary movement, which is not to say that conversion is uncritically accepted in those spheres. But it has had the effect of causing there to be a second look at the exclusive claims of Christianity, at proclamation as the means of propagating Christianity and at the call for people to convert to Christianity.

Inclusivist views, of one sort or another, are now in fashion. These views take many forms. They may argue, to give a few examples, that God has made himself known in all religions of the world through general revelation, although salvation is still to be found in Christ; or that sincere worshippers of other faiths are 'anonymous Christians' who receive the grace of Christ through responding to their own religions; or that our focus must shift from Christ as the centre of our concern to God who, it is believed, is the ultimate divine reality, being worshipped by the different but complementary faiths of the world. These positions lead to a great respect for other faiths and suggest that dialogue rather than proclamation is the more appropriate method of evangelism. Proclamation lacks humility. Dialogue seeks the truth together. If genuine dialogue takes place conversion could go either way but, at any rate, conversion should never be the centre of missionary concern and is culturally insensitive. Conversion is often popularly dismissed, sometimes with justification, as mere proselytism, that is, the making of converts by manipulative, pressurized or unworthy means.

Evangelicalism is associated with an exclusivist position and a proclamatory method, by which is meant that it teaches that salvation is to be found only in Jesus Christ (John 14:6; Acts 4:12) and that the task of evangelism is to proclaim the Gospel so that people might be converted to him. Consequently, it has found itself deeply unpopular.

The issues are complex.[46] No genuine evangelical would want to trade on the uniqueness of Christ as the exclusive means of salvation. As the Lausanne Covenant expressed it,

> We affirm that there is only one Saviour and only one Gospel, although there is a wide diversity of evangelistic approaches. We recognize that all men have some knowledge of God through his general revelation in nature. But we deny that this can save, for men suppress the truth by their unrighteousness. We also reject as derogatory to Christ and the Gospel every kind of syncretism and dialogue which implies that Christ speaks equally through all religions and ideologies. Jesus Christ, being himself the only God-man, who gave himself as the only ransom for sinners, is the only mediator between God and man. There is no other name by which we must be saved. ...[47]

If this is so, conversion must remain of central importance to missionary endeavour. Yet at the same time, evangelicals are displaying a greater openness to dialogue, not as a replacement for proclamation but alongside it, as a mark of humble listening and integrity.[48] Dialogue was not unknown in the scripture, nor in evangelical history. It does not require that those engaged in it lack conviction regarding the truth of what they believe. It does demonstrate a sensitive listening to one another, characteristic of Christ himself. Evangelicals are also sensitive to the methods of securing conversion. With the opening up of Eastern Europe the charges of proselytism, long heard elsewhere, have markedly increased. Popular evangelicalism, with the best of intentions, is unwittingly often culturally insensitive, confuses the benefits of conversion with the benefits of western civilization and must stand guilty as charged. As a free-enterprise form of faith there is no way to overcome this except to call evangelicals back constantly to model the integrity of their weak and servant King.

THE CRUCIAL CHALLENGE

For all the refinements which may be occurring to the idea of conversion, the final challenge is the most important of all. Do evangelicals still really believe and preach it? Evangelicalism often appears to have a public and a private face. In the mass crusades and overseas missions, evangelicalism speaks the public rhetoric of conversion. But increasingly people are called forward at evangelical gatherings for some less well-defined form of ministry rather than for conversion. Increasingly the idea of a gradual growth in understanding of the faith seems to be the order of the day rather than a more definite turning to God. Increasingly the concept of relief and social amelioration is taking over from evangelistic mission. Do evangelicals still believe that conversion brings about a radical transformation in the life of the one who turns to Christ? Although it is entirely mistaken to try to stereotype conversions, working for conversions, preaching conversions and testifying to conversions as a radical change which God makes in a person's life has always been at the heart of evangelicalism. Evangelicalism could no more be evangelicalism without the commitment to conversion than a car could be a car without an engine. The challenge remains to call people, in intelligible, sensitive and relevant ways, to turn to God.

8

THE CROWNING DAY IS COMING

Evangelicals and the last things

It was heady stuff. As a young boy I sat captivated, night after night, as ingenious preachers unravelled the mysteries of Daniel's visions, Ezekiel's prophecies and Revelation's mysteries, and showed how, centuries beforehand, the events of tomorrow's newspaper headlines had been foretold in the Bible. With one eye on my Schofield Reference Bible and the other on a diagram of prophecy, which looked a bit like an incomprehensible diagram of an electric circuit, these Prophetic Conferences provided me with my exact location in God's scheme of things and told me with complete assurance of the next steps in His timetable. It was completely enthralling.

I thought every true Christian thought this way and that this was *the* evangelical interpretation of prophecy. Only later did I discover that it was one evangelical viewpoint, known as premillennialism, and that other evangelicals, with equal sincerity and competence, interpreted what their Bibles had to say about the last things differently. A vision of the future has always been a mark of evangelicalism, at least until the present time. But the vision has differed over the years, and, between the different segments of the evangelical Rubik's Cube.

Where evangelicals agree

Evangelicals unite around one central truth. In the words of the Evangelical Alliance's *Basis of Faith*, they believe in 'The expectation of the personal, visible return of the Lord Jesus Christ in power and glory.' Move beyond that and the disagreements commence. Will He return before or after the millennium, or does it not matter? Will the church be 'raptured'? Will He come for His church and then come yet again to complete His work of judgment and re-creation? Will the new creation be heaven or a new heaven and a new earth? And what about hell? Will those who die without repenting be eternally punished or annihilated? And when will all this happen – tomorrow or later?

The disagreements should not blind us to the importance of what it is evangelicals agree about. The personal, visible return of Jesus Christ is not something all Christians affirm. To many the idea of his second coming is primitive. To avoid such crudity they interpret his second coming either as having already happened at his resurrection or at Pentecost, or, as a personal experience which occurs when the risen Christ comes to the believer. They see speculation about the future as irrelevant pipe-dreaming. So, to hold on to the idea that Christ will come again, cutting into history and winding up the present world order as we know it, is an evangelical distinctive.

The expectation derives its importance from the New Testament. W. Griffith Thomas, the Anglican theologian from earlier this century, pointed out, 'The Lord's coming is referred to in one verse out of every thirteen in the New Testament, and in the Epistles alone in one verse out of ten.'[1] If that is so, the doctrine clearly acquired a more important place than some other doctrines, such as that of the sacraments, which receive a great deal of discussion today, and evangelicals are right to give it careful attention.

Truth to tell, they have not always done so. It would seem that it was not until the 1820s that evangelicals came to believe that Christ's return would be a literal coming. The evangelical Bible commentator, Thomas Scott, claimed, in 1802, that there would be 'no visible appearance' of Christ. James Hartley Frere who wrote, *A Combined View of the Prophecies of Daniel, Edras and St John*, in 1815, believed the second advent to be imminent, but, even so, thought of it in spiritual and metaphorical terms rather than as a literal and visible appearing. Charles Simeon wrote in a letter, in 1830, that the matter did not occupy his thoughts.[2] But from the 1820s onwards, the expectation of a personal and visible return of Jesus Christ has been enshrined in evangelical thinking.

Basic agreement is to be found in the belief that his return will be personal, visible, sudden, unexpected, glorious and triumphant and that it will alter the course of creation-history for ever. It will be personal, 'For the Lord *Himself* will come down from heaven ..' (1 Thessalonians 4:16). It will be visible since, 'every eye will see Him' (Revelations 1:7, also Acts 1:11). It will be sudden, like a flash of lightning (Matthew 24:27), or 'a thief in the night' (1 Thessalonians 5:3). It will be 'a glorious appearing' (Titus 2:13) when he will come 'on the clouds of the sky, with power and great glory. And he will send his angels with a loud trumpet call, and they will gather the elect from the four winds, from one end of heaven to the other' (Matthew 24:30-31). It will be decisive: 'Then the end will come . . .' (1 Corinthians 15:24). The event will usher in the complete restoration of creation with its Creator (Colossians 1:20, 1 Corinthians 15:24,25); the recreation of heaven and earth (Revelation 21:1) and the final and full redemption of the saved (1 John 3:2, Revelation 22:1-5).

The millennium

It is when evangelicals move beyond that basic agreement and try to fill in further details that divergent views appear. The matter is not one on which it has ever been essential to have unity. The disagreements are considered legitimate since the Bible is less than clear on the details and the matter must, therefore, be of secondary rather than primary importance. The views diverge from one another essentially around the question of the millennium. The millennium is only mentioned once in the Bible, in Revelation 20, but how one interprets it, especially its place in relation to the second coming of Christ, determines what one believes about the events of the future. There are three basic positions: postmillennialism, premillennialism, which has a number of variants, and amillennialism or nonmillennialism, as it is sometimes called. [3] Each of these has been influential in evangelicalism at various times.

POSTMILLENNIALISM
Postmillennialism asserts that the second coming of Christ will take place after the millennium. The kingdom of God has been inaugurated and is currently at work in the world through the ministry of the Holy Spirit and the spreading of the gospel. That work will not only continue but increase until the climax of the present gospel age when there will be such a time of spiritual prosperity and peace, like that spoken of in Revelation 20, that Satan will be bound and the millennium will have arrived. At the end of the thousand years Satan will be released and a time of unimaginable tribulation and wickedness will follow which will be brought to an end by the coming of Christ. His coming will be the signal for the end. It will bring about the defeat of Satan, the overthrow of evil and trigger the resurrection, the judgment and the new creation.

Postmillennialism is essentially an optimistic view which encourages Christians both to spread the gospel and to engage in the reformation of society in order to hasten the dawning of the millennium. To pray, 'Thy kingdom come, thy will be done on earth as it is in heaven', is, for the postmillennialist, to receive a mandate for action in the present world. Although historians argue over who has held this view in the history of the church the evidence suggests that postmillennialism, or something akin to it, was the view of the Reformers and the Puritans.[4] It gave the Puritans the courage to intervene in the politics of their day and bring about a drastic revision of government.

It was from the Puritans that the early evangelicals derived their views which, coincidentally, provided them with a theology which exactly matched their own experience in the Great Awakening. Jonathan Edwards is usually said to be the key person in this regard. In his *History of the Work of Redemption* (1739) he wrote that the millennium would arrive through 'the preaching of the gospel and the use of the ordinary means of grace.'[5] And he saw the outbreaking of spiritual awakening as its early dawning. It led him to encourage Christians around the world to unite in extraordinary prayer for further revival and the advancement of God's kingdom, for, he said, Romans 11 tells us 'that the time is coming when the whole world of mankind, both Jews and Gentiles, shall be brought into the Church of Christ.'[6]

The universal dimension of the awakenings made him wonder whether God was about to do something even more glorious. 'It is not unlikely,' he wrote, 'that this work of God's Spirit, so extraordinary and wonderful, is the dawning, or, at least, a prelude of that glorious work of God, so often foretold in Scripture.'[7]

This view exercised a powerful influence on evangelicalism for most of the eighteenth century, and especially in the area of world missions.[8] But within a century it was to be replaced by premillennialism, an altogether different theology. Postmillennialism eventually suffered the fate of being secularized and became fused with the idea of progress. It continued to inspire the dream of America as having a special destiny in civilizing the world and, by a curious twist, in this way still exercises an implicit influence on premillennialists today, since premillennialism is often tied up with American nationalism, even while being rejected by them.[9] It is still current in some circles as a theology and was, to a considerable degree, rescued by the publication of Iain Murray's *The Puritan Hope,* in 1971.

PREMILLENNIALISM

Premillennialism comes in many forms, some of which require a fair amount of sophistication to understand.[10] Underlying them all is the belief that Christ's return will take place before the millennium. For premillennialists, the sequence of events looks like this. The world, far from getting better, is going to get progressively worse and be characterized by widespread unbelief, apostasy and wickedness, culminating in the reign of the Antichrist. At the end of this period

Christ will return to overthrow the Antichrist which he will do at the battle of Armageddon. Having done so he will establish his millennial rule of prosperity and peace which will end with a short rebellion by Satan – easily put down. It is then that the end will come with the resurrection of the dead and the judgment.

There are two schools of premillennialism. One argues that the prophecies of scripture chart the history of the church in symbolic form. Known as the historicist school, it leads to the eager decoding of Daniel and Revelation, by, for example, understanding 'days' to stand for 'years', so that the prophecies can be related to contemporary events and future dates predicted. The other school is the futurist school. This school teaches that the Book of Revelation does not unveil the course of the present but only relates to the 'last days', the short period immediately before the return of Christ. Whereas the first leads to a fascination with contemporary events, the second leads to a withdrawal from them. Among the many refinements to the futurist view is the question of what happens to the Christians during the period of the Great Tribulation. Some teach that they are to be raptured by a secret coming of Christ before the Tribulation commences, some midway through and some afterwards. Another refinement is dispensationalism, which owes its origins to the teaching of John Nelson Darby and the Brethren and is particularly common in the United States.

In the early nineteenth century, writings appeared which began to put forward premillennial ideas. Among them was James Hartley Frere's *Combined View* (1815) and a work by 'Ben-Ezra' entitled, *The Coming of the Messiah in Glory and Majesty* (1826). The latter, which purported to be by a converted Jew, received attention because it coincided with growing interest in the conversion of the Jews and was translated by the charismatic Edward Irving. Although initially opposed by evangelicals, premillennialism caught on. 'It was,' writes David Bebbington, 'part of the Romantic inflow into Evangelicalism. Christ the coming king could readily be pictured by poetic imaginations fascinated by the strange, the awesome and the supernatural.'[11]

The ideas gained currency through annual meetings held at Albury Park, Surrey, the country home of Henry Drummond, from 1826 to 1830. An influential participant was Edward Irving. After careful study of the Bible, which they interpreted with a great degree of literalism, they agreed six things about Christ's Second Coming: it would be cataclysmic; the Jews were to be restored to Palestine; judgment was to fall on Christendom; the coming would be prior to the millennium; the millennium would begin after the judgment and Daniel 7 and Revelation 13 applied to the French Revolution and the tumultuous events which they had witnessed subsequently.[12] That they were on the verge of new things seemed to be confirmed when the gift of tongues was restored to Edward Irving's church in 1831. It is easy to see how premillennialism was affected not only by Romanticism but by growing pessimism about the degenerating state of the world in the light of events in Europe. The views coincided with, and simultaneously reinforced, the growing belief in the Bible as inerrant and to be taken literally.

Of greater significance, long-term, was J. N. Darby, one of the founders of the Brethren movement. An erstwhile Anglican clergyman, Darby attended prophetic conferences hosted by Lady Powerscourt on her estate near Dublin and, from there, began to elaborate his views. He held that history could be divided into dispensations, periods which are marked off by the different ways in which God deals with people. So, for example, there were the dispensations of promise, from Abraham to Moses; of law, from Moses to Christ and of grace, from Pentecost to the rapture. He distinguished sharply between God's dealings with the Jews and with the church. Prophecies concerning the Jews were taken literally and so there was the expectation that the Messiah would restore David's throne. The timetable for all this could be found in Daniel's visions but, because the Jews rejected the Messiah, God had temporarily postponed that timetable and turned his attention to the Gentiles. The prophecies of Revelation would begin to be fulfilled only when the secret rapture of believers had taken place, prior to the Great Tribulation, thus, saving Christians from the suffering which would be involved. All these elements subsequently became characteristic of dispensational premillennialism.

By the middle of the nineteenth century historicist premillennialism was in decline. There had been too many failures in its predictions, due to faulty prophetic arithmetic, for it to remain strong. William Miller, for example, a Baptist preacher from Vermont who had almost a million disciples in the North-eastern States, had predicted that Christ would return on 22nd October 1844. He and his followers became laughing-stocks when it did not happen. Had it not been for this new form of premillennialism it might have died a death. But the new ideas became popular, aided and abetted by the growth of biblical literalism, and found circulation in a growing number of publications.

It was the revivalists who gave premillennialism its greatest platforms. D. L. Moody came into contact with premillennialism, probably through the Brethren, in the 1870s, and always preached once on the return of Christ towards the end of each of his campaigns. Like many others, the idea of the imminent return of

Christ to rapture the saints injected a note of urgency into the need to be saved. Moody warned that the coming could take place at any time, even before he had finished preaching. 'What if He were to come tonight and you were not ready? You would be left behind.' Moody proclaimed:

> I look on this world as a wrecked vessel. God has given me a life-boat, and said to me, 'Moody, save all you can.' God will come in judgment and burn up this world, but the children of God don't belong to this world; they are in it, but not of it, like a ship in the water. This world is getting darker and darker; its ruin is coming nearer and nearer. If you have any friends on this wreck unsaved, you had better lose no time in getting them off.[13]

Through Moody, premillennialism became established as the nearest thing to official doctrine in the revivalist strand of evangelicalism. Subsequent evangelists, like J. Wilbur Chapman and R. A. Torrey preached it. The summer conferences Moody established, held at Northfield, and frequently visited by F. B. Meyer and Henry Drummond, as well as those conferences held elsewhere, like those at Niagara or Mildmay, dwelt on it. Cyrus Schofield, a former lawyer whom Moody brought to Northfield to act as pastor, disseminated it widely through his Schofield Reference Bible (1909). The Moody Bible Institute, formed for the training of Christian workers, institutionalized it, in 1886, the same year as the Student Volunteer Movement was formed at Northfield. The founding of the Institute was significant in a number of ways. It poured forth volunteers to work in mission, spurred on by the urgency of the imminent return of Christ. It stood, too, as an enduring rebuke to the denominational seminaries where modern views of the Bible were encroaching, concern about the second coming was absent and the revival fires were dying. Those seminaries were, to many premillennialists, further evidence that the mainline church was on the road to apostasy, as their pessimistic prophetic scheme required.

Premillennialism also had a close connection with Keswick and with overseas missions.[14] With Keswick the connection was a little ambiguous. Premillennialism did not encourage people to believe that there would be a life of victory, nor a victorious church, in this world. None the less there was a great overlap in the networks they served and the preachers who serviced them, and the second coming of Christ was seen as an incentive to holiness. The connection with overseas mission is also ambivalent in theory but clear in practice. In theory, dispensationalism discouraged missions since it taught that the spread of the gospel would not succeed. In practice, it saw that the spread of the gospel around the globe was a sign of the second coming of Christ and, therefore, premillennialists were ardent missionaries. The zenith of Christian missions took place in the early decades of the twentieth century. The pattern was set by the China Inland Mission, which was founded by James Hudson Taylor, a premillennialist, and which recruited predominantly from their ranks. According to Kenneth Scott Latourette, the CIM resolved the tension inherent between premillennialist views and missions by desiring to spread the knowledge of the gospel throughout China as quickly as possible rather than being concerned primarily about winning converts or building churches.[15]

Not all was plain sailing in the premillennial channel. Despite some common concerns about the Bible, the Princeton theologians did not adopt premillennialism and spoke of it, or aspects of it, as 'unprofitable' or 'foolish'. Then, not all was well within the premillennialist ship itself. Around the turn of the century, splits occurred over the question of the secret rapture. The Niagara Bible Conference, which had been a major centre of the teaching, fragmented over the issue and announced that it would not meet again after 1901. But several factors were soon to contribute to premillennialism's rescue. The Welsh Revival of 1904 excited millennial hopes. Pentecostalism threw in its lot with premillennialism. The First World War seemed to confirm its pessimistic prognostications and the rise of modernism gave premillennialists a new cause to fight.

Ernest Sandeen has proposed that the fundamentalist reaction to modernism in the 1820s owes much to the existence of Bible Institutes and the premillennialism they taught.[16] Although most would believe he overstates the case, there was a connection. Lyman Stewart, who financed *The Fundamentals*, published between 1910 and 1915 was a firm advocate of Darby's dispensationalism. The editor was A. C. Dixon, pastor of Moody Tabernacle, Chicago, and half of the authors were known premillennialists, although their major concern was not with the future but with the Bible. Those who subsequently became influential in the leadership of fundamentalism were premillennialists. Indeed, William B. Riley called premillennialism 'the sufficient if not solitary antidote to the present apostasy.'[17]

Premillennialism remained strong in the 1930s but because of fundamentalists became increasingly tied to separatism. New evangelicalism, though never disowning it, distanced itself from it. Its leaders became passive premillennialists. Many of its details have now been forgotten by wider evangelicalism. But it remains strong in some institutions, such as, the Moody Bible Institute and Dallas

Theological Seminary. One aspect of it has been retained in the new evangelicalism, as well as surfacing in the Moral Majority, that is, its commitment to the Jewish people. Since the Jewish people are destined to play such a strategic role in God's future plan, their fortunes are followed with great care and their interests supported.

Whilst in Britain premillennial adventist teaching has ceased to be a feature of evangelicalism, even, to a large extent among the Brethren, the same cannot be said among popular, especially separatist, evangelicalism in the United States. According to one estimate, it has eight million adherents out of forty million evangelicals there.[18] The best selling Christian book in America has to be Hal Lindsey's *The Late Great Planet Earth* (1970) which, according to the 1992 edition, has fifteen million copies in print.

In a classic premillennial way Lindsey reads contemporary events into the prophetic parts of the Bible and traces the signs of the end of the age in the present time. Much is made of the rebirth of Israel, of unrest in the Middle East and the revival of interest in Satanism. But reading it twenty years after it was written demonstrates how precarious prophetic prediction is. It assumes the growing dominance of the USSR, since it is to be Gog, the northern nation which will attack Israel, spoken of in Ezekiel 38. America was to lose its leadership place in the world but a United States of Europe was to become more significant. The only problem is that events have not turned out as Lindsey assumed. The USSR has collapsed, America seems triumphant and the European confederacy, which was supposed to be made up of ten nations, in fulfilment of the fourth kingdom of Daniel 7, is now larger than that. This confederacy, it was prophesied, would share a common monetary currency by 1980, or sooner. The European Economic Community, it is true, is seeking monetary union but the goal seems strangely elusive. Of course, these things could yet come true. But, for the present, his fitting together of the prophetic puzzle, as Lindsey terms it, reads like a curious period piece. It was exciting, not to say sensational at the time of writing, but its speculations have been proved erroneous in part.

There are, too, more serious problems with it. Samuel Escobar has pointed out, 'The book's particular manner of handling the biblical material is clearly conditioned by an intensely conservative nationalism which is hostile to Europe, the Arab countries and communism. This hostility does not come from a specifically Christian stance, but rather stems from Americanism.'[19] He points to a passage when Lindsey bemoans the fact that American leaders have not had the courage to use their military capability decisively and seems to imply that a spiritual revival would lead to America not only being strong but militarily aggressive.[20] Not only does this appear a curious American-centred view of prophecy, but even more importantly, it seems, a long way from the Lord who rode into Jerusalem on a donkey and shunned the military options which he was offered, preferring, instead, the way of the cross.

Lindsey's premillennial approach to prophecy will doubtless recur and be of particular fascination to evangelicals of a speculative and sensational mind-set. But for the most part, it currently holds little sway in contemporary evangelicalism.

AMILLENNIALISM

The third view regarding the millennium treats Revelation 20 as symbolic. In this view, the millennium will occur neither before nor after the coming again of Christ, as a literal period of time, but refers instead to the present age of the church – the whole period of time between the first and second comings of Christ. The three great characteristics of the millennium, namely, that Satan is bound, Christians are bearing costly testimony but even so are reigning with Christ and that Christ is reigning in heaven, are all true of our present age. Satan has been publicly disarmed by the cross (Luke 11:21-22). Christians are already reigning with Christ (Ephesians 2:6, Colossians 3:1-3) and Christ is already exalted on the throne in heaven (Hebrews 1:3).

To understand this view it is important to realize that it does not fit into some linear sequence which is mapped out in Revelation but rather runs in parallel with the other visions in the book. Amillennialists believe that all these visions capture various aspects of the whole story of the time between the first and second comings of Christ, sometimes from an earthly and sometimes from a heavenly standpoint. Like the other views, it should be said, amillennialism is subject to a number of variations.

Tracing its roots to Augustine, its most influential expression in contemporary evangelicalism is found in William Hendriksen's widely respected interpretation of Revelation entitled, *More than Conquerors.*[21] Many evangelical leaders would put themselves within the amillennialist camp today, as John Stott has recently done.[22] It is wrong, therefore, to equate evangelicalism with premillennialist preaching as is often done.

THE PRESENT SITUATION

But there are more important issues to raise. The doctrine of the second coming of Christ has declined in importance among evangelicals since the middle of the century and consequently, for the most part, they no longer feel the need to be conversant with the finer details of prophetic schemes or to take sides in millennial disputes. The current attitude is summed up in an old story, which is probably apocryphal, about G. Campbell Morgan who, when once asked by a lady whether he was a premillennialist or a post-millennialist, answered, 'Madam, that question is pre-post-erous!' He clearly took a position similar to one leading present-day evangelical preacher who claims to be a 'panmillennialist' because he cannot make his mind up what he believes except that it will all pan out in the end.

The acceptance of agnosticism about theories of the millennium is in many ways to be welcome. Evangelicalism has displayed, all too frequently, an ability to self-destruct over issues which are unclear in Scripture and where, therefore, liberty of opinion should be granted. In so far as contemporary attitudes indicate a desire to shun dogmatism where it is unwarranted, or to shake off silly interpretations of Scripture which have brought the Bible and the gospel into disrepute, then it is a sign of maturity and is to be applauded.

But the suspicion is that there is more to it than that. Contemporary attitudes should alert us to a more fundamental, and less welcome, aspect of evangelicalism. It is not just that there is a decline in dogmatism about millennial theories, but rather that there is a decline in commitment to the doctrine of the second coming *per se*. Are evangelicals, at least those in the comfortable West, in the position where they no longer 'wait for the blessed hope – the glorious appearing of our great God and Saviour, Jesus Christ' (Titus 2:13)? Many give the impression that, rather than being their eager longing and expectation the second coming would be an interruption to their plans and ambitions for this world. Rather than welcoming it, they would welcome its postponement. Secularization fools people into thinking that this world is the only real world. Has secularization taken its toll and eroded evangelical belief in the world to come? Has life improved so much that many would want to dissent from Paul who 'desired to depart and be with Christ, which is better by far' (Philippians 1:23)? If so, then present attitudes to the second coming are not a sign of maturity but of weakness and a biblical distinctive has been lost.

John Wesley wrote, 'I desire to have both heaven and hell ever in my eye, while I stand on this isthmus of life, between these two boundless oceans; and I verily think the daily considerations of both highly becomes all men of reason and religion.'[23] I doubt whether Wesley would feel at home in today's evangelicalism in this matter.

The problem of hell

The doctrine of the last things properly covers the subjects of the return of Christ, death, judgement, heaven and hell. It is to evangelical belief in the last of these to which we now turn.

THE TRADITIONAL VIEW

Early evangelicals were clear in their views about hell. They believed in it, they believed it to be a place of never-ending torment and they used it to encourage the fear of God and to induce the experience of the new birth. They can probably be absolved from the charge that they persuaded people more by the fear of hell than the love of God. Even so, they were not embarrassed to preach hell without qualification. Wesley's defence against such an accusation was that it was better to terrorize people now than that they should wake up in hell.

The most famous sermon in the Great Awakening was preached by Jonathan Edwards in 1741, at Enfield, Connecticut, on the subject of 'Sinners in the Hands of an Angry God'. His text was Deuteronomy 32:35: 'It is mine to avenge; I will repay. In due time their foot will slip; their day of disaster is near and their doom rushes upon them.' The sermon portrayed the future punishment of sinners with graphic, firey imagery. 'Natural men', he urged, 'are held in the hands of God over the pit of hell.' The effect was electric. Before he had finished preaching, people fell under an awful conviction of sin, cried out that they were destined for hell and begged to know what they could do to be saved.[24]

Edwards was not alone in such preaching. Wesley may have been more restrained in his imagery but he was no less convinced of the importance of preaching 'the terrors of the Lord'. To him, it was a matter of straight-forward revelation in the Bible and was to be passed on literally. Either hell was a reality or God has perpetrated a fraud and if there was one such fraud then the whole of revelation fell as untrustworthy. It was an awful prospect. In his sermon on hell he stressed its unending nature. 'All those torments of body and soul are without intermission. They have no respite from pain; but "the smoke of their torment ascendeth up day and night" . . . and be their pain ever so intense, there is no possibility of their fainting away; no, not for a moment.' He insisted on the eternal duration of hell since the same word 'eternal' is used, for example, in Matthew 25:46, to describe both hell and heaven. So, 'It follows, that either the punishment lasts for ever, or the reward will come to an end.' He pleaded for people to flee from the wrath to come in words like these: 'And of this duration there is no end. What a thought is this! Nothing but eternity is the term of their torment! And who can count the drops of rain, or the sands of the sea, or the days of eternity? . . . What! Sufferings never to end!'[25]

One strand of evangelicalism has remained loyal to that traditional presentation of hell. It can be traced through the Princeton theologians to our own day. Charles Hodge asserted in his *Systematic Theology* (1873) that, 'It is an almost invincible presumption that the Bible does teach the unending punishment of the finally impenitent . . .' To the objection that the punishment was out of proportion to the crime, he replied that, 'We are incompetent judges of the penalty which sin deserves.' But he did concede, to those who had moral objections to the doctrine, that the final number of the impenitent may be small.[26] His son, A. A. Hodge, felt himself on equally firm ground and wrote, 'The ceaseless, hopeless, conscious suffering of those who die impenitent, both during the intermediate state before the resurrection and in the final state after the resurrection and judgment is asserted over and over again in every form, in the most definite language, and with the greatest emphasis possible.'[27]

The traditional doctrine of hell, as a place of perpetual and never-ending punishment, was asserted by others too. J. C. Ryle and C. H. Spurgeon were among those who did so in England. But its assertion was not confined to those of a more Reformed theology. Some revivalists and missionary statesmen also stressed it, since it was the most persuasive reason for propagating the gospel by evangelism and responding to the gospel in conversion. An example of the former can be found in R. A. Torrey. In *What the Bible Teaches* he argued that nothing less than the everlasting anguish of those who persist in their choice of sin would do justice to the perfect holiness of God and the infinite glory of Jesus Christ. He went on to write:

> If you really believe the doctrine of the endless, conscious torment of the impenitent, and the doctrine really gets hold of you, you will work as you never worked before for the salvation of the lost. If you in any wise abate the doctrine, it will abate your zeal. Time and again the author has come up to this awful doctrine and tried to find some way of escape from it, but when he has failed, as he always has at last, when he was honest with the Bible, and with himself, he has returned to his work with an increased burden for souls and an intensified determination to spend and be spent for their salvation.[28]

Missionary leaders were not above using the fate of the lost heathen in a way akin to emotional blackmail in order to motivate volunteers to the mission field. A powerful expression of that came from the pen of Amy Carmichael:

The tom-toms thumped straight on all night, and the darkness shuddered round me like a living, feeling thing. I could not go to sleep, so I lay awake and looked; and I saw, as it seemed, this: That I stood on a grassy sward, and at my feet a precipice broke sheer down into infinite space. I looked, but saw no bottom; only cloud shapes, black and furiously coiled, and great shadow-shrouded hollows, and unfathomable depths. Back I drew, dizzy at the depth. Then I saw forms of people moving single file along the grass. They were making for the edge. There was a woman with a baby in her arms and another little child holding on to her dress. She was on the very verge. Then I saw that she was blind. She lifted her foot for the next step . . . it trod air. She was over, and the children with her. Oh, the cry as they went over.

And over these gaps the people fell in their blindness, quite unwarned; and the green grass seemed blood-red to me, and the gulf yawned like the mouth of hell. Then I saw, like a picture of peace, a group of people under some trees, with their backs turned towards the gulf. They were making daisy chains. Sometimes when a piercing shriek cut the quiet air and reached them it disturbed them, and they thought it rather a vulgar noise. And if one of their number started up and wanted to go and do something to help, then the others would put that one down. 'Why should you get so excited about it? You must wait for a definite call to go! You haven't finished your daisy chains yet.'[29]

From the middle of the nineteenth century onwards, however, the evangelical consensus on hell began to crack. The major threat to it was simply that people ceased to emphasise it, as once they would have done. D. L. Moody is symptomatic. Through his acquaintance with a converted British pickpocket and boy preacher, called Harry Morehouse, Moody learned to preach the love of God rather than the fires of hell. Having listened to Morehouse preach for a week on John 3:16, Moody commented, 'I never knew up to that time that God loved us so much. This heart of mine began to thaw out; I could not keep back the tears.' From then on a loving gospel triumphed. It was not that Moody did not believe in hell as eternal punishment it was rather that, as he said, 'I believe that the magnet that goes down to the bottom of the pit is the love of Jesus.'[30]

Older style preachers might still appeal to the horrors of hell. Spurgeon did, allowing his imagination to run beyond Scripture. 'You have seen', he proclaimed, 'asbestos lying among red hot coals, but not consumed. So your body will be prepared by God in such a way that it will burn for ever without being desensitized for all its raging fury . . . the acrid smoke of the sulphurous flames searing your lungs and choking your breath . . .'[31] But such pictures no longer appealed to the popular imagination as once they did and evangelicals in the mainstream quietly marginalized the doctrine, referring only to the fact of judgment rather than the awful endless suffering which hell would entail.

Some went even further. T. R. Birks, the General Secretary of the Evangelical Alliance, published a book, entitled, *The Victory of Divine Goodness*, in 1867, in which he objected to the traditional doctrine of hell as 'the potential continuance of active malice' and asserted a form of universalism. He believed that the cosmic dimensions of future salvation should be considered and that, in the end, God would triumph over all evil. The condition of the lost, he admitted, was a mysterious paradox. They would 'combine, with the utmost personal shame and humiliation and anguish the passive contemplation of a ransomed universe, of all the innumerable varieties of blessedness enjoyed by unfallen spirits and the ransomed people of God.'[32] His universalist tendencies caused a hostile reaction among the Alliance's Council and he, wisely, resigned his post. But when steps were taken to have him removed as a member of the Evangelical Alliance insufficient support was forthcoming to do so. Most considered it enough that some form of eternal punishment was affirmed without requiring that it should be specified in greater detail. That one so close to the heart of British evangelical life could write such a book is, however, further evidence that evangelicals in the period had begun to reinterpret the doctrine of hell.

Apart from sheer neglect, there are two positions, other than the traditional doctrine of hell, which Christians hold. The first is universalism and the second, annihilationism or conditional immortality. The former has always been opposed by evangelicals whereas the second is one which they have flirted with over the years and which many are now coming to hold with increasing respect.

UNIVERSALISM

Universalism teaches that in the end all people will be saved. It is probably the most common popular view of the future but it also has some serious theological advocates. They point to texts such as Romans 5:18; Ephesians 1:10; 1 Timothy 2:3,4 and 4:10, to make out its case. The primary evangelical objection is that universalism flies in the face of many other passages of scripture which plainly assert a separation at the end of time and a judgment on the impenitent, such as, Daniel 12:2; Matthew 13:37-43,47-50; 25:31-46; Luke 16:19-31; John 5:28-29; and Revelation 20:11-15. Furthermore, universalism ignores the repeated connection in the Bible between eternal salvation and the exercise of faith (e.g., John 3:16,36; Acts 16:30,31; Romans 1:17 and 1 John 5:12).

A second objection is that none of the passages interpreted in a universalist way should rightly be interpreted in this way. Their inclusive statements are all defined by their surrounding contexts in such a way that their apparent universalism is qualified. The universalism of Romans 5:18, for example, is not only clearly qualified by verse 17, which defines those who have life as those who 'receive God's abundant provision of grace and of the gift of righteousness,' but also by the wider context of Romans. In the letter as a whole inclusivism generally refers not to the inclusion of every single individual but to the inclusion of Gentiles alongside Jews in the new covenant. On investigation, none of the verses quoted in support of universalism merit that interpretation. John Blanchard's conclusion is surely right. 'After centuries of trying to attach itself to Scripture, universalism comes unglued at every point.'[33]

In addition to these weighty objections there are moral and philosophical arguments against the suggestion that, regardless of evil, everything will work out all right in the end for everybody. It simply does not take wickedness seriously enough.

ANNIHILATIONISM

Annihilationism teaches that after death the impenitent will cease to exist. Akin to it, but not identical, is the idea of conditional immortality. That argument goes like this. God alone is immortal (1 Timothy 6:16). Men and women are mortal and dependent on God for the gift of immortality who gives it through Christ (2 Timothy 1:10). At the judgment those who are justified receive that gift whilst those who are impenitent phase out into extinction. Some argue that annihilation does not occur immediately but only after an appropriate period in Hades. The idea that each person has an immortal soul is said to be an import from Greek philosophy rather than a Christian idea.

The view has long been around. In fact, a clause was added to the expanded version of the Evangelical Alliance Basis of Faith in 1846, at the insistence of the Americans, specifically to counteract annihilationism and universalism because the ideas were gaining currency. R. W. Dale announced his commitment to it in 1874, but it first began to find more widespread public expression among evangelicals earlier this century (although doubtless this was voicing what many had long secretly believed). H. E. Guillebaud, a staunch defender of the evangelical view of the atonement, in his book, *Why the Cross?* went on to study the question of eternal punishment. In a work published in 1964, but written in the 1930s, he set out a conditionalist argument, as it is sometimes known. Around the same time, Basil Atkinson, a Cambridge scholar and redoubtable evangelical, published similar views.

Today the views are held by a growing number of evangelical leaders and scholars including Roger Forster, Clark Pinnock, John Stott, Stephen Travis and John Wenham. [34] Each of these has a high view of Scripture and desires to be faithful to it. With his customary lucidity, John Stott presents a four-fold argument in favour of annihilationism. Put with extreme brevity the argument is this. First, the natural meaning of many passages of scripture which use the language of death and destruction, as in Matthew 10:28, is that when destruction occurs, people are destroyed, that is, life is terminated. It seems strange to propose that, in the case of hell, to destroy, in fact, means not to destroy.

Second, the imagery used is that of fire and the 'main function of fire is not to cause pain but to secure destruction.' John Stott recognises powerful objections to this view since the image of fire does appear to be chosen to portray a picture of torment rather than destruction. But a careful examination of the objections suggests they are not insurmountable. Some occur because too much is being read into the text and others because the text is not read carefully enough. The oft-quoted Revelation 20:10, or 18:7,10,15, for example, refers not to the conscious suffering of individual people but to that of the devil, the beast, the false prophet and the harlot.

The third argument is that of justice. Everlasting conscious suffering seems disproportionate to the crime and, therefore, inconsistent with a God of justice who rewards people according to what they have done (Revelation 20:12). The final argument is more subtle. It is that 'the eternal existence of the impenitent in hell would be hard to reconcile with the promises of God's final victory over evil' or with the texts which speak of his universal triumph (for example, Ephesians 1:10; Philippians 2:10-11 and 1 Corinthians 15:58). These texts do not lead John Stott to universalism but they do lead him to the conclusion that they are easier to understand 'if hell means destruction and the impenitent are no more.' [35]

Evangelical annihilationists are hesitant about putting forward their views, not only because they contradict long-held opinions and may cause offence, but also for other reasons. Roger Forster points out that conditionalists do have problems with four texts, namely, Matthew 18:34; Mark 9:47 (the most significant one); Revelation 14:10-11 and 20:14. But the first is a parable about unforgiveness, not teaching about hell. The second says that the fires will not be quenched but does not imply that whatever is put on the fire is not destroyed. The third is 'a very strong way of describing the completeness and finality of their destruction'. And the most natural way to read the fourth is that death and Hades are thrown into the lake of fire in order to destroy them. Roger Forster concludes, 'If these problem verses are the only ones in Scripture which support the concept of eternal, conscious torment, then the conditionalist position raises serious questions that must be answered before we accept the dominant traditional establishment view as the only biblical one.'[36]

Wenham is hesitant on other grounds.[37] Although supporting the idea of annihilation, he fears it might be popular because of its natural appeal and merely a response to the spirit of the age. He notes that the modern origins of the concept lie with some strange bed-fellows for evangelicals, like Jehovah's Witnesses and Christadel-phians. Nor does it solve all the difficulties. And, in spite of its appeal to justice, it might well lead to the weakening of zeal for the gospel, as feared by R. A. Torrey. After all, if all that happens to our un-repentant neighbours at the end of time is that they cease to exist, why bother sharing the gospel with them? But this last reservation is not as serious as it seems for two reasons. It underestimates the awfulness of the punishment proposed by annihilationists. To be prevented from spending eternity with God and to be banished in extinction from his presence is an awesome punishment in itself. It is also to adopt an argument from an unnecessarily negative stance. The argument runs, 'We must tell others about the gospel so that they can escape hell fire.' Today, it is much more likely that evangelicals, as others, will respond to arguments framed in a more positive light, such as, 'We must tell others about the gospel in order that they might share in the benefits of eternal life now and heaven hereafter.'

THE CURRENT DEBATE

There is no shortage of advocates of the traditional viewpoint in contemporary evangelicalism.[38] They pose some powerful questions to those who believe in conditional immortality. Many have to be persuaded that annihilation is punishment, since it makes hell out simply to be a state of non-existence. Many need convincing that the traditional interpretation of the imagery was incorrect. Some need further satisfaction on the apparent contradiction involved if 'eternal' means 'of endless duration' when referring to the future life of the justified but does not mean that when referring to future destruction of the impenitent. Some say that if the Devil's torment in Revelation 20:10 is in perpetuity, then, so must be that of his followers. Still others argue that the words death and destruction carry the meaning of ruin or wrecking and do not mean to finish a life.

One recent work, *Whatever Happened to Hell?*, by John Blanchard, is a massive defence of the traditional position from a strictly biblical viewpoint. It refutes both universalism and annihilationism with painstaking detail. Its arguments cannot be dismissed lightly even though they will prove unpopular in this tolerant age. But nor will they be the final word in contemporary evangelicalism since they are not above criticism. Raising questions against the annihilationists' interpretation of texts is not thereby to establish the traditionalist cause. And because Blanchard's desire is to be tied narrowly to Scripture he cannot adequately refute the argument about the justice of God which is presented both on biblical and on wider moral and theological grounds. At times he does not give sufficient credit to other interpretations of the text, such as that the word 'eternal' in Matthew 18:8 and 25:41 may 'convey either the sense of "going on for ever" or that of "belonging to the age to come" '.[39] Not does he always convince that he has listened enough to the alternative viewpoint or credited those with whom he disagrees with integrity.

The debate about hell is currently a lively one, at least among evangelical teachers. It is good that it is since it demonstrates an evangelical commitment even to the most unpalatable aspects of the teaching of the Bible. It indicates a desire to grapple with how those unpalatable parts are to be communicated in a meaningful way in the late twentieth and early twenty-first centuries. The subject is not to be relegated to the concerns of yesterday since it actively impinges on so many other areas of belief, such as, the nature of salvation, God's triumph over evil and the fate of those who have never heard of the gospel.[40]

For all that, there is a suspicion that for the majority of evangelicals, as well as for the wider public, hell is no longer a meaningful concept. James Davison Hunter found in his survey of evangelical students that there was a measurable degree of unease with the notion of eternal damnation. Most would only affirm the existence of hell with some equivocation. 'It is clear,' he concluded, 'that they know what they "should" believe but with that they struggle.'[41]

So, in the light of the debate about hell, we must ask again, as we did regarding the millennium, whether contemporary evangelicals still really have a place for a doctrine of the last things, to anything like the degree that was evident among their predecessors?

GLORIOUS THINGS OF THEE ARE SPOKEN

Evangelicals and the Church

From the very beginning of evangelicalism as a modern movement evangelicals have differed over the Church. The stage which the Evangelical Revival entered was already strewn with several Protestant denominations, all of which claimed evangelicals in their membership. To these various denominations there was soon to be added Methodism, much to the sadness of John Wesley, who never had any desire to break from the Church of England. During the next century Anglican evangelicals were forced to define their views of the church more carefully in the light of the Tractarian movement. Others felt the church needed redefining in different ways and new forms of church, such as, the Brethren and the Salvation Army, emerged. The twentieth century added further evangelical pieces to the ecclesiastical jigsaw with the emergence of Pentecostalism, early in the century, and Restorationism, later in the century.

From the beginning, too, evangelicals have valued the structures of the church to different degrees. Wesley was a devout churchman and held a catholic view of the church to the last. Hence his sadness at the division between the Methodist societies and the Church of England. But Whitefield was far less concerned with ecclesiastical structures and united more easily with Dissenters who shared his Calvinism. The distance between these two perspectives became more obvious as evangelicalism progressed. Simeon and Ryle, for example, were churchmen. Moody and Hudson Taylor were not.

Evangelicals have always felt it legitimate to differ over forms of ecclesiastical government, the practice of baptism and the relationship between church and state.[1] Styles of worship have varied, from the liturgical to the spontaneous, although there have usually been common threads which have bound evangelicals together, such as, the place given to preaching and the relative lack of emphasis on the sacraments. None of these has ever been felt to be crucial to evangelical identity. Since this is so, what is there to say about evangelicals and the church? Does evangelicalism have any distinctive approach? In fact, despite the diversity, there are a number of factors which emerge to form a distinctive evangelical approach to the church.

Evangelical assumptions

With all Christians, evangelicals affirm the statement in the creed that the church is 'one, holy, catholic and apostolic.' But the interpretation given to those words may well differ from the interpretation others would give. Hugh McNeile set out the evangelical interpretation of them in his book. *The Church and the Churches; or, The Church of God in Christ and the Churches of Christ Militant Here on Earth*, in 1846. There, in Peter Toon's words:

> In four chapters he explained that this Church was in fact the invisible Church composed of all elect believers of all times and places. Its unity was in the union of Christ by the one Spirit; its holiness was that offered and provided in the work of the Holy Spirit; its catholicity was in virtue of the fact that the elect came from every tribe and nation; and its apostolicity was in the doctrine of the apostles by which the elect came to their salvation. [2]

Each of these leads to an evangelical distinctive about the church which Gerald Bray has outlined in a modified form. [3] He outlines four assumptions that form the evangelical view of the church.

THE AUTHORITY OF SCRIPTURE
Scripture is the final authority for evangelicals and not merely a useful resource to tell us how things were done in the early days of the church. Developments which have taken place since must be submitted to the authority of scripture and tested by it to see whether they are valid or not. Others argue that doctrine has developed since those days and certain practices or traditions have grown up, like the authority of the See of Rome, which should now be acknowledged. Evangelicals do not find this argument persuasive, although they recognize that you cannot write off two thousand years of church history. Developments must be submitted to the scrutiny of the Bible.

Evangelicals differ in detail at this point. Some argue that unless a practice is commanded in the Bible it should not be adopted. Others, in practice the majority, argue that unless it is forbidden in the Bible, or contradicts a biblical principle, it is permissible. This accounts for some of the ecclesiastical differences to be found among evangelicals. But this division of opinion is not nearly so wide as the gap between those who see the Bible to be their final authority and those who argue for the Bible plus tradition or other sources of authority.

It is often assumed that the place given to the Bible by evangelicals inevitably leads to narrowness. But this is not so for a number of reasons. On some matters, for example the structure of leadership in the church, it is evident that the New Testament presents a picture of diversity rather than a fixed blueprint. On other matters, it may be evident from the Bible itself that a certain practice was the appropriate way, in the culture of its time, of working out an abiding principle; but, today, the application of the same principle might lead to a different practice. Nearly all evangelicals would readily concede this in the case of foot washing and head covering but would still be in debate as to whether this applied to the leadership of women in the church or not. On yet other matters presently faced by the church the Bible may be silent. In these cases the evangelical will be concerned to go back to Scripture to discover relevant principles and doctrines which apply to the situation. In all these matters the concern is to discover what the Bible says, and to obey it.

The commitment to the authority of the Bible means that much evangelical thinking about the church has taken the form of Bible studies rather than wider theological reflection.[4] This has sometimes proved a limitation, especially in contemporary ecumenical discussions, when evangelicals have not been able to build adequate bridges between the early Christians and the present-day church. Serious theological, as distinct from biblical, work on evangelical ecclesiology is needed.

FLEXIBILITY
Gerald Bray's second evangelical assumption about the church is that of flexibility. The evangelical's primary concern is not with the fixed ecclesiastical structures but with people who are Christians whatever denominational label they wear or structure they inhabit. He cites as an example the welcome given by Anglicans to Billy Graham and their lack of concern about the status of his ordination or his denominational background. Evangelicalism has a great place for the rise of the charismatic leader who does not emerge from an institutional route. It recognizes that the Holy Spirit cannot be imprisoned within our structures and institutions.

Throughout their history evangelicals have demonstrated such flexibility. They have always given a welcome to revivalists and evangelists who were evidently used of God without quibbling over their ecclesiastical credentials. Moody was a layman. Sunday was eventually ordained as a Presbyterian minister but did not enter their ministry in a conventional way. Caughey, though a Methodist, was in constant tension with the Methodist authorities for not submitting to ecclesiastical discipline, and so on.

Lying behind this flexibility, which some would regard as indiscipline, lies an important principle. Evangelicals make a distinction between the visible and the invisible church. The distinction goes back to Augustine, was used by the Reformers, and has continued to be held by evangelicals. It was expressed fully, in 1851, by Edward Litton in his book defining the evangelical view of the church. He argued that:

> The one true Church, the holy catholic Church of the Creed, is not a body of mixed composition, comprehending within its pale both the evil and the good: it is the community of those who, whatever they may be, are in living union with Christ by faith, and partake of the sanctifying influences of His Spirit . . . The true Church is so far invisible as that it is not yet manifested in its corporate capacity; or, in other words; there is no one society, or visible corporation here on earth, of which it can be said that it is the mystical Body of Christ.[5]

If legitimate, the visible church, he explained, will contain the outward marks of the preaching of the word and the sacraments but, even so, will always be a mixed community, 'comprising hypocrites and nominal Christians, as well as true believers.' And so it will always be until the separation at the end of the age.

Since the visible structures are not the ultimate reality, evangelicals, whilst not ignoring them, also seek to identify with the invisible church. In practice, this leads evangelicals to find, support and unite with Christians wherever the gospel is preached, the Bible is honoured and the Spirit is moving, regardless of the niceties of church order.

SPIRITUAL UNITY

The same division between a visible and invisible church has a bearing on the evangelical understanding of unity. The flexibility of evangelicals is amply demonstrated by evangelical involvement in interdenominational missions and societies and the great evangelical gatherings, from Keswick to Spring Harvest, which are transdenominational and where participants feel they are all 'one in Christ Jesus'.

The oneness they espouse at such gatherings is based on the consciousness of what they share together. They are conscious of having been converted to Christ and desiring to live for him, as distinct from those who merely attend church or observe the outwards signs of baptism and Holy Communion.

As Gerald Bray points out, this has major implications for ecumenism. No section of the church is more genuinely ecumenical than the evangelical wing. But it is ecumenism of a different kind than that sought by the official ecclesiastical institutions. It is an ecumenism of the Spirit, derived from the Spirit himself who gives it as a gift (Ephesians 4:3). Consequently, evangelicals speak of maintaining and preserving, but not of manufacturing, unity. It is a spiritual, not an institutional unity. So, evangelicalism has always been 'an ecumenical church on the ground'.[6]

THE IMPORTANCE OF DOCTRINE

In line with evangelicalism's commitment to the Bible, it also takes its stand on the importance of doctrine. Unity cannot be at the expense of truth. Evangelicals frequently point out that in Christ's high priestly prayer, recorded in John 17, Jesus prays for both of these to be given to his church.[7]

The commitment to correct doctrine leads to some curious alignments and antipathies at times. It leads evangelicals to stand *with* Roman Catholics, from whom they would differ so much, on fundamental questions, such as the resurrection of Christ, but *against* those of their own denominations, who might call those fundamentals into question. The absence of a feeling of spiritual unity and crucial doctrinal differences particularly divides the evangelical from the liberal. The evangelical believes that, whilst the church must be an open place, it is not a place where anything may be taught legitimately or where one opinion, however misguided, is as valid as the other. The church must be a place where truth is both taught and practised, and the evangelical is committed to getting as close to that ideal as possible.

Evangelical weaknesses

Many critics of evangelicalism would argue that when it comes to the church the dominant characteristic of evangelicals is their indifference to it. When Robert Runcie, then Archbishop of Canterbury, spoke to the National Evangelical Anglican Assembly at Caister, Norfolk, in 1988, the main thrust of his address was that evangelicals needed to develop a more serious theology of the church. The charge was anything but new. When one examines an evangelical classic like R. A. Torrey's *What the Bible Teaches* and discovers a total absence of reference to the church one can see why the charge is made.

As a movement, evangelicalism does have a weakness about the church. But when that weakness is examined its features are seen to be the obverse side of evangelical strengths, as we hope to show. Five sources of weakness will be examined.

THE EMPHASIS ON PERSONAL GROWTH

The evangelical is so committed to personal conversion and personal spiritual growth, and so fearful of hiding in a disingenuous way in a crowd, that the church has usually taken second place in evangelical thinking. As a means of grace, personal Bible study and prayer have been exalted above the church. Michael Griffiths confesses as much, in his refreshingly illustrated book *Cinderella with Amnesia*. 'It is as though', he writes, 'most Christians expect to fly solo to heaven with only just a little bit of formation flying from time to time.'[8] For 'Christians' read 'evangelicals'. He writes of realizing that:

> There is a goal of congregational development and progress, which I may have been almost entirely overlooking. I had thought of the church primarily as something that will sometimes be of help to me. Now I began to realize that I have tremendous responsibilities to the congregation, because all of us are supposed to be developing and progressing together as a wonderful new community of God's people.[9]

But the personal and the corporate need not be in tension and there is increasing evidence that evangelicals are discovering the importance of the church not just as a means of growth for themselves but in the overall plan and purposes of God.[10]

THE PLACE OF PARACHURCH AGENCIES

A second strength of evangelicalism, which can have a detrimental effect on the church, is the strength of parachurch agencies. Unlike the church, which has all-round responsibilities, these agencies are usually committed to very specific goals in mission. We have seen how these developed in the nineteenth century until, today, they dominate the evangelical subculture. In contrast to the churches and denominations which, given their mixed natures, are often viewed with some suspicion by evangelicals, these agencies are often taken to be the true home of authentic evangelicalism.

D. L. Moody epitomized much of evangelicalism in substituting mission work, channelled through missions and parachurch groups, as the outward sign of faith in place of the church. Moody, as we have seen, is said by his biographer to have had no doctrine of the church.[11] R. W. Dale remarked on the difference between the old evangelicalism of Wesley, Whitefield and Edwards' era and the new, of the post-Finney era. 'The evangelical movement', he wrote:

> Encouraged what it called an undenominational temper. It emphasised the vital importance of the evangelical creed, but it regarded almost with indifference all forms of church polity that were not in apparent and irreconcilable antagonism to that creed. It demanded as the basis of fellowship a common religious life of an accidental and precarious kind. It cared nothing for the idea of the church as the august society of saints. It was an ally of Individualism.[12]

Ralph Winter has sought to find biblical precedent for parachurch societies in the apostolic bands sent out from Jerusalem and Antioch. But many dispute his conclusions and argue that they are an invention of the modern evangelical and missionary movement and that the New Testament knows of no dichotomy between mission agencies and church.[13] At Lausanne, Howard Snyder argued that 'the biblical church grows through proclaiming the Gospel, multiplying congregations, building the Christian community, and exercising spiritual gifts.' Parachurch structures, in which he included denominational structures, have their place in parallel with the community of God's people (the church) and are useful 'to the extent they aid the church in its mission, but are man-made and culturally determined.' As such they are expendable, in a way the church is not, when their task is done or they wear out.[14]

   The existence of such agencies have widespread implications for the church. According to one's standpoint: they channel zeal, or drain energy; they use gifts, or divert them; they release money, or siphon off funds; they are the all-absorbing call of God or a truncated vision of what the church should be. There is no doubt that much of the vitality and success of evangelicalism is due to the existence of parachurch groups. The spread of the gospel is, in large measure, a result of their work. But they can also be a liability and a distraction from an evangelical commitment to the church.

PERSONALITY CULTS
The obverse side of flexibility is that the evangelical movement is prone to gurus and personality cults. Without the restraint of church discipline anyone can set themselves up as an authoritative teacher and, if they are able communicators, they are likely to gain a following. Combine this with a desire not to criticize people around whom there is apparent spiritual action and the resulting cocktail can be dangerous. It must be admitted that because of this, on occasions, evangelicalism has made itself look ridiculous, not

least through the recent escapades of some televangelists.

Some argue that the place of personalities in evangelicalism is essential since in the absence of anything else which binds the movement together it is they who do so.

The dangers of the trend has been noted inside the movement, as well as outside. Alister McGrath has commented on the celebrity status accorded to televangelists and other preachers.[15] Gerald Bray has commented on a related theme – the way in which some churches, freed from the Papal authority, become subject to government by 'clique, party and pressure group'.[16] The greater the independence, the greater the potential danger of going off at tangents and even falling into heresy. In this light, Jon Braun, is one of several who have called for a renewal of church authority and of genuine discipline among evangelicals.[17]

SCHISM

The obverse side of the quest for a pure church, committed to truth, is that evangelicals are in constant danger of causing schism. It was a regular cry of Martyn Lloyd-Jones that evangelicals were too prone to take that course and should be wary of it. He regarded schism as a terrible sin. Schism occurred when people divided over issues which were not essential to salvation. On a number of occasions he referred to the church at Corinth as an illustration. There, divisions took place over personalities, over behaviour at the Lord's table and the practice of spiritual gifts. But none of these justified schism – a schism which occurred in their case without people actually leaving the church!

He was quite clear that evangelicals should refuse to tolerate heresy and leave churches where the essential truths of the Gospel were at stake. That could not be regarded as schism but was, rather, obedience to New Testament commands (see, for example, Galatians 1 and 1 John). It was because of this commitment to gospel truth, and his desire for unity, that, in 1966, he issued his famous call for evangelicals to leave their historic denominations which, he considered, were doctrinally and theologically compromised, and form a united evangelical church.[18]

In recent years evangelical churches have been riddled with schisms as people have divided over attitudes to the ecumenical movement, over the question of inerrancy or, even more, over issues associated with the charismatic movement. In some cases, people have left to go to a nearby church but not infrequently groups have left to establish their own church, often of an independent nature, nearby. Such behaviour is difficult for the universal church, which prizes outward unity more highly than evangelicals appear to do, to understand. It is behaviour which in the wider church would not only cause pain, as it has among evangelicals, but merit censure and discipline.

THE INVISIBLE CHURCH

The distinction between the visible and the invisible church is also simultaneously a strength and a weakness. Its strength lies in encouraging evangelicals to remain within churches which are less than ideal in encouraging unity with fellow Christians beyond denominational boundaries. Its weakness lies in undervaluing the visible church and a failure to take the visible institution as seriously as one should. This has a number of effects. It enables evangelicals to sidestep important questions, such as those posed by the ecumenical movement. It permits evangelicals to run away from discipline, which the Reformers thought to be the third mark of a genuine church, after the Word and the Sacrament. It encourages evangelicals to resort to division too easily, because the real church is not St Thingamajig's-down-the-road but the invisible church. And it leads, on occasions, to evangelicals coming close to having gnostic (secret and mysterious) views of the church in some places.[19]

But evangelicals are themselves demonstrating a capacity for self-criticism on this point. In reference, for example, to the concept of spiritual unity, to which the idea of the invisible church leads, F. Burton Nelson wrote, following the Chicago Call of 1977, which was an appeal to evangelicals, 'Evangelicals are being summoned in these latter years of the twentieth century to refuse to settle for these mere spiritualized concepts of church unity and to affirm the conviction that unity in Christ demands visible expression.' He pointed out that invisible or abstract unity 'costs no one anything.'[20]

Added together these are serious challenges to the evangelical view of the church, and evangelical history and present-day practice unite to suggest that they may not have given sufficient attention to the doctrine of the church.

Evangelical distinctives

For all that, evangelical views of the church have a number of distinctive emphases which could be of benefit to the wider church. Among them are:

- the idea of the priesthood of all believers
- the church as a body
- the priority given to mission

- the desire for purity
- the recognition of spiritual unity.

ROBERT W. ROSS

THE PRIESTHOOD OF ALL BELIEVERS
Evangelicals note that the New Testament applies the word 'priest', in the singular, only to Jesus Christ. There is a total absence of anything like the Old Testament order of priesthood as a separate order of ministry within the New Testament church. Evangelicals look, therefore, on some recent debates within the institutional church about priesthood with bewilderment, if not astonishment. Why should the contemporary church consider matters to be of such significance when there is a total absence of reference to anything like today's priesthood in our normative documents? In fact, those documents present a very different model of leadership than is currently practised, one which is based on servanthood.[21]

What evangelicals do find in the New Testament is a clear picture that all believers are called to priesthood (1 Peter 2:5,9; Revelation 1:6 and note the sacrificial language applied to all believers in Romans 12:1-2 and Hebrews 13:15). It teaches that all believers have a right of equal access to God, that no human mediator is necessary and that the duties of the Old Testament priest to offer worship and intercession have devolved upon us all. It is true that evangelicals have often misapplied the doctrine and assumed it means either that all are equally gifted and so anyone should be able to lead, or, that all are equally knowledgeable and anyone should be able to teach.[22] But evangelical misapplication should not detract from the importance of the priesthood of all believers nor from the challenge it presents to the present-day church. The evangelical commitment to the priesthood of all believers rightly challenges the clerical dominance of most churches and its preoccupation with questions of hierarchy, status and order.[23] It leads to a recognition of the equal worth and varied giftedness of every member who should be released for service.

THE CHURCH AS A BODY
The doctrine of the priesthood of all believers has sometimes become confused with the idea of the church as the body of Christ. The picture of the body teaches that the church is a living organism not a formal organization. Furthermore, each member of the body has, according to 1 Corinthians 12, been endowed with a spiritual gift with which to contribute to the upbuilding of the church as a whole. If this model of the church is adopted it leads to it being run on very different lines than is customary if an organizational model is adopted. Members, for example, will be used according to their

gift, rather than merely according to organizational need. A conscious effort will be made to value the involvement of all people in the life of the church and, again, to shun clerical dominance, as if all gifts belonged to the clergy alone.

The evangelical church has consistently been committed to the principle that the church was a body composed of gifted members, as its history demonstrates. Wesley encouraged the use of (and trained) lay leadership. Other revivalist streams gave great public expression to the gifts of the laity, whether male or female. The concept was prominent among the Brethren, and evident in many other ways too. Falling on hard times, the principle was given renewed emphasis, and fresh application, by the charismatic movement and is a powerful feature of the contemporary evangelical church. It has affected the nature of leadership; broken the dominance of 'one man ministry' or the clerical monopoly, which seemed to assume that the clergy had all the gifts; affected forms of pastoral care and had widespread implications for the conduct of worship.[24]

THE PRIORITY OF MISSION

Historically, evangelicals have always emphasized mission. The priority of mission in the church, taken to its logical, and many would say unbalanced, conclusion, can be seen in the formation of the Salvation Army. Not for nothing have mission halls been an evangelical substitute for churches. Wherever one looks in evangelical literature about the church one is immediately struck by its emphasis on mission.[25] The church is God's agent for change in the world both through evangelism and social action. God's Kingdom is wider than the church and his sovereign power is not limited to the church. But that does not detract from the church as God's primary agent of change.

The church, then, does not exist for its own sake, nor even just for worship but for service. As Clause 6 of the Lausanne Covenant put it:

> We affirm that Christ sends his redeemed people into the world as the Father sent him, and that calls for a similar deep and costly penetration of the world. We need to break out of our ecclesiastical ghettos and permeate non-Christian society. In the church's mission of sacrificial service evangelism is primary. World evangelisation requires the whole church to take the whole gospel to the whole world. The church is at the very centre of God's cosmic purpose and is his appointed means of spreading the gospel. But a church which preaches the cross must be marked by the cross. It becomes a stumbling block to evangelism when

it betrays the gospel or lacks a living faith in God, a genuine love for people, or scrupulous honesty in all things including promotion and finance. The church is the community of God's people rather than an institution, and must not be identified with any particular culture, social or political system, or human ideology. (John 17:18; 20:21; Matthew 28:19,20; Acts 1:8; 20:27; Ephesians 1:9,10; 3:9-11; Galatians 6:14,17; 2 Corinthians 6:3,4; 2 Timothy 2:19-21; Philippians 1:27).[26]

It is not surprising that evangelicals are fond of quoting William Temple's comment that, the church 'is the only society on earth which exists for the benefit of non-members,' and equally, of quoting Emil Brunner's statement that, 'The church exists by mission as fire exists by burning.'[27] It is also logical that the close tie between God's action in the world and the role of the church in mission should lead to an interest in leadership which is functional in orientation, rather than theological, and to an interest in the study and principles of church growth.

It is equally consistent with the emphasis on mission that churches should develop along the lines of Willow Creek Community Church, Illinois. That church has moved its Sunday worship and teaching activities to the middle of the week and on Sundays presents a highly professional seekers' service, which is geared to those who are not used to the Christian subculture and free from ecclesiastical baggage. They have done so after discovering that Sunday morning is the time, in their community, when 'unchurched Harry' is most likely to want to come. Although criticized by some evangelicals for this move it is but one contemporary, if bold, expression of the evangelical practice of the church down the centuries. The church exists for mission and its structures and programme should be geared to that end.

THE DESIRE FOR PURITY

Most evangelicals readily understand that the church on earth is bound to be a mixed community of true believers, nominal believers and even unbelievers. But the evangelical prizes the purity of the church and seeks to move the church as near to the ideal as possible. The quest for purity takes place in the areas of doctrine, morality and relationships. The basis for the quest arises from the New Testament teaching that the church is the bride of Christ (Ephesians 5:25-27,32; Revelation 19:6-9) and builds on the extensive imagery in the Old Testament of Israel as betrothed to God. All would recognize that the church will never be 'without stain or wrinkle or any other blemish, but holy and blameless' until Christ returns. But that hope imposes a serious responsibility on the church to prepare for it as best as she can now. That is why Paul wrote to the church at Corinth, 'I am jealous for you with a godly jealousy. I promised you to one husband, to Christ, so that I may present you as a pure virgin to him' (2 Corinthians 11:2), and encouraged them to aim for perfection (13:11).

Some evangelicals have considered that the logical outworking of this position is to separate from churches which seem to compromise themselves by their very constitution, such as, an established church which allies itself to the state, or, one that embraces all, whatever their spiritual standing, who live within a defined geographic area in its membership. These form 'gathered' churches or 'believers' churches. A pronounced form of such churches are 'separatist' churches who often demonstrate a great suspicion about the spiritual credentials of any church but their own. But other evangelicals have found it perfectly possible to justify being part of a state church without feeling any sense of compromise.[28]

The desire for purity has frequently given evangelicalism an apparently stern face and a reputation for denouncing others. This countenance may be seen in the writings of J. C. Ryle, but he is representative of many others. In *Holiness*, he included a chapter, entitled 'Visible Churches Warned', where an address based on the letters to the churches in Revelation 2 and 3 is applied as a warning to:

- All who are living only for the world, to take heed what they are doing
- All formalists and self-righteous people to take heed that they are not deceived
- All careless members of Churches to beware lest they trifle their souls into hell
- Every one who wants to be saved, not to be content with the world's standard of religion
- Every one who professes to be a believer in the Lord Jesus, not to be content with a little religion.[29]

In his book *Knots Untied* he included many further admonitions to churches, so much so that selections from it were subsequently reprinted under the title of *Warnings to the Churches*. Here he included a chapter on idolatry where he labours the point that, 'natural proneness and tendency in us all to give God a sensual, carnal worship, and not that which is commanded in His Word . . . in fact, idolatry is all natural, down-hill, easy, like the broad way. Spiritual worship is all grace, all up-hill, and against the grain.'[30] He then mounts a sustained attack on the Church of Rome as a church in error, which reaches its climax in the five-fold repetition of the sentence ... 'I say there is idolatry in the Church of Rome!'[31]

Some of this portrays the unlovely face of evangelicalism. It can lack love and humility. Yet the quest for purity need not put on such an unsmiling face. In recent days, none has been more concerned about the purity of the church that Francis Schaeffer but he combined a robust plea for doctrinal purity, in the tradition of J. Gresham Machen,[32] with an equally robust plea for love. He spoke of the beauty of human relationships. To fight, he argued, for doctrinal purity without love is to put oneself in the position of a wife who is never unfaithful but never shows love to her husband. 'What God wants from us is not only doctrinal faithfulness, but our love day by day. Not in theory, mind you, but in practice. Those of us who are children of God must realise the seriousness of modern apostasy; we must urge each other not to have any part of it. But at the same time we must be the loving, true bride of the divine bridegroom in reality and in practice day by day . . .'[33]

The desire for purity in the church obviously has implications for evangelical involvement in the ecumenical movement and explains some of the caution evangelicals demonstrate towards it – a subject to which we shall return at the end of this chapter.

Although evangelicals need to be aware of all the pitfalls, in seeking to be true to the New Testament they rightly value the purity of the church and justifyably stand amazed at those churches which seem to tolerate denials of basic Christian truths or morality, on the part of some of their leaders, without moving to discipline them.

THE RECOGNITION OF SPIRITUAL UNITY

The matter may be briefly dealt with since it has already been introduced as a major 'evangelical assumption' about the church and the weakness of the position confessed. At the same time, the principle is of great contemporary relevance. The recognition that unity must have a spiritual basis erects major question marks about the path taken by the contemporary ecumenical movement with its apparent concern for organizational unity. Evangelicals believe that greater attention needs to be given to spiritual unity if it is to be of any worth. To many of them so much of the present ecumenical movement smacks of a modern business deal where the concern is with the small print and where institutional matters – matters of property, status, clerical orders, and rights – predominate. Many evangelicals, but not all, are happy to rejoice in the variety that there is within the church, providing there is spiritual unity. For them, there is no need to press for institutional mergers. Others believe that spiritual unity must find expression in organizational unity.

Most rejoice that the latest ecumenical developments in the United Kingdom have gone some way to recognising this and seek to base their growing relationship on mission. But that begs other questions about the nature of the mission in which we are to engage and the gospel we are to proclaim together.

Evangelicals and ecumenism

One of the great facts of modern church life, alongside the charismatic movement, is the ecumenical movement. Evangelicals have a reputation for being cautious, at best, about the movement. Relations between evangelicals and others have been described as like porcupines making love. It is not even unusual to suggest that evangelicalism and ecumenism are polarized.[34] It is true that there are certainly tensions, but to present them merely as polarized is misleading and simplistic.

ANTI-ECUMENISM
Some evangelicals, out of a desire for purity in the church, will have nothing to do with ecumenism and suspect fellow evangelicals who are involved of inevitable compromise.

A recent example of that position can be found in the booklet, issued by the British Evangelical Council, formed in 1952, during the process which began at Swanwick and led up to the latest ecumenical arrangements in Britain. The booklet was called, *Holding Hands in the Dark*. It expressed fear:

- That unity would be given precedence over truth
- That absolutism in doctrine would be further eroded
- That the doctrinal basis of the Swanwick process was weak
- That the Roman Catholic Church would be further accepted
- That pressure would be put on evangelicals, especially at local level, to be involved
- That evangelicals' relationships would be strained
- That many would be deluded into thinking that they were 'pilgrims' when they were not.[35]

The evangelical tradition in which the BEC booklet stands looks back to the courage of the Protestant Reformers who stood for truth against the error of the Roman Catholic Church and draws on those elements of evangelical history where evangelical truth has been vigorously defended against the corrosive effects of Liberal or

Catholic advance in the church. So, for example, frequent reference is made to Spurgeon's role in the Downgrade controversy with the Baptist Union. With the development of the ecumenical movement in the twentieth century fears of union with false teachers and amalgamations with erroneous churches have been common. The anti-ecumenical stance has affected all mainline denominations, especially the Baptists, although usually it has been a position held by a small minority within them. Its chief expression has been in the independent churches.

E. J. Poole-Connor, the founder of the Fellowship of Independent Evangelical Churches, was a forthright advocate of this position. A constant critic of the World Council of Churches, he wrote a number of booklets against it. To him, the desire for one church was an ungodly conspiracy which was deceiving those in Protestant churches who should know better. The following words, written in 1958, give the flavour of some of his writings.

> Doctrines which in earlier years would have been regarded as the gravest of heresy are now accepted with scarcely the lift of an eyebrow. Meanwhile, the dazzling vision of One Church in One World becomes ever clearer in outline; and the day seems not far distant when Babylon the Great, masking doctrinal confusion under external pomp and power, will again enter upon the stage of history in a new and perhaps final form.[36]

Not all who oppose ecumenism do so from the standpoint of Poole-Connor about the future!

PRO-ECUMENISM

But not all have adopted this stance and many committed to evangelicalism are involved ecumenically at a local, national and international level. This is especially true of those who already belong to comprehensive denominations, since, as *Holding Hands in the Dark* recognized, involvement in the process would not entail as great a change for them as it would for those in more separatist churches. Evangelicals have been involved in the recent 'Swanwick pilgrimage' and many have contributed to the World Council of Churches over the years.

An examination of the evangelical Anglican position shows that they have made significant contributions to ecumenical discussions at every stage. The Anglican-Methodist proposals were subjected to constructive critique in *All in Each Place*, edited by J. I. Packer. Then, J. I. Packer and Colin Buchanan, with E. L. Mascall and Graham Leonard, put forward both a critique of, and proposals for, ecumenism, in *Growing Into Union* in 1970. The Ten Propositions of the 1970s, 'and particularly the whole project of multilateral talks from which they spring,' were welcomed by The National Evangelical Anglican Congress which met in Nottingham in 1977. At the same time it was acknowledged that some Free Church evangelicals saw such proposals as 'harmful to the gospel' and promises were made to 'keep the closest and friendliest possible contact with them.'[37] Subsequently they were involved in the Swanwick process and the new ecumenical arrangements which resulted. On the international front, ARCIC, the Anglican–Roman Catholic International Commission, has had several evangelical participants.

Many evangelicals, deriving their views from John 17 and Ephesians 4, see involvement in ecumenism as their responsibility before God and as the consistent outworking of a long-standing evangelical commitment as, they believe, evangelical history demonstrates. Among those who put forward this position are the group who met in Chicago in 1977 and issued an appeal to evangelicals to discover their historic roots and shun shallow evangelical experience. One clause in their appeal was a call to church unity. They wrote:

> We deplore the scandalous isolation and separation of Christians from one another. We believe such division is contrary to Christ's explicit desire for unity and impedes the witness of the church in the world. Evangelicalism is too frequently characterized by an ahistorical sectarian mentality. We fail to appropriate the catholicity of historic Christianity, as well as the breadth of the biblical revelation.[38]

They point to 'the ecumenical concern of the Reformers and the later movements of evangelical renewal' as the basis for 'renouncing sacred shibboleths' whilst recognizing that 'God works within diverse historical streams'. They are far from indifferent to the need for correct doctrine but even so believe that unity must have 'visible and concrete expressions'.

ECUMENISM IN EVANGELICAL HISTORY
Roger Martin has written about some of those movements of evangelical renewal which reveal a deep commitment to ecumenism.[39] Jonathan Edwards wrote a tract entitled, *An Humble Attempt to Promote Explicit Agreement and Visible Union of God's People in Extraordinary Prayer* (1747). It resulted in much united prayer for revival and overseas missions. By the end of the eighteenth century the possibility of union between Christians led to the

founding of the London Missionary Society, the British and Foreign Bible Society, and the Religious Tract Society, among many other societies, on a pan-evangelical basis. Each of these sought to shun denominational differences and work on the basis of a theology of consensus for the sake of the gospel. The spirit of the times was summed up by David Bogue. Speaking to the first annual meeting of the London Missionary Society, he told the assembled company that they were there 'with one accord to attend the funeral of bigotry.'[40] His words were greeted with general shouts of joy.

The history of these societies shows how difficult the quest for unity was going to prove. LMS never really achieved its objective but there can be no doubting the sincerity of its founders nor the influence they exercised both on church relations and overseas missions. The British and Foreign Bible Society was the most ambitious pan-evangelical organization of the period and gained the support of most active evangelicals to start with. But it was to undergo a sad division when a dispute between evangelicals polarized over the question of the Apocrypha from 1825 onwards. The Religious Tract Society also underwent a number of internal tensions but managed to ride the storms more successfully than the Bible Society because they were handled differently. But they, no less than the others, found the actual achievement of unity elusive. The difficulties, however, should not blind us to recognizing how deep the commitment of these evangelicals was to union – a commitment that derived from the study of Scripture.

Roger Martin attributes the passing of this phase to a number of factors. Political changes had their affect. Theological differences emerged when it was discovered that working on the basis of a few centrally-agreed affirmations about the gospel was not always satisfying or practical. There were other matters people held dear which could not always be relegated to a secondary position. Then, too, the rise of denominationalism took its toll on the spirit of union and inevitably changed the course of ecumenical relations, as greater national organizations were formed, for instance, among Congregationalists and Baptists from the 1830s onwards.

In spite of that the ecumenical vision, however, has been a persistent theme among evangelicals, even if the way in which unity was envisaged was to change as circumstances in the wider church changed. The Evangelical Alliance was formed, in 1846, 'to realize in themselves and to exhibit to others that a living and everlasting union binds all true believers together in the fellowship of the Church of Christ.' It saw itself as expressing the essential unity of the church, given by God himself, rather than creating it. Yet the

Alliance was formed, it must be admitted, as an alliance in opposition to Romanism and Tractarian developments in the Church of England.

Much of the ecumenical vision of evangelicals was diverted into the non-denominational channel of Keswick and mission work. But that is not the whole story. Many, like F. B. Meyer, were at home both in evangelical non-denominationalism and in the more official structures of the church. He actively supported both Moody and Keswick and, at the same time, in his denomination and the National Council of Evangelical Free Churches – a body which was formed in 1896 so that by their union they might strengthen the witness of the Free Churches in national life through evangelism and social action. Other expressions of the vision for unity are seen in the emergence of the Brethren. The writings of J. N. Darby frequently referred to this theme. In 1828, he wrote that Christian believers are 'so to be all one, as that the world might know that Jesus was sent of God; in this we must all confess our sad failure.'[41] The desire was clear, even if its practical application was somewhat deficient.

Then, too, one of the significant streams flowing into the Edinburgh Missionary Conference of 1910, which is often cited as the beginning of the modern ecumenical movement, had its source in the Student Volunteer Missionary Union, which subsequently led to the Student Christian Movement. The passionate commitment of John Mott, a YMCA and Student Volunteer Movement worker and the key figure of the Conference, was 'the evangelisation of the world in this generation'. Unlike evangelical ecumenism, the ecumenism which flowed out of Edinburgh was to be inter-denominational rather than undenominational. Rather than calling its participants to set aside their denominations, the modern ecumenical movement has worked ever since on the principle of participants representing their denominations.

The evangelical contribution to ecumenism, then, should not be underestimated. In the early history of their movement evangelists had a genuine commitment to seeking union, borne out of a sense of the will of God, as found in the Bible and the work of God as they observed it in their world. It is the route of inter-denominational union which the ecumenical movement has taken which has made it harder for those who cherish doctrinal purity to be committed to ecumenism in the way in which evangelicals once were. Yet, many admit involvement to be the only realistic, and ultimately biblical, route. John Stott, for example, in expressing reservations about much that is seen in the current ecumenical movement and the belief that submission to scripture is the way to ecumenical progress, writes:

Nevertheless, I am also disturbed by the blanket condemnation of ecumenical activity which is expressed by a large section of the evangelical constituency. It is clear to me that we cannot simply dismiss the whole non-evangelical section of Christendom as if it did not exist, or, since it does exist, regard it as non-Christian and resolve to have nothing to do with it. Besides, Jesus our Lord prayed that his people might be one in order that the world might believe (John 17:20-23), and his apostle urges us to 'make every effort to keep the unity of the Spirit in the bond of peace' (Ephesians 4:3).[42]

It is too simplistic, then, to identify evangelicalism with an anti-ecumenical stance. There is, in fact, a spectrum of views about ecumenism to be found among evangelicals. One end of the spectrum draws on the more Protestant elements of the Reformation and the other the more Catholic elements. Both can appeal to pages of evangelical history for support, but both must realize that circumstances have changed since those pages were written, in order that they address the ecumenical question as it now is, rather than as it once was.

The ecumenical movement, I believe, needs to show a greater understanding of the evangelical perspective and to appreciate that its concern for truth is not to be regarded as secondary to the concern for unity but must run in parallel with it. Likewise, it would do well to appreciate the alternative ecumenism of evangelicalism rather than denigrate it.

In conclusion, evangelical Christians have much to learn about the church from other sections of Christianity. But they also have much to offer. Evangelical Christians may place the church in the category of matters which are of secondary importance in comparison with the Bible and the gospel but that does not mean they have nothing distinctive, and nothing of significance, to say about it. The emphasis on the Bible and the gospel leads them to work for a pure church and a spiritual unity, free from the restrictions which often characterize humanly-created institutions, where all are priests and all have gifts which can be used to further the church's mission. Beyond that, a diversity will be found, reflecting the diversity found in the wider ecclesiastical jigsaw. But it has never been felt of first importance to eradicate that diversity. On many matters evangelicals consider liberty to be the right attitude. Among them, admittedly, tensions will be discovered, especially in regard to involvement in comprehensive denominations and the ecumenical movement, which it is difficult to resolve. But what binds evangelicals together is ultimately of far greater significance than what occasionally divides them. The evangelical position was expressed by Richard Baxter, long ago.

> In things essential, unity;
> In things non-essential, liberty;
> In all things, charity.

TREAD ALL THE POWERS
OF DARKNESS DOWN

Evangelicals and social action

One of the most persistent misconceptions of evangelicalism is that it has no social concern. There are a number of reasons for this. It is conservative in theology, so it is assumed to be conservative in politics and, therefore, to be happy with the *status quo*. It is committed to converting sinners, so it is presumed to be indifferent to changing society. It is characterized by individualism, as seen in its stress on personal conversion, so it is imagined to lack a social ethic. It is concerned about heaven, so it is thought to have little concern with earth. But this is a myth, albeit one which evangelicals at times have been in danger of believing themselves. Their story, however, suggests reality is different.

Early reformers

THE CLAPHAM SECT

The Clapham Sect[1] was so called because they were a group of influential evangelical laymen who lived at Clapham, worshipped at the parish church under the ministry of John Venn, who had a remarkable impact on British society. The dominant personality of the Clapham Sect was William Wilberforce. Converted at the age of twenty-six, he was an eloquent speaker and close friend of William Pitt, the youngest Prime Minister in British history. The sect's great cause was the abolition of slavery. One of their number, Grenville Sharp, won an early victory when, in 1770, he obtained the judgement that as soon as slaves set foot on English soil they were free. But subsequent victories were to prove hard to obtain and they demonstrated a persistence which stands to their eternal credit. They faced immense opposition because of the economic interests involved. They fought opposition with painstaking research but also with a new weapon, that of public agitation. Although Parliament voted to regulate the number of slaves on transporter ships in 1789, it showed reluctance to go further. So, in 1792, Wilberforce 'fanned the flame' by organizing a series of public meetings against the slave trade. Petitions came to the House of Commons from all over.

From 1794 to 1804 they faced many defeats. Unsettlement at home and events surrounding the French Revolution did not encourage the British Parliament to take radical steps like the ones Wilberforce was proposing. In 1804, however, the circumstances and mood changed and promising votes were won which prepared the way for the Commons voting, by 283 votes to 16, to abolish the Slave Trade, in 1807.

Clapham then turned their attention to the abolition of slavery itself. Again, they used public opinion as a weapon, presenting a petition to Parliament on one occasion containing one million signatures. Again, they engaged in careful, detailed preparation of their case. Again, they faced many set-backs and much opposition, not least when slaves rebelled in the West Indies. As the campaign wore on the leaders of the Clapham Sect were either dead or ageing but the cause was taken up by Thomas Fowell Buxton, another evangelical. An Anti-Slavery Society was formed. Motions were introduced in the House of Commons with Buxton arguing that slavery was 'repugnant to the principles of the Christian Religion and the British Constitution.' On 29th July 1833, the day on which Wilberforce died, slavery was abolished throughout the British Empire.

The abolition of the slave trade and of slavery was not accomplished by evangelicals alone; others, especially the Quakers, played a part. But they were the prime movers in the cause. Motivated by their faith, they saw slaves as human beings and brothers. Their cause was fed by their commitment to missions, which provided them both with information about the lot of slaves and an incentive to abolish the system of slavery because it was a hindrance to the spread of the gospel.

Slavery was not their only cause. They were committed to education. John Venn, Vicar of Clapham, was the first to introduce Parish Schools. The lay members of Clapham supported schools both at home and in Sierra Leone, a colony for freed slaves founded in 1808, in which they had much influence. Since education could lead people to read seditious literature, they turned their efforts to the publishing of tracts and Bibles so the newly educated would have good literature to read.

They were also concerned about the 'reformation of manners' and engaged in a host of efforts to remove vices, such as drunkenness, lotteries, bear-baiting and sabbath-breaking, from the lower classes. Here they were less successful and received much ridicule for their puritanical attitudes. They saw poverty, not as a problem to be solved, but as a situation deserving of sympathy. They started the

Society for Bettering the Condition and Increasing the Comforts of the Poor in 1798 and a number of other related works. They sought improvement in the lot of the blind, debtors, prisoners and the destitute, and supported factory reform.

William Wilberforce and his colleagues at Clapham were men of their age. They were conservative in many respects but in reactionary days they were far from being the most conservative. They were prepared to co-operate with men who did not share their evangelical convictions in order to achieve reform. They were hard-working, practical politicians, who lived their faith with integrity. Free from avarice, they gave away much of their wealth. When Wilberforce died he had no house of his own.

REVIVALISM AND THE ABOLITION OF SLAVERY

Although long neglected or misrepresented by historians, revivalism played a key role in social reform in the United States. The contribution of the revivalists in the first half of the nineteenth century is so impressive that it is to them that Timothy Smith traces the origins of the later social gospel movement.[2]

Jonathan Blanchard spoke for the revivalists in a commencement address at Oberlin College in 1839 when he said, '. . . every true minister of Christ is a universal reformer, whose business it is, so far as possible, to reform all the evils which press on human concern.'[3] Slavery, was one such sin. Jonathan Blanchard was subsequently a worker for the American Anti-Slavery Society, an American vice-president of the World Anti-Slavery Convention, the pastor of what was known as 'the nigger church' in Cincinnati and President of Wheaton College. A social activist to the core, his evangelical credentials were beyond dispute.

Charles Finney was a convinced abolitionist and called slavery an 'abominable abomination'.[4] Resistance to reform and taking a wrong stand on human rights issues were among the greatest hindrances to revival in Finney's view. Churches that did so caused the Holy Spirit to depart from them. One of Finney's converts and assistants became the chief advocate of abolition. Theodore Weld adapted revival techniques to the anti-slavery cause and took many a courageous stand for the cause of abolition. He wrote a book, called *Slavery As It Is*, which was influential in the writing of the anti-slavery best-seller, *Uncle Tom's Cabin*, by Harriet Beecher Stowe. He was associated with Lane Seminary and it is no coincidence that a third of the agents of the Anti-Slavery Society came from there.

When trouble erupted at Lane, many transferred to the recently formed Oberlin College, where Asa Mahan was President and Charles Finney was on the staff. It came to espouse very revolutionary views, arising from its evangelical commitments. Donald Dayton has detailed their radicalism.[5] They were in the vanguard of abolition and educational reform, they practised a radical communtarian life-style, they contributed to the cause of feminism on the basis of Galatians 3:28, they supported the peace movement, they had a fund for fugitive slaves, they engaged in civil disobedience and harboured escaped slaves. The backing for Oberlin came from two wealthy brothers, Lewis and Arthur Tappan, the founders of Dun and Bradstreet. They may have been described personally as severe and humourless evangelicals but they were adventurous in their support of evangelical radicals. Arthur Tappan was the first President of the Anti-Slavery Society.

This is only one illustration of the social concern of American evangelicals during the period. Methodism, to begin with, took an abolitionist stance but later divided over the issue. Many other revivalists could be cited as advocating abolition.[6] And slavery was only one issue. For, as William Hosmer stated, 'The work of conversion is, and must be, an indiscriminate war against sin, all sin – sin of every kind and degree.'[7] Evangelicals wanted to 'tread all the powers of darkness down'.

Another evil which much concerned them was that of poverty. Phoebe Palmer was one of the few revivalists to be silent on the question of slavery but she was active in the fight against poverty. She contributed much of her own money to help the poor and became involved with the New York Female Assistance Society for the Relief and Religious Instruction of the Sick Poor. In 1850 she founded the Five Points Mission to provide housing for the poor. Shortly afterwards Lewis Pease opened up property nearby to supply them with jobs. The work rapidly grew and was soon housed in a six-storey building providing a shop and schoolroom as well as a chapel and living quarters. Many others imitated this initiative.

Not all evangelicals welcomed such social involvement. The Old School pastors and Princeton professors advocated that Christians should be concerned about the narrower concerns of 'old time religion' like personal salvation and the preaching of the cross. Some even provided justification for slavery, arguing that it was to be found in the Old Testament and was not opposed by the New. But they were a minority. For the most part evangelicals were anything but other-worldly. That was left to groups which were anti-revival and liturgical in interest.

Why was revivalism so socially revolutionary? The answer is to be found in the combination of the elements it brought together. It never lost its stress on the need for personal conversion. Conversion led to a radically transformed and ethical life. Society could only ultimately be changed through changed persons. But that did not stop it from having a wider vision of social reform and an ideal society for which to work. Sheer individualism was considered unchristian. Holiness teaching urged it to work for the eradication of all sin. Armenianism taught revivalists that power to change lay within their own hands. The Bible, which they took with the utmost seriousness, taught them that every human being had value and that Christ must be King over all. And, most importantly, at this stage their views of the future were unitedly postmillennial. They had a vision of a coming kingdom to which they were advancing. God was imminent and was waiting to transform the world by the outpouring of the Holy Spirit. As William Arthur, Methodist author of the holiness book, *Tongues of Fire*, put it, 'Nothing less than the general renewal of society ought to satisfy any soldier of Christ . . . the gospel is come to renew the face of the earth.'[8]

The Age of Societies and Missions

GREAT BRITAIN

In 1884, the Earl of Shaftesbury told his biographer, 'I am essentially and from deep-rooted conviction an Evangelical of the Evangelicals. I have worked with them constantly, and I am satisfied that most great philanthropic movements of the century have sprung from them.'[9] It is a judgment from which no serious historian would dissent. Evangelical faith became the mainspring of what we now, misleadingly, call 'humanitarian action'.

Shaftesbury himself, as we have seen,[10] had played a leading role in many philanthropic causes but he was representative of the evangelicals of his day, rather than unique. Kathleen Heasman estimates that 'three-quarters of the total number of voluntary charitable organisations (in Britain) in the second half of the century can be regarded as evangelical in character and control.'[11] Ian Bradley gives an insight into what this would mean in saying that, since the Clapham Society started the 'Bettering Society' in 1798 six new charitable societies were started each year. By mid-century there were 500 of them and they continued to grow![12]

It is the extent of the evangelical philanthropic empire which is truly staggering. In addition to the work of the churches and of missions, like the Salvation Army, evangelicals involved themselves in relief, reform and improvement work in every area where social evil was to be found. Ragged Schools were founded to teach the children of the poor who could not afford education. Hand in hand with the teaching they supplied went food, clothing and training for employment so that destitute children could become useful members of society. When the Ragged School Movement closed, in 1890, the Shaftesbury Society took over its welfare work.

Orphanages were started, by George Müller, Charles Spurgeon and Dr Tom Barnardo, among others. They offered homes to children on the basis of need rather than subscription. And they provided accommodation which was more homely than the old strict and barrack-like asylums of former days. Smaller groups of children were cared for by house parents. Special care for disabled children was first put into operation in an evangelical home. The big British societies which care for children today, all had their origins in evangelicalism.

Young people were provided for through the Young Men's Christian Association, which had close links with D. L. Moody and played a significant role in the 1858 Revival in America. A supporter of Moody, Quintin Hogg, started training young men in technical skills so that they could enter a trade. Evening classes were soon added to morning sessions and from these beginnings Regent Street Polytechnic (now the University of Central London) was to emerge. The Boys' Brigade and Church Lads' Brigade catered for others.

Temperance work began in local groups in the 1820s. Two national societies were formed in the 1850s. Only then did Gospel Temperance take hold in Britain, owing to visits from temperance workers from America, where it was more developed. Drink was a social evil which needed to be eradicated. Total abstinence became more fashionable and by 1882 one million people sported a blue ribbon as a signal that they had signed the pledge. A Band of Hope was started for the young. Non-alcoholic public houses were opened. And work was undertaken to care for alcoholics.

Care of prostitutes was the province of both evangelicals and the High Church, but the evangelical approach was less penitential than that of their co-labourers. Ellice Hopkins saw the need not only to rescue those already engaged in prostitution but also to rescue their children who would otherwise follow in their footsteps. Preventative measures were taken. Societies for 'friendless girls' were started in addition to the Bridge of Hope, which provided girls from brothels with education. Evangelicals broke the Victorian conspiracy of silence about sexual matters and saw the need to deal with man's role in prostitution as much as the woman's. In 1885 the age of consent was raised to sixteen, thanks to the work of Bramwell Booth.

Evangelical approaches to prison work laid stress on the reform rather than the punishment of the criminal. They continued in the tradition of John Howard and the Quakers who had laboured for reform. A Reformatory and Refuge Union was started in 1858. But most energies were spent on Prison Gate Missions, Prison visiting, writing letters to prisoners and an early form of probation work.

Medical Missions were formed. Work to care for the blind and deaf was not only undertaken by evangelicals but significantly developed by them. Evangelicals agitated for state pensions for the elderly as well as setting up societies for caring for them themselves. Other special groups, like soldiers and sailors, were provided for through a number of religious and welfare societies which still function.

What is to be made of all this evangelical philanthropy? It provides ample evidence that evangelicalism is characterized by activism. But was the activism well founded?

Heasman offers a sympathetic evaluation of these efforts.[13] She recognizes that others played their part but that evangelicalism was responsible for the lion's share of reforming societies. Their chief motive was undoubtedly compassion. Although it must be admitted that they were also motivated by guilt, the desire for conversions and the availability of surplus money and time, especially among women. Their faith had taught them to value each individual and consequently their approach was a personal one. This personal perspective coloured the type of work they undertook. They have been criticised for duplication of effort but a Charity Organisation Society was set up in 1869 to ensure co-ordination. And, in any case, informal co-ordination was already provided by evangelical networking to some extent. They rarely resorted to legislation, except on a few occasions to prevent some course of evil activity. They rarely went beyond tackling the symptoms of social evil to address their cause. But it is easy to impose our modern understandings of society on people of a different age and judge them by unreasonable criteria. Even if they did not turn their social action into social policy, at least they raised the issues in the national consciousness. In many ways they laid the foundations for, and set out the principles of, the social services which were to become a feature of the twentieth century welfare state. It is a record for which we must be thankful.

David Bebbington has pointed out some additional features which must be borne in mind if we are to understand their work in a true perspective.[14] It is his analysis that leads to the suggestion that we should be cautious about calling their work 'humanitarian'. Their target was clearly sin. Three classes of wickedness called forth evangelical action:

- They wished to remove obstacles to the spreading of the gospel – slavery was such an obstacle because slave owners prevented missionaries from preaching the gospel to them lest it should ferment sedition, so slavery had to go

- They opposed substitutes for the gospel, such as Roman Catholicism, and participated widely in educational matters to ensure that the Christian faith was taught
- They attacked 'sins' such as sexual immorality, drunkenness and Sabbath-breaking.

They usually had a clearer sense of what they wanted to stop than a positive vision of a society they would like to create. Agitation was therefore an appropriate method for their campaigns. Their focus on sin also led them down the path of moralism, which did not always make them popular. Their achievements were not without risk, but were none the less substantial. They were brought about largely by people becoming specialists, being prepared to do detailed work and knowing their way around the world of politics or of vice, whichever their cause necessitated.

THE UNITED STATES

Social action among evangelicals in the United States continued after the era of Finney, taking on much the same complexion as that in Great Britain. Norris Magnuson[15] has documented the work they undertook there between 1865 and 1920, in the areas of food and shelter, rescue homes for women, unemployment initiatives, prison philanthropy, the liberation of women, attitudes to Black Americans and overseas philanthropy. He discovered the same busy pattern of activity, motivated by spiritual convictions and married to a wider social critique, as was evident in the United Kingdom.

He builds his picture on several major evangelical institutions: the Salvation Army, the Christian and Missionary Alliance, the Water Street Mission, New York, The Door of Hope and the Florence Crittenton Association. In 1880 George Railton and seven young army lassies left England to establish the Salvation Army in the United States. In 1887, by which time they had 300 corps and twice that number of officers, William Booth's children took over its leadership and established widespread social work in all the areas mentioned above. In 1896 the Army split and gave rise to the Volunteers of America. But both the Army and the Volunteers continued their strong commitment to social work.

The Christian and Missionary Alliance was formed in 1897 from two groups started by the Revd Albert B. Simpson after he left the Presbyterian ministry in 1880. The purpose of these groups was for Gospel work 'particularly among the neglected classes, both at home and abroad.' But no sooner had Simpson started his new work than they were running a rescue home for women, a college for Christian workers, a home for rest and healing, an orphanage, work with immigrants from Germany and several rescue missions.

Jerry McAuley was converted in Sing Sing Prison and, after a relapse, responded to the gospel again in 1868 and underwent the transformation which was to lead him into rescue mission work. In 1872, with the aid of a Wall Street Banker called A. S. Hatch, he acquired a property in Water Street, New York, which became 'the most important American centre in the rescue mission movement.'[16] Jerry McAuley went on to found the Cremorne Mission in the worst area of the city. Later, Samuel Handley, a drunk converted under McAuley, and descendent of Jonathan Edwards, took over the leadership of the Water Street Mission. He is reported to have led 75,000 persons to faith in Christ whilst the Water Street Mission as a whole reported totals of between 3,000 and 5,000 converts annually.

Wealthy evangelicals also took direct steps to engage in social action. Among them were Sidney and Emma Whittenmore, who were converted in the unlikely setting of the Water Street Mission, and Charles Crittenton. The former couple opened a 'Door of Hope' in 1890 to provide food, clothing and medical care, in an accepting atmosphere, for fallen girls. They later opened the Florence Mission and a large chain of homes, as a result of his visits to the slums, which were to be influential in evangelical social work far beyond their own doors.

There is no disguising the fact that all these social agencies saw sin as the heart of the problem and conversion as the indispensible basis for reformation of life. Even so, they were not guilty of narrow interpretations of social problems nor of superficial spiritual answers to complex social problems. Take unemployment as an example. The Whosoever Gospel Mission, Germantown, Pennsylvania, offered employment to 8,000 men by 1897 manufacturing brooms and shoes and engaging in woodcutting, upholstering, printing and chaircaining. Woodyards became a typical feature of many missions providing people with temporary employment whilst looking for something more permanent. In 1890, William Booth had recommended the establishment of farm colonies in his book *In Darkest England and the Way Out*, a book of deep social criticism. By 1899 three such agricultural communities were established by the Salvation Army in America. Their fortunes declined once Booth-Tucker vacated the leadership of the Salvation Army but others took up the challenge. Salvage brigades became common and training in skills, like blacksmithing, metal work and wheelwrighting were frequently offered at missions.

In 1895 the Salvation Army went further and set up Labour

Exchanges. In Boston they had 300 applicants in the first three weeks. In New York they received 2,600 applicants in their first year and managed to place 1,975. Booth-Tucker's aim was for a national network of employment bureaux. Others could not reach the scale of the Army but followed their example with local initiatives none the less. Their attitude to unemployment is instructive. Whilst avoiding sentimentalizing the unemployed they did not pin the blame for it, nor for its effects, on the individual. There was no shame in honest poverty. Most would fall into moral problems if they had to endure the lot of the poor. It was reckoned that 90 per cent were willing to work, if only the work were available and they refuted the belief that you could find work if you wanted to. At the same time, dignity as well as sympathy was given to the unemployed individual. But there was to be no coddling of them, to use General Booth's word. Indiscriminate charity would only lead to further pauperization. So, hand-in-hand with charity went an active encouragement to work and practical steps were taken to enable work to be found.

The great reversal

From the 1920s onwards a very different picture of evangelicals and social action is to be found. A 'great reversal', as it has come to be called,[17] swept over them and evangelicals withdrew from involvement in the world, except to convert it and to challenge it in regard to one or two issues, like evolution in the United States and ritualism in the United Kingdom. Energies were directed towards self-preservation rather than social transformation. The proud record of social action which had been theirs became but a distant memory. Why was this so?

The causes were numerous, but they had their roots in the nineteenth century, even if their fruit only became apparent in the twentieth. Among them was the sheer magnitude of the problems faced which were multiplied by the explosive growth of urbanisation, especially in the United States. Grand visions gave way to the tackling of specific problems. A sense of defeatism was felt, which was only aggravated by the horror of the First World War.

Revivalism had seen social action as an ally of evangelism: if the body was fed, people would be more prepared to listen to the gospel. D. L. Moody had never believed that, but others did. Moody believed the world was a wrecked vessel from which people needed rescuing by conversion. When the alliance between social amelioration and evangelism noticeably failed, others like A. C. Dixon, got back to the 'first principle' of preaching the gospel. Evangelists began to attack 'false evangelism, which hoped to save society in bulk by means of humanitarian work.'[18] Billy Sunday, who had his own list of reforms, believed that the only real way to change society was to change individuals.

Evangelical converts and sponsors of evangelical missions became wealthier and consequently more socially conservative. Unrest in the labour market caused concern among industrialists upon whom Moody, and subsequent evangelists, depended. Preachers were not therefore going to make statements which upset the proverbial apple cart.

Reformist statements came to be associated more with socialism and even to have revolutionary overtones. Evangelicals therefore drew back. Those who came to adopt a more liberal theological persuasion, like Washington Gladden and Walter Rauschenbush, took up the torch to light the path where the evangelicals dropped it and to illuminate the way to reconstruct economic and social relations at a fundamental level. Rauschenbush, the theologican of the social gospel movement, wrote a number of books setting out concrete proposals for the transformation of society into the kingdom of God. To him, the evils to be abolished were not drunkenness and adultery but the gap between the rich and the poor, an economy centred around competition, profit and greed and the failure to grant power to the labour unions. The Kingdom could be brought about by political change. Society, not individuals, was to be the object of redemption. All this drove evangelicalism right out of the field of social reform.

But evangelicals were predisposed to neglect social action because of another change they had undergone during the course of the nineteenth century. It was a change which altered the direction of their vision. The social action of Finney, and those like him who opposed slavery, was driven by a millennial hope. They believed that the day was coming when God's Kingdom would arrive and God's will would be done on earth as it is in heaven. They foresaw the time when wars would cease, divisions would be overcome, sin would be banished and justice prevail. The church was advancing towards the millennium which was to take place before the second coming of Christ. But when evangelicals began to adopt premillennialism, things changed.

There was a shift from optimism to pessimism, from the social to the individual, from earth to heaven, from grand visionary reform to limited, specific improvements. Evangelicals adopted a more hopeless stance towards the world. Premillennialism taught that Christ's return, which would take place before the millennium, would be preceded by a period when the state of the world would get worse. If the world was to get worse before Christ came and if evil was to be unleashed in an unprecedented fashion, why do anything to reform it? In so far as it was redeemable it would only be redeemed by individuals being converted and transformed who, in turn, would have a bearing on society through their personal lives. Attacking social evil or seeking to transform society became lost in the preoccupation with the individual's preparation for the second coming of Jesus Christ. The earth receded into the background, only having value as a preparation for heaven, in which direction all eyes were now firmly fixed. Many would have agreed with the sentiment of Arno Gabelein, when he wrote, 'The world, to which we do not belong, can do its own reforming without our help. Satan, I doubt not, wants to reform his world a little, to help the deception that men do not need to be born again.'[19]

Some have contended that premillennialism was not as disabling to the evangelical social consensus as that. Timothy Weber[20] has argued that, in practice, moderate premillennialists did get involved in the world. F. B. Meyer and the Salvation Army would be cases in point. Keswick, which adopted a premillennial stance, was not without elements of a social gospel for a substantial part of its first fifty years.[21] Many premillennialists simply refused to accept the logic of their position. Since no date for the return of Christ could be set premillennialists were forced to live in the tension of being members of this society whilst waiting for the next. This led to continuing involvement, especially in the area of rescue missions and prohibition. These causes were ideally suited to premillennialism since they dealt with individual needs and provided opportunities for evangelism without leading premillennialists to engage in the long-term reconstruction of society. But some premillennialists went further and advocated socialist solutions. It is a valiant argument but one which, after 1920, is less convincing.

Evangelicals, betrayed their heritage and withdrew from any real, meaningful social reform. It is to this period we owe the mistaken and disastrous impression that evangelicals have no social conscience or concern. It was a period from which evangelicals were only slowly to recover.

The path to recovery

It is true that evangelicals never quite forgot their social responsibility. Even *The Fundamentals* acknowledged it. The twelfth volume included an essay by Charles Erdman which called for a new emphasis on the social teaching of the gospel and argued that the New Testament had as much to say about the believer's relation to his or her neighbours and the state as to Christ himself. T. C. Hammond wrote a companion volume to *In Understanding Be Men*, his much-used volume on Christian doctrine, called *Perfect Freedom* (1938) which dealt with ethics and devoted a third of its space to social ethics. It was a conservative work, but none the less declared that 'the true self was the social self' and it advocated that Christians should consider choosing politics as a career. But for the most part evangelical social consciences went underground.

PRE-LAUSANNE DEVELOPMENTS

The rediscovery of the evangelical social conscience was not really to begin until the emergence of the new evangelicalism after the Second World War. Carl Henry issued a clarion call to evangelicals to think again in *The Uneasy Conscience of Modern Fundamentalism*, published in 1947. He pleaded for the implications of the gospel both for individuals and society to be made clear. He reasoned that the gospel was a world-transforming message that fundamentalism had made into a world-resisting message by divorcing individual salvation from social responsibility.

In the years to come, Henry's plea was to prove fruitful. A trickle of writings began to emerge in the 1960s showing that the evangelical social conscience was being reawakened. Sir Frederick Catherwood wrote *The Christian in Industrial Society* (1964) and, later, *The Christian Citizen*. Carl Henry contributed again with *Aspects of Christian Social Ethics* (1964). David Moberg wrote *Inasmuch* (1965). Sherwood Eliot Wirt penned *The Social Conscience of the Evangelical* (1968). J. N. D. Anderson offered *Into the World: The Need and Limits of Christian Involvement* (1968). They were limited works, but the debate had begun.

Evangelicals were slowly beginning to stir into action once more. The Evangelical Alliance established a relief agency (TEAR Fund) in 1968. A workshop on evangelicals and social concern was held in Chicago in 1973 which issued a declaration and led to the formation of Evangelicals for Social Action. The work of evangelicals in inner city London attracted attention and the question of how the gospel applied to such an area was tackled by David Sheppard in his much acclaimed work, *Built As A City* (1974).

The evangelical Anglicans, meeting at Keele in 1966, stressed the need for responsible involvement in the world once again. Student missionary conferences and regional evangelism conferences[22] found the issue on their agenda and more radical notes began to surface once again. Tom Skinner, to cite just one example, speaking at the Urbana Conference in 1970 on the subject of race, challenged evangelicals as to whether the doctrines of creation and providence were sufficient for the social action to which they were now committing themselves. That basis, he claimed, led to *laissez-faire* attitudes. Rather we must see that the kingdoms of the world are in the grip of Satan. He called on Christians to become infiltrators, 'fifth columnists in Satan's world for the purpose of preaching liberation to oppressed people.'[23]

LAUSANNE

When the Lausanne Congress on World Evangelicalism, the most significant gathering of evangelicals this century, met in 1974 it was inevitable that the relationship between evangelism and social action would be much debated. John Stott's paper,[24] in which he argued that Christians were called both to the fulfilment of a great commission (Matthew 28:19-20) and a great commandment (Matthew 22:39), set the scene. The contribution of those from Latin America was electrifying. A radical group met spontaneously wishing to go much further than the official conference statement was likely to do. Its statement, which was welcomed by the drafters of the official statement and included in the official documents, spoke of the gospel as 'Good News of liberation, of restoration, of wholeness, and of salvation that is personal, social, global and cosmic.' It confessed the cultural captivity evident in evangelicalism and evangelical failure to treat people in the totality of their being and situations. It called for a condemning of societal and instutionalized sins, not just personal ones. And it glimpsed, once again, a millennial dawn in declaring, 'It is certain that the kingdoms of this world shall become the Kingdom of our God and of His Christ. He shall reign for ever, Alleluia.'[25]

In fact, the official statement contained a clause which has become a classic expression of evangelical social responsibility in the late twentieth century. Clause 5 reads:

> We affirm that God is both the Creator and the Judge of all men. We therefore should share his concern for justice and reconciliation throughout human society and for the liberation of men from every kind of oppression. Because mankind is made in the image of God, every person, regardless of race, religion, colour, culture, class, sex, or age has an intrinsic dignity because of which he should be respected and served, not exploited. Here too we express penitence both for our neglect and for having sometimes regarded evangelism and social concern as mutually exclusive. Although reconciliation with man is not reconciliation with God, nor is social action evangelism, nor is political liberation salvation,

nevertheless we affirm that evangelism and socio-political involvement are both part of our Christian duty. For both are necessary expressions of our doctrines of God and man, our love for our neighbour and our obedience to Jesus Christ. The message of salvation implies a message of judgement upon every form of alienation, oppression and discrimination, and we should not be afraid to denounce evil and injustice wherever they exist. When people receive Christ they are born again into his kingdom and must seek not only to exhibit but also to spread its righteousness in the midst of an unrighteous world. The salvation we claim should be transforming us in the totality of our personal and social responsibilities. Faith without works is dead. (Acts 17:26,31; Genesis 18:25; Isaiah 1:17; Psalm 45:7; Genesis 1:26,27; James 2:9; Leviticus 19:18; Luke 6:27; James 2:14-26; John 3:3,5; Matthew 5:20; 6:33; 2 Corinthians 3:18; James 2:20).[26]

In John Stott's commentary on the clause he drew attention to four doctrines that shaped it: those of God, man, salvation and the Kingdom.[27] An echo of earlier generations of evangelicals who were socially involved began to be heard again.

Since Lausanne evangelicalism has reacted in a number of different ways. Some have regarded the elevation of social responsibility to a status alongside evangelism as a regrettable mistake which will divert evangelicals from their task of preaching the gospel.[28] But they are a minority voice and evangelical history proves them wrong. As we have seen, it was precisely when evangelicals were most concerned about social issues that they were most effective in evangelism and revival.

Others have engaged in debate, much of it arid, on the precise relationship between evangelism and social action. Which is primary? Some refuse to answer the question since both are essential aspects of the one mission. The 'Response to Lausanne' issued by the Radical Discipleship group at Lausanne stated, 'We must repudiate as demonic the attempt to drive a wedge between evangelism and social action.'[29] A consultation called to discuss the matter by the Lausanne Continuation Committee met in Grand Rapids in 1982 and reached an inclusive conclusion. Social activity is a consequence of evangelism, since the convert is saved for good works. It is also a bridge to evangelism, since it often opens the door for the gospel. But most of all social activity and evangelism are partners, 'like the two blades of a pair of scissors or the two wings of a bird.'[30]

Still others have pursued the matter more creatively. In England, Leadership 84, sponsored by the Evangelical Alliance, issued a statement, entitled *Converted to Wholeness*[31] which called for local churches to express social concern, especially in peace-making and confronting justice. Salt and Light consultations have developed issues further. In several places evangelicals have begun to clothe words with actions. The Ichthus Fellowship in London, for example, demonstrates its commitment to holistic evangelism, that is evangelism by words, works and wonders, by not only vigorously proclaiming the gospel and practising signs and wonders but also by running a life skills course, a launderette/coffee bar, pre-school facilities for single mothers, a pregnancy counselling service, an accommodation service, a credit bank and it encourages its members to active political involvement.[32] They argue that a gospel of words, which addresses only the spiritual, is a biblically deficient gospel. Oasis Trust, also in London, is another model of holistic evangelism where words stand in equal partnership with works in the proclaiming of the gospel. The Evangelical Alliance has run an employment scheme and currently runs a Community Initiatives Unit. There are other models that could be named.

Preachers, like Tony Campolo, demonstrate an impressive blend of, and balance between, speaking evangelistically and prophetically on matters of social justice. Creative writing and thinking has been emerging. Christopher Wright[33] has written an excellent book which looks freshly at Old Testament ethics and applies its teaching faithfully and maturely to areas such as economics, politics and crime. It is a good example of contemporary evangelical biblical scholarship which is committed to the authority of the Bible and yet does not interpret it naively. It sets out a ground plan, involving a theological angle (God), a social angle (Israel) and an economic angle (the land) by which to understand the Old Testament ethical teaching and has much to say of direct relevance to social questions today.

Athol Gill, in *Life on the Road*,[34] provides an evangelical exposition of gospel passages which set out an alternative, messianic lifestyle which is free from concerns about possessions and emphasises that if we are to walk with Jesus we should have special responsibilities towards those who are poor and oppressed. Solidly based in scripture, it calls people to a lifestyle which is a far cry from that which often characterizes evangelicalism with its pre-dominantly middle-class ethos. Richard Longenecker has written a more academic treatise, laying the groundwork for *New Testament Social Ethics for Today*,[35] which revolves around Galatians 3:28. Each of these illustrates the way in which evangelicals are trying to grapple with the Bible as a guidebook for contemporary social involvement.

And even statements of faith, so sacrosanct to evangelicals, have begun to reflect some of the emphasis on social responsibility.

Scripture Union, for example, in a revised statement adopted recently, included clauses which would have been absent before. They expressed the mission of the church in these terms:

> We acknowledge the commission of Christ: to proclaim the Good News to all people, making them disciples, and teaching them to obey him; and we acknowledge the command of Christ: to love our neighbours, resulting in service to the church and society, in seeking reconciliation for all with God and their fellows, in proclaiming liberty from every kind of oppression; and in spreading Christ's justice in an unjust world . . . until he comes again.

Having said all this about post-Lausanne developments, mention has yet to be made of the greatest contribution to recent evangelical social thinking which is to be found in John Stott's *Issues Facing Christians Today*. It is a thorough outworking of the Lausanne position and an urgent plea for Christians to be involved in their world and its problems. The theological reason for involvement is found in the five-fold framework of God, Man, Christ, salvation and church.[36] A full doctrine of God will lead us to see that he is a God of nature as well as religion; of creation as well as of covenant; of justice as well as of justification. Christianity leads to a high value being placed on human beings and, 'The higher our view of the worth of human beings, the more we shall want to serve them.' A fuller understanding of Christ, 'who did not stay in the safe immunity of heaven', will lead us to renounce comfort and security and engage in costly incarnational mission. A fuller doctrine of salvation will lead us not to separate the Kingdom of God from salvation, nor Jesus the Saviour from Jesus the Lord, nor faith from love. A fuller doctrine of the church will help us to appreciate that its distinguishing marks should be both 'holiness', that is, its calling out of the world, and 'worldliness', that is, its being sent back into the world to serve.

John Stott steers a steady course through three obstacles put in the path of evangelical social involvement. The complexity of issues sometimes causes Christians to fear that they cannot think straight and so they do not bother to think at all. Pluralism intimidates them and they shrink back lest they are accused of imposing their views on others. Alienation marks our society, and leads to the feeling that we are powerless to effect change. Christians, therefore, ask, 'Have we any influence?'

Convinced that these obstacles can be negotiated, John Stott leads the reader through a *tour de force* of issues which must be on the contemporary agenda. His selection is noticeable for its balance between global, social and sexual topics. Globally, his concern lies with the bomb, the environment, the North-South divide and human rights. Socially, he details work and unemployment, industrial relations, racism, poverty and wealth. Sexually, he covers men, women and God, marriage and divorce, abortion and homosexuality.

His writing is compassionate, soaked in scripture and yet thoroughly conversant with the contemporary situation. It is not lacking in practical suggestions and solutions yet ends with a plea for a renewed vision to be combined with a sense of industry, perseverance, service and discipline. *Issues Facing Christians Today* will serve as a worthy guide in the area of social involvement for some time to come.

The way forward?

As far as social action is concerned evangelicals are on the road to recovery. They are learning that the test of right doctrine is right practice; that an orthodoxy that does not issue in compassion and a commitment to working for justice is in error.[37] Whilst some might still be concerned to argue over minute points of theology, which are often contentious because they are expressed in the left-over language of previous generations, most are healthily learning to live in the real world with a passion for mercy and justice.

Older evangelicals have fears, perhaps because of their memory of the social gospel movement, which strayed from the authentic gospel into a gospel akin to socialism. They question whether it is possible to hold at one and the same time both to the preaching of personal salvation and social transformation without the latter taking over the former. But they must be encouraged to look to an earlier generation of evangelicals for their model, rather than to evangelicals of the early twentieth centuries. Earlier in the nineteenth century, both in the Anglican evangelicalism centred around Clapham and in the revivalist evangelicalism of the United States, evangelicals maintained a balance, with a vigorous commitment both to evangelism and social reform in which neither was compromised.

The question we should be facing lies, I think, elsewhere. Early evangelical social action was generated by a belief in certain doctrines. They believed that God had revealed himself in the Bible, not just to Christians but to all humankind. They believed that Jesus should be King over all. They believed that every person was made in the image of God and therefore, though fallen, deserved respect, dignity and should be free from oppression. They believed that sin, in all its forms, should be eradicated. They believed that *all* the powers of darkness should be trodden down. Above all, they were inspired by a vision; the vision of the coming millennium.

Whilst contemporary evangelicals share some of these perspectives they do not seem to be driven by the same grandness of vision. By comparison with earlier generations, some recent debates concerning the relationship between evangelism and social action have demonstrated a poverty of imagination and of faith, and a lawyer's quest for precision. The question is whether the renewed commitment to social action is based on a sufficient foundation. Evangelicals have begun to talk about the Kingdom of God again, but often in a loose way, insufficiently related to the gospels. Other doctrines and images, especially that of salt and light, are quoted. But an overarching vision and a prophetic hope, such as that supplied by postmillennialism, seems to be lacking. Do they really believe in the redemption of the whole of creation or just of individuals? In this light it must be asked if the reservoir of evangelical activism is sufficiently deep to sustain its commitment to the world, or whether it will run dry all too soon, leading to discouragement, a lack of perseverance and a withdrawal from the world once more?

World Vision?

O FOR A CLOSER WALK WITH GOD

Evangelicals and spirituality

'Spirituality' is not a word which would have been found on the lips of evangelicals until recently. It more naturally belongs to other Christian traditions. Many would even question whether evangelicals have much to offer by way of spirituality. Evangelicalism appears to be such an activist faith that the essential characteristics of spirituality can too easily appear to be squeezed out. From a distance it can look as if evangelical spirituality consists solely of 'the quiet time', a daily devotional time of Bible reading and prayer, before the Christian rushes out to get on with life. But there is much more to it than that, as, to take but one item, the concern for holiness, which has been such a major preoccupation of evangelicals down the centuries, suggests.

What is spirituality? The word is used in a number of different ways but some common threads can be identified. Spirituality has to do with the inner life, the vision of God, encountering God in mystery and devotion, mystical theology, contemplative prayer and loving knowledge. It is designed to bring the head and the heart together, to encourage a spiritual journey and to lead to spiritual formation.[1]

The major components of this interior spiritual life lie outside of evangelicalism in the writing of mystics like Teresa of Avila or in the spiritual exercises of Ignatius Loyola. A significant place is given to the role of a spiritual director, which evangelicalism, with its robust individualism, has traditionally resisted, suspecting that putting another human being in such a place may undermine both the sole mediatorial work of Christ and the priesthood of all believers.[2] Contemplative retreats are much used, which stand in tension with evangelical activism. And use is made of aids to devotion, particularly aesthetic aids of symbol and art, which have often been held suspect by a word-centred evangelicalism.

And yet, within recent years evangelicals have shown a great interest in spiritual disciplines which come from outside their own immediate family and have begun to adopt practices which would have been foreign to previous generations. There are a number of explanations for this, to which we shall return, but the move does suggest a dissatisfaction with evangelical spirituality as it stands, or, more precisely, as it is understood by contemporary evangelicals. Perhaps, part of the answer at least, is that evangelicals have not sufficiently understood their own heritage in spirituality and have been made to feel unnecessarily inferior when brought into contact with those of other traditions.

What is evangelical spirituality?

Evangelical spirituality is not a tight-knit system. It is a living tradition which down the centuries has been marked by flexibility, tensions and responsiveness to its context but which none the less displays some clear common themes. It shares, with other Christians, a trinitarian perspective but is also marked by a number of distinctive emphases. Its spirituality has always expressed and replenished itself in singing, and so much can be discovered about evangelical spirituality from the hymns and songs which belong to it.

Among the themes are those of grace, assurance, holiness, the Bible, prayer and obedience. [3]

GRACE

If there is one word which captures the heart of evangelical spirituality it is 'grace'. P. T. Forsyth spoke of 'grace unspeakable' [4] to describe God's amazing love to undeserving sinners in making salvation possible through the cross of Christ. Down the centuries evangelicals have preached, contemplated and worshipped a God of grace. This single starting point breaks into a number of separate paths before coming full-circle to be the finishing point too.

Because of grace, evangelical spirituality is Christ-centred. John Newton wrote:

> How sweet the name of Jesus sounds
> In a believer's ear!
> It soothes his sorrows, heals his wounds,
> And drives away his fear.

> Jesus! my shepherd, brother, friend,
> My prophet, priest and King;
> My lord, my life, my way, my end,
> Accept the praise I bring.

Charles Spurgeon, who unusually for an evangelical, used the word 'spirituality' to mean devotion, dwelt on the loveliness of Jesus.

Typically, in a sermon on Song of Songs 5:16 he said, 'All loveliness meets in Him. He is the gathering up of all sorts of loveliness. He is the climax of beauty . . . He has within himself an unquenchable flame of love, unexplored and unexplorable.'[5] He went on to speak of the loveliness of Christ on Calvary, ever the centre of his message, and the way in which the cross makes us, the unlovely, 'comely'. He commented on the balance of the loveliness of Christ. 'You never find his kindness lessening his holiness, nor his holiness eclipsing his wisdom, nor his wisdom abating his courage, nor his courage injuring his meekness.'[6] From this writing alone, which could be duplicated by many others, we can see that it is not for nothing that Spurgeon has been called a great evangelical mystic.[7]

In less sentimental style, but none the less on the same theme and in an attitude of similar devotion, John Stott has written on the centrality of Christ to evangelical spirituality. In *Focus on Christ*, John Stott explores the prepositions used to describe the believer's relationship to Christ. He speaks of the need to rediscover a passion for Christ which has always characterized the saints, if the church is to be brought to health and the believer to vitality. He writes:

> As we start following him, we discover to our increasing and delighted surprise, that a personal relationship to Christ is a many-sided, many-coloured, many-splendoured thing. We find that he is our mediator and our foundation, our life-giver and our Lord, the secret and the goal of our living, our lover and our model. Or, bringing together the presuppositions . . . we learn that to be a Christian is to live our lives through, on, in, under, with, unto, for and like Jesus Christ. Each position indicates a different kind of relationship, but in each case Christ himself is at the centre.[8]

Because of grace, evangelical spirituality is Cross-centred. Donald Bloesch has written:

> The atoning work of Christ is the basis of a biblical, evangelical spirituality . . . True spirituality views the Christian life as primarily a sign and witness to the atoning work of Christ. The imitation of Christ is a token of our gratitude for his incomparable work of reconciliation and redemption on Calvary. It is not to be seen as a means to gain additional merits, insuring us a place in heaven.[9]

Nothing encapsulates evangelical spirituality more than Isaac Watts' hymn:

> When I survey the wondrous cross
> Where the young Prince of glory died,
> My richest gain I count but loss,
> And pour contempt on all my pride.

> See from His head, His hands, His feet,
> Sorrow and love flow mingled down:
> Did e're such love or sorrow meet,
> Or thorns compose so rich a crown?

> Were the whole realm of nature mine,
> That were a present far too small,
> Love so amazing, so divine,
> Demands my soul, my life, my all.

The evangelical 'cloud of witnesses' that meditatively centre on the cross is crowded. A few witnesses only can be called. John and Charles Wesley saturated their hymns with the cross. To quote just one is to introduce the flavour of their wonder at it:

> 'Tis mystery all,; th' Immortal dies!
> Who can explore His strange design?
> In vain the first-born seraph tires
> To sound the depths of Love divine.
> 'Tis mercy all! Let earth adore!
> Let angel minds enquire no more.

Simeon's Christian experience was described as 'the religion of a sinner at the foot of the cross.' He said, 'The cross is so extensive a field for meditation that though we transverse it ever so often, we need never resume the same track: and it is such a marvellous fountain of blessedness to the soul that if we have drunk of its refreshing streams, we shall find none other so pleasant to our taste.'[10]

For Spurgeon, 'there (was) nothing worth thinking of or preaching about but this grand truth, which is the beginning and end of the whole Christian system, namely, that God gave His Son to die that sinners might live.' 'As for me,' he proclaimed, 'God forbid that I should glory save in the cross of our Lord Jesus Christ, since to me the cross is identical with Jesus Himself. I know of no Jesus but He who died, the just for the unjust.'[11]

For Moody it was the same. 'The moment a man breaks away from the doctrine of the blood, religion becomes a sham, because the whole teaching of the book is of one story . . . that Christ came into the world and died for our sins . . . It is sheer love which gave Christ for us . . . if you want to know how much God loves you you must go to Calvary to find out.'[12]

Passing over the riches of others like Horatius Bonar, Robert Murray McCheyne, James Denny and P. T. Forsyth and coming to our own day we come again to John Stott. Writing on Galatians 6:14,

'May I never boast except in the cross of our Lord Jesus Christ', he comments. 'There is no exact equivalent in the English language to *kauchaomai* (boast). It means to boast in, glory in, trust in, rejoice in, revel in, live for. The object of our "boast or glory" fills our horizons, engrosses our attention, and absorbs our time and energy. In a word, our "glory" is our obsession.'[13]

Because of grace, evangelical spirituality is conversion-centred. David Gillett rightly asserts, in his recent exploration of evangelical spirituality, that, 'In essence, evangelical spirituality begins with conversion, when the individual responds to the gospel of Christ.'[14] It is therefore a 'twice-born' spirituality. It stresses the need for a person to experience radical personal change, to have their sins forgiven and to become a new person in Christ. It focuses, therefore, on redemption rather than creation. Without the 'change which God makes' spirituality fails to find its starting point.

So evangelicals have always preached and if spirituality is to be evangelical it must always maintain this distinguishing mark. Again, it is expressed in many evangelical hymns, the classic of which must be that written by John Newton about his own conversion:

> Amazing grace! How sweet the sound
> That saved a wretch like me!
> I once was lost, but now am found,
> Was blind, but now I see.

ASSURANCE

Frances van Alstyne's hymn, which became something of an evangelical national anthem through its use in Billy Graham crusades, voices the next aspect of evangelical spirituality:

> Blessed Assurance, Jesus is mine:
> O what a foretaste of glory divine!
> Heir of salvation, purchase of God;
> born of his Spirit, washed in his blood.
>
> > This is my story, this is my song,
> > Praising my Saviour, all the day long.

Assurance is an aspect of evangelical experience much misunderstood by others and often mistaken for presumption or arrogance, into which it can easily degenerate. But that is not the essence of it. When assurance is rightly based on God's grace rather than our merits it will lead to a confidence which is inevitably blended with humility.

It was in the evangelical revival of the eighteenth century that the note of assurance was rediscovered and sounded with ringing clarity. John Wesley's own experience typifies the new departure. Of his conversion he wrote, 'An assurance was given me that he had taken away my sins, even mine, and saved me from the law of sin and death.' He went on to preach that those who had faith should seek assurance as their 'common privilege'. It was to be expected that the Holy Spirit would make such an 'inward impression on the soul' as to 'evince the reality of our sonship'. John Wesley could say, 'I never yet knew one soul saved without what you call the faith of assurance; I mean a sure confidence that, by the merits of Christ, he was reconciled to the favour of God.' Charles Wesley put it like this: 'No condemnation, now I dread, Jesus, and all in him, is mine!'[15]

That assurance was a humble acceptance, by faith, of the teaching of Scripture and the example of the saints of the Bible. Assurance was a gift of God obtained by 'standing on his promises'. Job (19:25-26); David (Ps 23:4) and Isaiah (32:17) are examples of it, whilst the use of words like 'persuaded', 'confidence', 'know', as well as the word 'assurance' itself, in the New Testament (e.g., Romans 8:38-39; 1 Timothy 3:13; 2 Timothy 1:12; Hebrews 10:22; 1 John 3:14; 5:13,19) show it to be God's desire for his children.

The Puritan stream, from which evangelicalism drew, injected a note of realism into talk about assurance. Puritanism had previously stressed the struggle the soul experienced both before and after knowing Christ, but not to the exclusion of teaching assurance. J. C. Ryle, who exemplified this tradition after the evangelical revival, stood firm on the conviction that assurance is 'a true and scriptural thing' and no 'mere feeling'. He nevertheless believed that 'a person may have saving faith in Christ, and yet never enjoy an assured hope, such as the Apostle Paul enjoyed ... All God's children have faith; not all have assurance.' Faith is the essential requirement. Assurance, though part of the believer's birthright, may not be experienced. There were reasons why this might be so, and Ryle believed that steps could be taken to remedy the condition. He thought it could arise from a defective view of justification; from lack of diligence in pursuing spiritual growth; or from an inconsistent spiritual walk.[16]

So, lack of assurance should not be accepted with resignation but action should follow to enable the believer to enter into their full inheritance.

In our own day, Charismatic renewal has brought the doctrine of assurance to life once again. Although always asserted by evangelicals, David Gillett is right in saying, 'By the middle years of this century assurance of salvation had become more a doctrine to be taught than an experience to be encouraged.'[17] He speaks of the lower expectations of the Spirit which characterised evangelicalism at that time which often led to a credibility gap between what was professed and what was experienced. But, not surprisingly in view of the connection made in Romans 8 between the Holy Spirit and assurance, when the Holy Spirit moved again one of the results was a new sense of assurance. The witness of the Spirit to the believer's adoption as a child of God again became prominent and led many to call God 'Abba, Father' with renewed confidence and intimacy. Head-knowledge was once again becoming heart-knowledge.

Why is assurance so important to evangelicals? It is important primarily because they believe it to be taught in Scripture and part of the package of salvation God has designed. It would seem strangely incomplete on God's part to want to make us his children and yet withhold our enjoyment of the fact. But, secondly, it is important for its effects. Assurance prevents the believer from looking inward all the time in a state of insecurity, questioning their acceptance by God. It removes uncertainty from them and provides them with a settled peace which frees them to work for Christ energetically, to pray to the Father confidently, to pursue holiness through the Spirit expectantly and to anticipate the new creation eagerly.

HOLINESS

Visions of holiness may differ among evangelicals but a passion for holiness has always been a marked feature of evangelical spirituality.

Again, hymns disclose the evangelical desire for holiness. Two of which might be cited:

> May the mind of Christ my Saviour
> Live in me from day to day,
> By his love and power controlling
> All I do or say.
>
> *Katie Wilkinson*

> Take my life and let it be
> Consecreated, Lord, to thee;
> Take my moments and my days,
> Let them flow in ceaseless praise.
>
> *Frances Ridley Havergal*

In his classic on the subject, J. C. Ryle listed the essential characteristics of holiness.[18] Holiness is:

- The habit of being of one mind with God;
- The endeavour to shun every known sin and to keep every known commandment
- A striving to be like our Lord Jesus Christ
- Meekness, longsuffering, gentleness, patience, kind tempers, government of the tongue
- Temperance and self-denial
- Charity and brotherly-kindness
- Purity of heart
- The fear of God
- Humility
- Faithfulness in all duties and relations in life
- Spiritual mindedness.

J. I. Packer, who has contributed much to an evangelical understanding of spirituality through his many writings in our time, has recently addressed himself to this topic. Insisting that holiness has to do with our heart, temperament, humanness and relationships, he summarizes holiness like this:

> Holiness is a matter both of action and motivation, conduct and character, divine grace and human effort, obedience and creativity, submission and initiative, consecration to God and commitment to people, self-discipline and self-giving, righteousness and love. It is a matter of Spirit-led law-keeping, a walk, a course of life, in the Spirit that displays the fruit of the Spirit (Christ-likeness of attitude and disposition). It is a matter of seeking to imitate Jesus' way of behaving, through depending on Jesus for deliverance from carnal self-absorption and for discernment on spiritual needs and possibilities. It is a matter of patient, persistent uprightness; . . . of single-minded, wholehearted, free and glad concentration on the business of pleasing God.[19]

Holiness is union with Christ, a joining with him in dying to self and rising to walk in new life. The agent of holiness is the Holy Spirit. He produces it within us.

Within that common framework evangelicals have differed in their more detailed understanding of holiness in a number of respects. The differences give rise to quite different versions of holiness and a variety of tensions.[20] These deserve greater attention than it would be helpful to give in this preliminary survey of evangelical spirituality so we will return to them later in the chapter.

THE BIBLE

Within evangelical spirituality, after grace, a prominent place is given to the Bible, as the channel through which God speaks to his people and by which they listen to him. Taking their stand on 2 Timothy 3:16–17, evangelicals not only believe the Bible to be the inspired word of God, but also that it is sufficient to equip the Christian for holiness. It is a rich mine which endlessly yields precious truths, resources and insights for believers and therefore evangelicals have, down the centuries, shown a love for, and devotion to, it.

> Lord, Thy word abideth,
> And our footsteps guideth;
> Who its truth believeth
> Light and joy receiveth.
>
> Who can tell the pleasure,
> Who recount the treasure,
> By thy word imparted
> To the simple hearted?
>
> *H. W. Baker*

The Bible performs many functions in evangelical spirituality:

It is *the source of truth*, determining what is believed. Consequently, evangelicals are always concerned to establish their positions by reference to the teaching of Scripture and seek to do so even when they disagree with one another. In their hymns about the Bible, G. W. Briggs could assert, 'God hath spoken by His prophets, spoken his unchanging word', and Charles Wesley could pray, 'Unlock the truth, Thyself the key, unseal the sacred book'.

Secondly, the Bible is *a source of nourishment*. It is frequently compared to the 'bread of life' or the manna by which the Children of Israel were kept alive in the wilderness. It is the daily spiritual food which Jesus spoke of as necessary for a person to live (Matthew 4:4) in addition to ordinary daily bread.

Thirdly, it is *a source of direction*. One of the best loved texts is Psalm 119:105, 'Your word is a lamp to my feet and a light to my path'. (In fact, the whole psalm which is a celebration of the glories of God's word expresses a typical evangelical devotion to the Bible.) In seeking answers to both the moral and personal questions of life the Bible proves a wise guide.

Fourthly, it is *a source of protection*. Just as Jesus quoted it to fend off the temptations of Satan, so the evangelical believes it to be a weapon in the fight against sin. It is 'the sword of the Spirit, which is the word of God' (Ephesians 6:17). Recalling it to mind in moments when evil is encountered, and living by it daily, provide the best protection. As Baker wrote in another verse of his hymn:

When our foes are near us,
Then thy word doth cheer us,
Word of consolation,
Message of salvation.

Fifthly, it is *the source of change*. It is not a magic tool, there is no
automatic formula at work, but by reading it with faith (Hebrews 4:2)
it transforms the believer to be like Christ. James (1:21), Peter (1 Peter
1:21-2:3) and Hebrews (4:12) combine to speak of the Bible as a living
and active agent of change in the life of the believer.

The foundational role of the Bible in the evangelical
understanding of holiness has led to the adoption of the practice of
reading it daily, systematically and completely, and also of
memorizing parts of it. When the routine of the 'quiet time', as it
is called, is maintained but the motivation lost it can become a
barren ritual, as many would testify. But when approached in the
right manner, with unhurried devotion and vision it can still lead
to a daily encounter with God. Whitefield's prescription still holds,
the Bible should be read 'devout and daily'. But it is never an end in
itself. The evangelical hymnwriters were never in any doubts that the
purpose of Bible reading was to bring the reader closer to their Lord.
H. W. Baker, again:

O that we, discerning
Its most holy learning,
Lord, may love and fear thee,
Evermore be near Thee.

Or, Anne Steele, who concludes her hymn, 'Father of mercies, in Thy
word':

Divine instructor, gracious Lord,
Be Thou for ever near;
Teach me to love Thy sacred word,
And view my Saviour there.

The stress on the Word, which achieved even greater significance
once the view of the Bible's full verbal inspiration gained currency,[21]
has often led to a devaluing of other means of grace and to a cerebral,
even rationalistic, feel to evangelicalism. More recently, evangelicals
have come to appreciate the value of symbol, dramatic action and
picture, the last particularly through the charismatic movement, as
means by which God communicates. But none of these forms of
communication carry the precision of words and if spirituality is to

be genuinely evangelical it must forever remain committed to the
Bible as central.

Two voices from the past give us a concluding glimpse of the place
of the Bible in evangelical spirituality. Robert Murray McCheyne,
who devised a plan by which the Bible could be read through in a
year which is still used by some, wrote in a letter to Horatius Bonar,
'I love the word of God and find it sweetest nourishment to my
soul'.[22] J. C. Ryle, wrote, 'The man who has the Bible, and the Holy
Spirit in his heart, has everything which is absolutely needful to
make him spiritually wise.'[23]

PRAYER

In evangelical spirituality, prayer goes hand in hand with the Bible.
It is the means by which believers speak with their God. But again,
evangelicalism has been marked by a distinctive emphasis in the
discipline of prayer. With true understanding David Gillett has
written, 'In evangelicalism, so committed to seeing God in action,
intercession is at the very heart of prayer'.[24] The characteristic
vehicles of prayer among evangelicals are not only personal prayer
in the quiet time but the prayer meeting, and days or nights of prayer
in which spontaneous intercession, energized by the Holy Spirit, is
poured forth, and more recently prayer marches or concerts. Prayer
diaries or journals are encouraged. A characteristic evangelical saint
would be a 'prayer warrior' who regularly and fervently sets aside
much time to pray for others.

Intercession has been particularly linked to the missionary work
of the church, especially overseas, but at home too. 'McCheyne used
maps and missionary intelligence to widen the scope of his and his
people's prayers, convinced that prevailing prayer and mission are
profoundly connected in the divine purpose.'[25] Handley Moule spoke
of the need for prayer to be 'reverent, unhurried, detailed, confident
and expectant.'[26] Consistent with this is the way in which prayer is
much spoken of as hard work. Such an approach matches the activist
character of evangelicalism. It is prayer that leads to getting things
changed and getting things done.

Whilst adoration and praise have always been a part of evangelical
prayer it has been transposed into a new key by the charismatic
movement. In some circles the soprano note of praise is sung almost
to the exclusion of other notes, even of intercession.

Whilst meditation on Scripture has always been encouraged,
silent, meditative and contemplative forms of prayer have not been
common among evangelicals. However, there is currently a
broadening of appreciation of other forms of prayer among
evangelicals with many finding value in retreats or more contemp-

lative forms. James Houston, in his work *The Transforming Friendship: A Guide to Prayer* makes the desire to be filled with God the centre of the life of prayer. In his book he remarks, 'Homesickness for God is a mark of the life of God.'[27] Richard Foster, who in an earlier book, *Celebration of Discipline* set out a rich evangelical spirituality, has recently published *Prayer: Finding the Heart's True Home*[28] through which many will be introduced to other traditions of prayer.

The key questions here for evangelicals lies elsewhere, however. Given the secular atmosphere in which we now live, and the pressure many endure in their jobs and family life, how much praying, of any kind, is still done? Prayer meetings are now less well attended than they were, family prayers rare and individual quiet times often cut short. Prayer marches take place but are, in practice, more committed to singing than praying. House groups include prayer, but not in the concentrated form of the prayer meetings. Several intercessory prayer organizations exist and concerts for prayer are arranged from time to time. Even so, from a general viewpoint the doubt remains as to whether evangelicals pray as once they did. Will the evangelical enterprise of the next generation be sustained by prayer as that of previous generations has been?

Perhaps the old evangelical hymn about prayer has never been more apt:

> What a friend we have in Jesus,
> All our sins and griefs to bear!
> What a privilege to carry
> Everything to God in prayer!
> O what peace we often forfeit,
> O what needless pain we bear –
> All because we do not carry
> Everything to God in prayer.
>
> *James Scriven*

OBEDIENCE

Evangelical spirituality then is about doing as well as being. True to its activist nature, evangelicalism cannot separate action from spiritual growth. Rather, growth is both manifest in action and takes place through action. It is not action for the sake of it. Action results from a desire to be obedient to the Lord. Grace is news to be shared, not simply to be privately enjoyed. Assurance frees one from preoccupation with oneself in order to be useful. Holiness is seen in the bearing of fruit. The Bible contains commands to be obeyed. Prayer is the engine of mission and service. Disciples do not truly learn in the classroom or the chapel but only as they are on the road and on the job.

Evangelical obedience has particularly been expressed in mission and evangelism, both at home and overseas. But it has also been seen in loving service to the community and world. To the evangelical, a spirituality which does not lead to such usefulness is suspect.

An evangelical hymn, popular with a former generation, sums it up:

> There's a work for Jesus
> Ready at your hand,
> 'Tis a task the Master
> Just for you has planned.
> Haste to do His bidding
> Yield Him service true;
> There's a work for Jesus,
> None but you can do.
>
> > Work for Jesus, day by day.
> > Serve Him ever, falter never, Christ obey.
> > Yield Him service, loyal, true:
> > There's a work for Jesus none but you can do.
>
> *Elsie Duncan Yale*

The evangelical means of spirituality

Recent writers about evangelical spirituality have, rightly, expressed caution about saying too much about the mechanics of spirituality. The kernel of evangelical spirituality consists of the grace, assurance, holiness, Bible, prayer and obedience outlined above. The means are the husk that come to surround them. What often happens is that in transmitting a tradition to a second or third generation the kernel gets lost and the husk remains. Sadly, that has been all too true of evangelicalism. So many have found the quiet time a legalistic chore, perhaps because they have never truly grasped the meaning of grace. Others have encountered holiness as a list of things from which they must abstain or places they dare not go. Prayer has become a ritual where the words have bounced back from the ceiling. This is the inevitable fate of those who only encounter the means of evangelical spirituality without a true understanding of its heart.

Even so, a mention of the means is legitimate and may be briefly done. In an essay on the spirituality of William Wilberforce, Murray Pura and Donald Lewis have identified from his *Practical View*

(1797) the means he used. They are characteristic of the evangelical tradition at its best and demonstrate a balance between the individual and the corporate, the active and the passive, the personal and the social and the present and the future which is sometimes lacking.[29] They were:

- Daily self-examination
- Prayer
- The Eucharist
- Continual communion with God
- Morning devotions
- The careful observance of providence
- The importance of solitude
- Evening devotions
- An expectancy of heaven
- Benevolence to humankind and usefulness.

Richard Foster speaks of another balance which needs to be maintained in the area of means: that of the balance of celebration and discipline. Disciplines can so easily degenerate into burdensome laws. But the answer is not to reject the disciplines, since, 'God has given us the disciplines of the spiritual life as a means of receiving his grace. The disciplines allow us to place ourselves before God so that He can transform us.'[30] Rather, the answer is to refuse to let them deteriorate into external laws, especially laws which we wish to impose on others as a means of control, by healthily blending the disciplines with celebration. 'Celebration brings joy into life, and joy makes us strong. Celebration is central to all spiritual disciplines. Without a joyful spirit of festivity the disciplines become dull, death-breathing tools in the hand of modern Pharisees. Every discipline should be characterized by carefree gaiety and a sense of thanksgiving.'[31] In a day which exalts easy 'how to' practical programmes and when the mood is to go after systems, it is good to make sure that it is the inner dynamics of the spiritual life which remain uppermost in our thinking.

Tensions in Evangelical Spirituality

Historically, there have been a number of tensions within the overall framework of evangelical spirituality. Furthermore, contemporary evangelicals show not a little dissatisfaction with inherited patterns. It is to these conflicts we now turn. Much relates to the idea of holiness.

ACTIVE STRUGGLE OR PASSIVE RECEPTION?

Is holiness to be achieved by active struggle or passive reception?[32] The question has been on the agenda since the earliest days of evangelicalism but came into sharp focus with the emergence of Keswick. The debate can be seen clearly by reference to two spokespersons, J. C. Ryle and Handley C. G. Moule.

J. C. Ryle is representative of evangelicals who owe much to Puritanism and see growth in holiness to be the result of active struggle. The believer is called to a fight in which his opponents are the world, the flesh and the devil. It is a fight in which faith is the key and not an unaided contest. Even so, it is a real fight in which the believer must engage with his or her wholehearted commitment. To Ryle, and those who adopt this position, the struggle is highlighted in Romans 7 where, it is argued, Paul is talking about his experience as a Christian, still doing the things he does not want to do and still finding it difficult to do the things he does.

In his book on *Holiness*, written to challenge the teaching of Keswick, Ryle questioned the wisdom of talking about holiness by faith alone, of teaching about perfection, and of the possibility of a sudden and mysterious transition to a state of entire consecration. Rather, struggle would be characteristic of the Christian, a struggle that must be held in tension with the equally true experience of assurance. It was through this struggle that a gradual growth in holiness would occur. 'A deep sense of struggle, and a vast amount of mental discomfort from it, are no proof that a man is not sanctified. Nay, rather, I believe they are healthy symptoms of our condition, and prove that we are not dead but alive. A true Christian is one who has not only peace of conscience, but war within.'[33] The Christian will be known by inward warfare as much as by inward peace.

The other approach is to argue that holiness is a gift of God, implicit in our salvation; the believer obtains it, not by active exertion on their own behalf, but by giving up the struggle and restfully trusting God for it. Faith was the key to a successful Christian life. Bishop Handley Moule, the scholarly leader of the Keswick Convention, is representative. The starting point was to argue that Romans 6 taught that the believer was already dead to sin. It was an accomplished fact. The believer's need was to live according to that status, looking to, submitting to, yielding to Christ who already had the victory over sin, which, itself, was neither necessary nor inevitable in their life. Effort would not bring victory about, for self could not crucify self.

In this view, Romans 7 does not speak of normal Christian experience but of a Christian who is not living as he should. His struggles arise because he is failing or reverting to his old way of life, living in his own power and struggling with the flesh and the law, rather than relying on the power of the Holy Spirit. As Handley Moule put it, 'The man does not adequately use God – as he ought to do, as he might do, as he will ever rise up afresh to do. And when he does not, the resultant failure . . . is to him sorrow, burthen, shame.'[34] The answer, then, is to move out of Romans 7 into Romans 8, to move from the chapter which does not mention the Holy Spirit to the one which is saturated by the Spirit, to move to the 'higher life'. To do so requires the Christian to have a resting faith and this would, in all likeliness, come as a sudden experience or a second blessing. Keswick, then, taught holiness to be much more of a crisis than a process, a crisis of submission to God rather than a process of struggling with sin.

Each position has strengths and weaknesses. Keswick teaching, though it raises many pastoral questions, became mainstream evangelical teaching and displaced the older classical view of holiness as a process of struggle. In a modified form which suggests that total consecration is needed to enable a believer to engage in the fight, and with some affinities to the Charismatic movement, it still exercises much influence among evangelicals although the other view is still current among them too.

PERFECTION OR NOT?

A second area of difference is that of perfectionism. John Wesley taught, albeit in a somewhat confusing fashion, that it was possible for a Christian to attain perfection in this life, although it was more usually reached at the moment of death. It meant that the root of sin had been taken out of his or her life, which would then be one full of concentrated love for God and others. He believed it was brought about by an act of faith and, therefore, was attained 'in an instant'. But he qualified it by allowing the importance of 'gradual work' preceding and following its attainment, since, although it was a state which could be achieved, it was not a static state. So, he also accepted that people could, having achieved it, fall from the state of 'perfect love'.

Full-blown belief in perfection is rarely found among evangelicals, although some fringe groups teach it from time to time. Both Scripture and experience seem to call it into question. Some elements of the teaching were adopted in a modified form by Keswick which called Christians to adopt 'a higher life' through a second blessing experience. J. I. Packer aptly describes Keswick's position as a half-way house.[35] Keswick's concern is that the average experience of the Christian life is not necessarily the normal

Christian life and that the believer can have the victory over *known* sin. In the words of one of its exponents:

> No matter what may or may not have occurred in the past and no matter how inadequate my understanding, if my relationship with God is one of unconditional surrender and confident expectation that he will keep His word, I can experience a life of consistent victory over temptation and growth towards His own likeness, I can see His purpose for my ministry substantially fulfilled and, above all, I can daily experience loving companionship with my Saviour.[36]

But, though scriptural holiness remains an ideal set forth by evangelicals, few would argue that it is reachable in this life where sin and temptation sadly remain a part of the normal believer's experience.

HUMAN BEING OR SPIRIT?

A further tension arises over whether the goal of holiness is to make one more fully human or whether it lies in a more mystical direction where the spirit triumphs. The alternatives have some very practical implications. The former route stresses that living in obedience to Christ leads to a celebration of the physical gifts which God has given, like the celebration of sexual love and intimacy seen in the Song of Songs. The latter runs away from such things seeking union with God through the spirit. The former looks to the transformation of the whole life in Christ, the latter speaks the language of 'saving souls'. The former values creation as good, though fallen, and to be enjoyed. So the benefits of culture, of art, music and intellect can be pursued and appreciated. The latter shuns the world and poses a sharp distinction between sacred and secular. The former works with the natural order and is relaxed about natural gifts. The latter stresses God's supernatural working and supernatural gifts. The former tends to involvement with the world, the latter to withdrawal.

The tension raises some important spiritual questions. For example, what did Paul mean by saying in Galatians 2:20, 'I have been crucified with Christ, and I no longer live but Christ lives in me'? What is the place of the self in the Christian life?

Underlying the tension are two conflicting world-views and philosophical systems. The former is the Judaeo-Christian world-view which believes that God created the world to be good and, although it is marred by sin, it is the arena of God's redemption, accomplished through the incarnation when Christ assumed a human body, and that the resurrection we anticipate will be a resurrection of the body. It has, therefore, a large space for creation and the material. The second is that of Greek philosophy, based on Plato, who argued that reality was made up of two distinct realms, the material and the spiritual. The material is an imperfect and transitory realm. The spiritual, consisting of ideas and the forms which stand behind the visible world is the real, lasting and perfect realm. Death transports us finally to the spiritual realm where the soul lives. In a platonic understanding of things, the person who wants to be spiritual will devalue the ordinary and natural and escape to the other realm as fast as they can.

The tensions are, in fact, much manifest in popular spirituality. In recent days *L'Abri*, the work associated with Francis Schaeffer, has drawn attention to the question and argued that much popular evangelicalism is based more on a platonic foundation than a biblical one.[37] Illustrations of this can be found in some of the writings of Watchman Nee, where he talks of the release of the spirit, in some aspects of the charismatic movement, especially where there is a devaluing of the mind and of natural gifts, and some forms of evangelical spirituality that have a commitment to mystical ways of seeking union with God.

Evangelicalism in its origin was thoroughly grounded in the biblical world-view and showed a concern with the whole of life, not despising the physical, nor devaluing the cultural and intellectual life, but cultivating the growth of the spiritual in the fullness of human life and in the world which God made.

PERSONAL OR SOCIAL, WITHDRAWAL OR INVOLVEMENT?

The fourth area where different emphases are seen lies in how holiness is clothed in practical application. What does it mean to be holy today? At times, as in the preaching of Charles Finney, F. B. Meyer and others, evangelicalism has demonstrated a balance between personal and social concerns when talking of holiness. Personal purity and social justice have stood shoulder to shoulder. But, with the rise of premillennialism and the dominance of Keswick as the main channel of holiness teaching, personal and inner purity came to be stressed almost to the exclusion of any social dimension. So, great concern was manifest about a sober way of life where the temper, tongue and spirit were under control and all directed well away from those activities or relationships which might disturb the calm and tempt the flesh. Alcohol and sex became key sins and places which might cause the Christian to fall prey to them, like the public house or the dance hall or other places of entertainment, became taboo. With that went a withdrawal from the world, and from concerns with social justice.

The culture of evangelicalism today is still marked by that legacy, but those issues do not feature unchallenged, nor in such prime positions as once they did. Television culture and the greater openness in society have inevitably had their impact on evangelical understandings of holiness. Evangelicals cannot live in the ghetto culture of yesteryear. From the 1960s onwards, a greater involvement with the world began again and personal holiness began to be balanced a little more with concerns for social justice and righteousness in society. However, on the whole, the individualism within evangelicalism still means that there tends to be a natural bias within it to a holiness which is personal rather than corporate or social. Thus, though many evangelicals are concerned and involved in questions of poverty, homelessness, or oppression, the greater number are more concerned with pornography, abortion and homosexuality.

In this respect evangelicals are less than true to the Scripture they exalt, which constantly reveals God's concern to be both for personal purity and for social justice, and for a *shalom* which means that individuals, communities and the environment are rightly related to him. Too often they separate what God has joined.

Contemporary evangelical spirituality

Mention has been made of signs of dissatisfaction among some evangelicals today with their spiritual inheritance. It seems to fail to satisfy their innermost longing and to be shallow in comparison with other traditions. Elements of those other traditions are, then, being grafted onto an evangelical spirituality, not always comfortably, and people are drifting away from evangelicalism to other folds. What should be made of this?

There are several things to be said. First, it has already been mentioned that often the kernel of evangelical experience has been mistaken for the husk of evangelical method. And where it is an empty method which is passed on it is not surprising that people should quickly look elsewhere for more nourishing food.

Secondly, David Gillett,[38] helpfully points out that in this area, as in other areas, evangelicalism has never been static and if other traditions can provide sources of on-going spiritual renewal for evangelicals then why not enrich the evangelical tradition by them? Facing the onslaught of contemporary secularism, we need to be open to all the resources which God may provide.

Thirdly, evangelicals cannot help but be affected by the

environment in which they live. They always have been and, as we have seen, evangelicalism is a living tradition which has always changed and adapted to its context without losing its own identity. Today's environment affects evangelical spirituality in a number of ways. The environment is pluralistic. We no longer live in a world where there is a narrow range of options; still less, one where there is an agreed view of religion or morality. We live in a world which is peculiarly open and where we are acutely aware of alternatives, multiple options and other viewpoints. Evangelical spirituality inevitably encounters other spiritualities as previous generations may not have done. It is not surprising, therefore, that some should wish to explore alternatives and come to appreciate them. Indeed, it may be a God-given opportunity that they do so and lead to an enrichment of evangelical spirituality.

Then, the environment in which we live shapes the kind of people we are. In a recent study of the religion of the baby-boomer generation, Wade Clark Roof[39] has shown how the generation born after the war are a generation of seekers, suspicious of institutions and organized religion, and, are those who, for a good time, turned inwards for spiritual answers and self-fulfilment. Indeed, they speak of religion as a matter of preference rather than obligation and find the word 'spiritual', with its looser connotations and overtones of feeling and experience, preferable to 'religious'. It would be surprising if these characteristics did not find expression among evangelical baby-boomers and it is essential that evangelicalism provides a spirituality that meets the needs of today rather than yesterday.

Further, as a particular illustration of the last point, one aspect of the baby-boomer's spiritual quest is a greater awareness of the earth and the need to care for it and, as some would say, to be in tune with it. In the light of this, it is not surprising that the creation theology of people like Matthew Fox has some appeal. But that leads us to the final important point.

Contemporary pluralism and change should also be greeted with caution. It is easy in today's world to come up with a hybrid spirituality which is no longer evangelical or to transform the evangelical tradition so much that what results ceases to be evangelical. The challenge then is so to breathe life into tradition that it does, as it can, answer the deepest inner searches of contemporary seekers and provide a clear but humble pathway through the supermarket variety of spiritualities on offer.

If it is to be an evangelical spirituality we should be able to satisfy ourselves on the following points:

- Does it lead us to a deeper understanding of God's grace?
- Does it encourage our sense of acceptance and assurance?
- Does it lead us to holiness?
- Does it deepen our respect for the Bible and its teaching?
- Does it deepen our life of prayer?
- Does it lead us to active and altruistic obedience?
- Does it lead us to know God?

It may be that some contemporary quests fail the test. Contemporary evangelicalism, for example, does not give the impression of being as concerned for holiness as previous generations were. When it comes to spirituality, that is an acid test.

PART THREE

CONTEMPORARY EVANGELICALISM

THE LORD HAS YET MORE LIGHT AND TRUTH

Evangelicalism today and tomorrow

This chapter reviews some of the crucial issues facing contemporary evangelicalism and suggests pointers for future directions in the light of evangelical history.

Commentators are divided over whether evangelicalism is on the verge of widespread revival or total collapse. The former speak of it as leading to the conversion of the nations and eclipsing all other forms of Christianity. The latter point to its growing fragmentation and internal secularization and predict it cannot survive. The truth is probably more mundane. History suggests that although evangelicalism's fortunes may fluctuate neither extreme is likely. Consequently, rather than engaging in unwise speculation about the future, it is better to address some of the significant issues of the present with a view to producing an evangelicalism which is marked by greater maturity.

Unity and diversity

Today, much is made of the fragmentation of evangelicalism and people look back in the belief that it was once a more coherent movement. The fragmentation is said not only to jeopardize the future of the movement but to call into question its present integrity, if not existence. Given the diversity, what is cohesive about it?

Although there have been moments of glorious unity among evangelicals it is important to remember that the evangelical movement has never been anything other than diverse. Evangelical Anglicans were cautious about Wesley, whose movement eventually had to form a separate church. Wesley and Whitefield had their doctrinal differences. These ensured that the Calvinist-Armenian tension was implicit in evangelicalism from the beginning. Dissenting evangelicals were looked on suspiciously and, in turn, looked suspiciously at evangelicals in the established church. Co-operation was sometimes hard to find.

As evangelicalism developed, so did the causes of diversity. As evangelicalism encountered each new wave of intellectual change some adapted but others did not. So the impact of the Enlightenment, of Romanticism and of Modernism was to cause a further fracturing of evangelicalism. Some remained old-style Calvinists whilst others adopted New School Theology. Some adopted the new measures of Finney whilst others resisted. Some imbibed Romantic influences and translated them into holiness teaching. Others stuck with the old ways of Puritanism. Some responded to the challenges of Darwinism and biblical criticism by outright opposition but others took more moderate lines. In our own time some have been influenced by (cultural) Modernism whilst others have been insulated from it. The history of evangelicalism has been one of constant reformulations of old doctrines and realignments of old movements.

These are only broad brush strokes. The finer detail would reveal yet further diversity. In reference to the Bible, for example, evangelicals have differed over the method of its inspiration, whether it is best described as inerrant or not, whether critical approaches are legitimate and, if so, which ones, and, most recently, over the subject of hermeneutics. These have led to different views regarding the historical value of parts of the Bible, and over numerous doctrinal matters, such as, baptism in the Holy Spirit, water baptism and the place of women in the church. All these divergencies have occurred despite evangelicals sharing a common reverence for the Bible and believing it to be the revelation of God's word for the world.

Although diversity has always been characteristic of evangelicalism, some suggest that fragmentation has accelerated rapidly in recent years. New issues, such as those raised by the ecumenical movement, the charismatic movement and the feminist movement, have caused division. New churches have been formed. And parachurch societies, which were already a colourful mosaic, have been added to in plenty, leading to the impression that the mosaic is now formed of a million pieces. It would be surprising if the picture did not get more complex as time went on, adding to the impression of greater chaos. New pieces added and new interpretations adopted do not necessarily mean old pieces and old interpretations being subtracted. So the picture inevitably grows in complexity. Furthermore, by its increasing fragmentation evangelicalism is mirroring the greater options available in society generally and the deep commitment to pluralism which is evident in the post-war generation.[1] Choice, in religion as much as anything else, matters to the baby-boomers.

John Wesley told George Whitefield that their differences were small in comparison with their agreements. If doctrine divided they were united by a common experience of God's grace. But even in their doctrinal disagreements they were closer together than they sometimes thought in the heat of controversy. They believed essentially the same.[2] Furthermore, the differences between them were nothing in comparison with the difference between evangelicals and others. And so it remains.

If evangelicalism is to have integrity it must have *unity in essentials*. The essentials have always been, first, a reverence for the Bible as the authoritative and trustworthy Word of God. Evangelicals may differ over methods of inspiration, questions of inerrancy and much else to do with the Bible but once it is no longer accepted as the revelation of God's word to humankind, once it is no longer accepted as a reliable guide and a trustworthy revelation, once it is no longer accorded the place of supreme authority in matters of doctrine and practice, the boundary line of evangelicalism has been crossed.[3]

A second essential is a commitment to the gospel. The heart of the evangelical gospel is the atonement made by Christ on his cross and through his resurrection. Inseparably connected to that is the call to conversion and to the radical transformation of life which that new birth entails. These two essentials are of such consequence that they are sufficient to lend a diverse movement coherence.

Second, if the evangelical movement is to have integrity it must have *unity in relationships*. Evangelicals from across the spectrum must meet and respect one another. All too frequently a section of evangelicalism has chosen to define evangelicalism in its own image and to question the authenticity of those who do not conform. Thus, some emphasize its Reformed roots and question the right of those who are not Reformed to claim the title. Others define evangelicalism according to churchmanship and suggest that unless one is a separatist one cannot be truly evangelical. Others seek to impose particular interpretations of certain doctrines, for instance, those connected with the last things, as the only legitimate position which may be held by evangelicals. But history amply demonstrates such restrictiveness to be unwarranted. Evangelical unity calls on all its participants to refuse to elevate secondary issues into places of primacy and to accept the biblical integrity of those with whom they may differ on such issues.

Such recognition and understanding of one another is only likely to develop if evangelicals come out from behind their self-imposed barricades and meet with one another in genuine spiritual fellowship, free from either superiority or defensiveness. Relationships matter.[4]

Third, if the evangelical movement is to have integrity it must have *unity in reality*. The world is suspicious of words and it is really no longer possible to shelter behind notions of spiritual unity and an invisible church as sufficient answers to the question of our disunion. The reality of our unity must be pursued at every level. Evangelicals in the local church must shun schism. Evangelicals setting up new organizations must question, long and hard, why another separate organization is necessary. Evangelicals in comprehensive denominations and in separatist traditions must work at their relationships. And, beyond evangelicalism, too, the question of the wider unity of the church must not be shirked.

Where there is an inability to work together, or lack of respect for those from whom one differs, evangelical diversity must be called into question. But for the most part, providing evangelicals are united around essentials, loving in relationships and real in their pursuit of unity, it may be welcomed as a positive feature of the movement and no necessity need be felt to impose a strait-jacket on the movement.

Doctrine or ideology?

A further issue which cries out for attention is whether evangelicalism is a movement united around a few essential doctrines, allowing liberty elsewhere, or whether it is, in reality, not united by its doctrines at all, but by prescribed behaviour patterns. Is it any more than a religious subculture, held together by external and often restrictive codes of conduct? That is the view put forward by Kenneth A Meyers, who writes:

> Modern evangelicalism has always tended to be a subculture concerned more with doing than knowing. Evangelicals have disagreed on the nature of the atonement, on the meaning of the sacraments, on whether or not one could lose salvation, on eschatology, and many other doctrines significant to the lives of individual believers and to the church. Yet they agreed that to be a good Christian meant that you didn't play cards, go to movies, or drink alcoholic beverages. *Behaviour patterns not even discussed in Scripture become more 'the tie that binds' than belief systems that are the entire substance of Scripture.* (Emphasis mine.) One is most trusted in evangelical leadership if he adheres to social, cultural, and political conservatism, regardless of whether or not he can define 'justification', which, according to Martin Luther, was 'the article by which the church stands or falls'.[5]

This is a stunning critique. It captures how many feel about evangelicalism and is the sort of charge not infrequently heard from those who encounter evangelicalism but do not stay within it. Randall Balmer's recent exploration of American evangelicalism lends credence to it.[6] In so far as it is true, it is a shocking indictment of a movement which claims, above all else, to seek to be biblical in behaviour and belief.

It may be argued that the picture is dated and that today's evangelicals do not inhabit such a circumscribed subculture. That is only partly true and, in any case, care needs to be taken with such an argument. The subculture described is largely composed of legitimate responses to yesterday's issues being fossilized and held up as the behavioural test for evangelicals in today's, different, world. Each new generation meets new issues and responds to them as best as they know how. It is all too easy for those responses to become frozen and held up as the test for the next generation. That is no less true of the evangelicalism of the baby-boomer generation than it was of their parents' generation. What sort of subculture is evangelicalism today constructing for the world of tomorrow?

But the emphasis on behaviour is only one half of Meyer's complaint. The other half is the relative unimportance given to doctrine. Again, present-day evangelicalism cannot be easily acquitted. Without wishing to retract from the position that evangelical unity must be found in essential truths, it is also accurate that many evangelicals show indifference to doctrine of any kind. Experience has been exalted above doctrine and serious study of important matters is often given short shrift.

Since evangelicalism seeks to be nothing else than true to Scripture it must constantly test its life against Scripture and re-evaluate its practices in the light of what is discovered. If this were done, many of the shibboleths of the evangelical subculture would quickly be demolished and weightier matters, such as truth, love and justice, would be put in their place. The evangelical subculture is in urgent need of reformation by a fresh submission to the Word of God.

Arrogance or humility?

John Stott once wrote, 'It is the contention of evangelicals that they are plain Bible Christians, and that in order to be a biblical Christian it is necessary to be an evangelical Christian. Put in this way, it may sound arrogant and exclusive, but this is a sincerely held belief.'[7] Many evangelicals sincerely hold to the connection between the Bible and their faith but, then, regretfully, fall into the temptation of arrogance to which John Stott alludes.

Because evangelicalism entails holding religious convictions it has frequently been dogged by arrogance. Witness the remarks of L. E. Elliot-Binns, in 1928: 'A lack of trust and a spirit of suspicion has been one of the gravest faults of evangelicals throughout the whole history of the movement.' As evidence, he cites the divisions which took place in the Church Missionary Society, which resulted in the formation of the Bible Churchmen's Missionary Society a few years before he wrote. He went on, 'Much of the spirit of suspicion arises from a narrowness of mind which insists on making its own spiritual experience the standard by which to test all mankind. He concluded that some had fallen into dreadful arrogance, that they were narrow and undervalued anything which did not have a direct bearing on the soul and were so narrow as to be unable to join in the church constructively. [8]

From a different angle, James Barr also notes the arrogance of evangelicalism. The characteristic is seen in their only listening to 'sound' speakers and reading books from 'sound' publishers and in dismissive attitudes to those who hold other positions. One aspect of his complex picture is worth highlighting. He comments that, for all their claim to be true to the Bible, at the end of the day they are not interested in what the Bible says but in the achievement of dominance for the evangelical tradition. [9] The quest for power is often the fruit of arrogance.

There can be no doubt that other sections of the church have frequently encountered the arrogant face of evangelicalism, and been both mystified and hurt. That face has sometimes been displayed in the local church and sometimes in national or ecumenical negotiations. But wherever it has been displayed it should be a cause of repentance. There can be no place for pride in evangelical faith for the God whom the evangelical worships 'opposes the proud but gives grace to the humble,' the Lord whom the evangelical follows exemplified humility and the Bible which the evangelical believes enjoins it. Furthermore, the failure of evangelicalism to live up to its own ideals, let alone Scripture itself, gives us no possible grounds for arrogance. Other sections of the church have often much to teach evangelicalism about how to put the Bible into practice seriously in today's world. Grace is needed to learn from others.

Evangelical convictions need to be infused with a spirit of humility. [10]

Change or decay?

Some speak as if evangelicalism were a fixed and immutable position in the church. The truth, as we have seen, is that evangelicalism is a living tradition which has regularly undergone changes during the two and a half centuries of its existence. There have been reinterpretations of its doctrine, realignments in its structures and relationships and reformulations of its behaviour patterns. Without change, evangelicalism would now be relegated to being an interesting exhibit in some museum of ecclesiastic history. But change always causes tensions and frequently causes divisions, and understandably so. Change is never easy and, in the case of evangelicalism, special discernment is needed to ensure that change does not strike at the roots of evangelicalism with the result that a living tradition withers. Unfortunately, disagreements take place over what strikes at the roots and what does not.

Several positions can be discerned in contemporary evangelicalism with regard to change. The first two are common but unwise.[11] The third is a more creative way forward.

The first position is that of *resistance*. It takes a number of forms. Some want to go 'back to the Reformation', or, 'back to the Puritans', or, 'back to Wesley, Whitefield, Moody, or Spurgeon, or whoever'. There is much to learn from these godly people and phases in church history, but it is not really possible to go back to them. The world has moved on since they lived. The thought forms are different. Life is dramatically changed. Christianity no longer occupies the place it did in their world. Religious assumptions are not shared by others as they were then. To return to them would require entry into some form of time machine, with the result that once transported to where they were, we would be unable to communicate meaningfully to the world in which we now live. So much would just not connect. It would be like trying to spend foreign currency. It needs changing into the currency of the country where you are. So evangelicalism needs changing into the currency of the day.

Another form of resistance is that of separatism. This approach seeks to resist change by insulating itself from the mainstream church. Aiming for a pure church, it is sectarian in nature and idealises the past. It creates a ghetto mentality and, as Donald Bloesch comments, 'is characterized by a preoccupation with issues that no longer trouble the church at large. Some of these issues should be left buried in the past.'[12] Like all 'strong' religions it is capable of generating a great deal of energy and loyalty. When clear boundaries mark a church's relationship with the world, rigorous ethical and financial demands are made on its members, absolutism characterizes its teaching, discipline is exercised and evangelistic zeal evident, churches can grow and call forth remarkable commitment on the part of some.[13] These characteristics are to be found in many separatist churches. But on both pragmatic and theological grounds it should be questioned. Pragmatically, it is cut off from the wider community and church and fails to have any major transforming influence on society. Separatist churches are often seen to back themselves into an evangelical cul-de-sac. Theologically, its view of the rest of the church is subject to question, especially in view of the New Testament teaching about the unity and catholicity of the church and freedom brought about by the gospel.

The second major, but unwise, response is *accommodation*. In this response the church sees the need to adapt itself to the world around it but does so by capitulating to the values, philosophies and standards of the world. Although more characteristic of the liberal wing of the church than the evangelical wing, accommodationism is not unknown in evangelicalism. Perhaps the most significant popular example of accommodationism in the contemporary evangelical church is to be found in the translation of the gospel into a form of psychological therapy. The gospel according to psychological therapy does not teach that the Lamb of God came to take away the sins of the world but to remove the psychological discomfort of the individual. In popular evangelicalism the gospel is now frequently subjected to a psychological captivity.[14] Other forms of accommodation can be seen in the prosperity gospel, with its emphasis on wealth and health, in exclusively allying it to specific political positions or programmes or subordinating it to philosophical and intellectual trends. Accommodation does not translate the gospel into contemporary language – it comes up with a different gospel.

The third, and wisest, response is to work for change by *renewing the tradition*. This response welcomes change, but is discriminating about it. It is aware of the need to hold fast to apostolic doctrine, as Paul exhorts Timothy to do (2 Timothy 1:13-14; 3:14; 4:2-5). No new revelation will be added to that already received. Even so, apostolic truth needs restating in every age and new illumination of it may be had.

In 2 Timothy 1:13 Paul instructs Timothy to keep 'the pattern of sound teaching' which he had received from the apostle. The word 'pattern' may refer to an architect's drawing and gives us a clue as to what our approach should be. The architect's plan could be faithfully built at a number of times in history but whenever it is so built new techniques and new materials would be used to do so. The building built in the sixteenth century would be the same as that built in the twentieth century but adaptations, which did not affect the essential nature of the building, would inevitably and legitimately be made. In a similar manner the teaching of the Bible must be faithfully reproduced in every generation. But, without altering the pattern, changes will occur, and rightly so, since each generation lives in a new day and addresses its message to a new context.

John Stott has listed three areas where renewal is needed.[15] First, there must be *renewed understanding* of the old message. No fresh revelation can be expected, but the Holy Spirit is always our contemporary interpreter of the old revelation and so new illumination might be expected. The old message must never be abandoned. But new light may be shed on it.

Second, there must be *renewed application* of apostolic message. The evangelical subculture, as we have seen, is often in danger of fossilizing its interpretation of Scripture and therefore of rendering it quaint and irrelevant. But every generation is called to make a fresh application of the Bible's truths and principles so that the word of God may be ever relevant.

Third, there must be a *renewed experience* of the ancient message. The mere recitation of old forms can become an empty ritual. For that reason, as we have argued, many have found evangelical spirituality a barren path to tread. Each generation needs to experience the holy grace of God for itself, in ways which are fresh and appropriate to its day. Again, it is the same holiness and grace of God which is to be experienced as ever was. But the experience of it, and consequently the expression of it that follows, must be always new. In the light of this it is not surprising that Puritanism could be refashioned into evangelicalism, which subsequently could find its chief expression through the holiness movement and, later still, be influenced by the Pentecostal movement and affected to such a degree by charismatic renewal.

Lancelot Andrews, at the beginning of the seventeenth century, stated, 'we are renovators, not innovators'. That is what we are called to be. Those who resist change are preservationists who have no interest in either renovation or innovation. Those who too readily accommodate to change are innovators and neither preserve nor renovate. But those who welcome change with discernment, renewing and restating the evangelical faith for their own time are renovators. In this way that which is old is ever made new and that which is changing is always kept true to the original revelation. The mainstream of evangelicalism has shown a remarkable capacity to renew itself like this down the centuries. We need discernment to aid that renewal in our own day.

The list of areas where renewal is needed, or, in process, is long. The authority and trustworthiness of the Bible needs maintaining whilst a credible way of handling it at the turn of the twenty-first

century is worked out. New ways of talking about the atonement are
required whilst retaining the view that its heart is to be found in a
God of holy love substituting himself, in Christ, for us sinners and
bearing the penalty for our sin. A credible doctrine of the last things
is urgently wanted in order that we might understand the nature of
our hope. Whilst holding on to some important distinctive
evangelical insights into the church, evangelicals must urgently
think afresh about the church with a view to having an
understanding which takes its oneness and catholicity more
seriously. The evangelical tradition of social action needs renewed
commitment and to be inspired by a grander vision. Evangelical
spirituality demands to be taught again and, even more, to be
experienced afresh.

In addition to the task of renewal there is the need to go deeper.
Evangelicalism has been particularly noted for suffering from the
problem of the second generation in an acute form. The sons of the
Clapham Sect did not follow in their fathers' footsteps, but found
greater spiritual satisfaction, instead, in more catholic sections of
the Christian church. In our own day a number of Anglican Bishops
who now hold to liberal or catholic understandings of the faith began
as evangelicals. Others have failed to have their faith sustained at all.
Why should this be so? Part of the answer may lie in the false
substitution of the evangelical subculture for dynamic evangelical
faith. But part of the answer may also lie in evangelicalism's
commitment to activism rather than to thinking. In all the areas
mentioned above, and in other areas too, there needs to be deeper
and richer thinking on the part of evangelicalism in order to satisfy
the legitimate questions and pilgrimages of those belonging to it.

Fixed or Progressive?

There are four significant areas, at least, where evangelicals are
currently grappling with new illumination of old truth. It may be
argued that these are areas where changing practices in the world
have infiltrated evangelicalism and that evangelicals are now seeking
some theological justification for changes which they have already
adopted in practice. Even if that were so, it is to the credit of
evangelicals that they both want their practices, however revised, to
conform to Scripture and that they are willing to look at Scripture
afresh on these issues. Evangelicals have always believed that
revelation was progressive, not in the sense that new revelation
would be given, but in the sense that new understandings of old
apostolic teaching was possible. They have not seen it as so fixed and

static that they were unable to adapt the application of unchanging truths or the working out of unchanging principles to an ever-changing society. Nor have they seen themselves as having arrived at such a perfect state of understanding that they could not correct past imbalances, give attention to past neglects or concede that their understanding of Scripture may have been wrong.

The four areas we might briefly mention are those of the Holy Spirit, the place of women, the nature of the family and the nature of mission.

THE HOLY SPIRIT

Much has been said, at least indirectly, about the Holy Spirit in previous chapters. Our purpose here is to bring the Holy Spirit into focus in his own right.

Evangelicals have always been trinitarian. Older evangelical understandings of the Holy Spirit stressed His role in bringing about new birth (regeneration) in the sinner and holiness (sanctification) in the believer. Most evangelicals' writings would have concerned one of these two themes. There was also some acknowledgement of the Holy Spirit's role in world mission, but not really any interest in his role outside the church. Evangelical arguments, as we have seen, particularly centred around the way in which the Holy Spirit produced holiness in the believer, although all would have agreed that in some measure He indwelt believers and imparted the life and truth of Christ to them, producing within them the fruit of godly lives.

So, the place of the Holy Spirit in evangelicalism was secure in theory. In practice it was a different matter. Looking back at older evangelical theologies the Holy Spirit is clearly not on a par with the Father or the Son. A. A. Hodge's *Evangelical Theology* (1890), is typical in hardly mentioning Him. There is no single chapter on the Holy Spirit although there are four on Christ and two on Scripture. Others were more balanced. Louise Berkhof's *Systematic Theology* (1939) subsumes the doctrine of the Holy Spirit under the work of grace. R. A. Torrey's *What the Bible Teaches* (1957, but much older) corrects the balance but devotes itself to the themes mentioned above.

In reality the Holy Spirit was not much mentioned in evangelicalism this century until the mid 1960s. Since then the Holy Spirit has been given much greater priority on the evangelical agenda, and the understanding of His work has also developed. Concern is not only now with His role in regeneration and sanctification but in empowering and gifting believers and in His supernatural workings. This has caused issues like miracles, prophecy, speaking in tongues, baptism in the Spirit, deliverence, physical and inner healing, visions, dreams and words of knowledge to be looked at afresh. Many evangelicals have discovered whole tracts of Scripture which were previously ignored becoming important. The Acts of the Apostles and 1 Corinthians, as well as other references to the miraculous work of Jesus and the on-going work of the Spirit, are being read with fresh eyes.

Many uncertainties and disagreements exist among evangelicals. Some disagreements are disagreements of fundamental principle, such as, whether the charismatic movement is purely a worldly response to changing culture, or whether it is of God, or, whether the Spirit or the Word has priority in Christian understanding and experience, or, whether gifts of the Spirit were purely for the Apostolic age or for all time. Other disagreements are over proportions. Many evangelicals want to embrace much of the teaching of the charismatic movement and confess that the Holy Spirit has been subject to unwarranted neglect by evangelicals previously. But they are unhappy about some of the absolute claims made, some of the excesses which the movement seems to generate and by the way in which everything seems to be hijacked, in some circles, by certain views of the Spirit.

Positions have changed remarkably since the start of the charismatic movement and much learning and *rapprochement* has taken place. It is an issue of on-going debate and one where evangelicals are tested most as to their humility, love and freedom from arrogance.

THE ROLE OF WOMEN

The debate on the role of women in evangelical circles gives rise to passionate emotions on all sides. Evangelicalism is traditionally patriarchal and, on the basis of verses which seem plain to some, such as 1 Corinthians 14:33–35 and 1 Timothy 2:11–12, they have not been permitted to have leadership or teaching roles within the church. Their changing role in society, however, has posed the question as to whether the subordination of women is the correct understanding of what Scripture teaches about their position. Within the Church of England many evangelicals have examined the issue anew and as a result of a fresh examination of the text have changed their views. It was because many evangelicals, but by no means all, had changed their views that the Church of England General Synod has recently voted to allow the ordination of women. Elsewhere in evangelicalism, for example, among some streams in the restoration movement, there has been a resurgence of teaching on the submission of women.

Even though much of evangelicalism remains patronizingly patriarchal today, evangelical practice has not always been consistent with the theory that women should not teach or lead in the church. Indeed, in her study of feminism, Olive Banks,[16] traces one source of the rise of feminism to the evangelical revival and its successors, especially in the United States. She points not only to the enormous charity work in which they were engaged but to a journal founded, as a result of Finney's preaching, called *Advocate of Moral Reform*. The journal was the organ of the New York Female Moral Reform Society formed in 1834. What was significant about it is that it was edited, written, administered and typeset wholly by women and attempts by men, in 1837, to take it over were 'indignantly repulsed'.

Although, with sad inevitability, women have not figured large in the public history of evangelicalism, their contribution has been enormous and evangelicalism has often given them a status and opportunity denied elsewhere. The experience of evangelical conversion where men and women are on an equal footing before God, the desire to convert others and the sense of purpose among evangelicals which leads to movements of moral and social reformation all release the energies of women and free them for action. Many revivalist movements, such as Primitive Methodism, gave a platform to women preachers and prophetesses. The work of Hannah More had profound affects on the nation of her day. Phoebe Palmer and Hannah Pershall Smith were among the most significant of people in the rise of the Holiness Movement. The Salvation Army treated women as of equal worth and ability from the beginning so that the names of Catherine Booth, Evangeline Booth, Mrs Bramwell Booth, to name just a few, are as famous as those of their male counterparts.

Women have made significant contributions in evangelicalism in four other areas, some of which point up the paradoxes involved in the evangelical approach to women. First, they have been prolific hymn-writers. Whilst many evangelicals have been unwilling to listen to female preachers they have not had difficulty singing their hymns, without apparently realizing the educative role which hymn-singing occupies. The names of Frances Ridley Havergal and Christina Rossetti are outstanding in this connection but, also, representative of many other female hymn-writers.

Second, women have frequently led the way in reform and rescue work as the names mentioned in the chapter on evangelical social action just begins to hint. A close examination of the work undertaken both in the United States and in the United Kingdom would show just how enormous their part has been and how little would have been achieved if left to the men.

Third, they have also played the most significant part in the Sunday School movement. The ban on their teaching does not apply to their teaching of children, where, it is traditionally argued, they have a special and natural role to play because of their maternal calling. It is curious that women have been encouraged to teach at this level so much, which is arguably the most important point at which a person is educated, but denied the opportunity elsewhere.

Fourth, they have contributed a disproportionate amount to overseas missions. Here they have not only demonstrated a pioneering spirit and physical and spiritual stamina often lacking in men, but also had to accept the full range of leadership and teaching responsibilities sometimes denied to them at home. Many of the greatest missionaries of all time, like Gladys Aylward, Amy Carmichael, Helen Roseveare and Jackie Pullinger have been such women. But they stand for countless numbers of unnamed women who have responded courageously and selflessly to the call of world mission.

For all that, feminism is often dismissed by evangelicals today as a dangerously radical movement and its origins attributed to secular, even pagan, sources. But should this be so? The key issue for evangelicals is clearly, 'What does Scripture say?' In the recent prolific debate[17] about the role of women in the Bible three themes can be identified:

1   There has been some discussion about submission and headship. Whilst some assert the issue is straightforward others point out that the Bible's teaching is far from simple. They suggest the Bible teaches the subordinate role of women resulted from the fall (Genesis 3:16) but is not part of God's original intention. Therefore we should have no desire to perpetuate such fallen relationships in the renewed community of the church anymore than we desire to perpetuate any other effect of the fall. There has, too, been a closer examination of the way in which the Bible uses the term 'headship' (for example, 1 Corinthians 11:3) to refer to the place of men in relation to women. Some evidence suggests that the meaning of headship does not lie in terms of authority but in terms of source, as in the source of life or the source of a river. If this is so, overtones of domination or subordination have little to do with the point Paul is making in 1 Corinthians.

2   Attention has been given to the actual role of women in the New Testament. For too long evangelicals have presented only a partial picture of their place there. Jesus

manifestly liberates women and gives them a status denied to them by the religious and social conventions of his day. It is clear from the Acts and elsewhere they had adopted some very significant roles. Lydia hosts a church in her house. Priscilla presumes to correct and teach Apollos. Phoebe is commended for her work. It may even be that there were female apostles in the early church (Romans 16:7) though we cannot be sure. They do not seem to have been the passive spectators in the New Testament church which has sometimes been suggested.

3 Careful exegetical work has been done on key passages like 1 Corinthians 14:33–35 and 1 Timothy 2:11–15. This work has not only sought to understand the meaning of the words used but to interpret these scriptures in the light of other scriptures and to set them in the social context of their day. When this is done many conclude that it is possible to read these texts in a way which does not imprison women in a silent or subordinate role for all time without dismissing the texts as either Paul's personal views or saying that they applied merely to the culture of his day.

The issue is complex and its subterranean roots run in all directions. It is a further issue where evangelicals need to demonstrate not only an ability to grapple with the hard reality of the contemporary world but also to speak and listen to one another with love and humility.

THE FAMILY

Evangelicals have a special place for the family and much of their energies are directed into courses, conferences, books, videos, films and counselling about the family. Early evangelical writings on social ethics, in the 1960s, gave special prominence to the family as a divine institution and the matter has been kept firmly in the evangelical consciousness by the writings of James Dobson and the work of CARE, among many others.

The popular image which evangelicals present is that they wish to rediscover the traditional family in which the husband is the bread-winner, the wife stays at home to look after the house and children, the foundation of love is strong enough to withstand any storm, faithfulness is unquestioned, discipline is strong and consistent, family prayers are practised and romantic love is evident. The family is the place where emotional needs are to be met and where feelings unite people in the first place and bind them and their dependants together subsequently, whereas the wider troubles in society can be traced to trouble in the family. That may be a parody but that is how many read the evangelical ideal. The difficulties with that ideal, however, are enormous.

The shape of the family is changing in our contemporary world and whilst many evangelicals lament the changes and trace our ills to them many others within evangelical churches represent its changed shape. In many churches the traditional pattern of an isolated nuclear family is no longer in the majority. One quarter of all households in the United Kingdom are occupied by one single individual. These do not belong to the isolated nuclear family. Cohabitation before marriage has become the norm. Approximately one in three marriages end in divorce with 150,000 children, under 16, experiencing the break-up of their parents marriages every year in the United Kingdom alone. One quarter of all births take place outside of wedlock. Fourteen per cent of families have a lone parent, usually the mother. 'Reconstituted' families are becoming common. On a wider front, people are living much longer and so the aged and the very aged are becoming an increasing proportion of society and all the additional responsibilities and stresses which fall to the family as a result need to be recognized. Women are increasingly going out to work.

Give this picture of family life being caught in a vortex, the evangelical response has usually been to reassert the traditional pattern of family life as an ideal. But there is evidence that not only does that not connect with contemporary society as it is but that an increasing number of evangelicals do not have confidence in that approach.[18]

The root problem is that by upholding the isolated nuclear family as an ideal, evangelicals have imposed one model of family life on Scripture and read all of Scripture in the light of it. But the isolated nuclear family is not to be found in Scripture. The situation in the Bible is a good deal more complicated if we are honest. Various models of family can be found there including, in the Old Testament, one which we would strongly resist today where in strongly patriarchal societies a husband could take more than one wife and also have concubines. In the New Testament most small family units of mother, father and children, were tiny elements in a much larger extended family network where relationships, as well as geography, were close and dependent. Others belonged to households which, again, were large inclusive units incorporating not only family members but slaves, employees and clients as well. To read the commands of the Bible regarding family life without taking this into account may well be causing more problems than it cures.

Furthermore, the evangelical ideal of traditional family life is a recent invention as history shows. Families have usually been economic units rather than units designed for emotional satisfaction. Privacy was non-existent until comparatively recently. Childhood was not considered a distinct period of life to which special attention should be paid. Puritan children were often brought up in other people's homes. Families have been both patriarchal and matriarchal. Survival, rather than affection or emotionalism, was the name of the game. Evangelicals have wrongly tended to evaluate one model of family life, a typical nineteenth-century bourgeois family, as the biblical model of the family.

Industrialisation privatized the family and the pressures of capitalist economies have often gnawed into family life. By separating the work place from the home, families were put in the private, left-over, compartment of life. By forcing many to move, in order to get a job or give into the demands of a career, small family units have been isolated from the larger extended family. By elevating the impersonal nature of the work place, modern industrial society has caused people to look to the family as a place of refuge, of personal fulfilment and emotional renewal. There may well not have been enough investments made in the family for the emotional withdrawals we have wanted to take from it. The family, then, had more and more demands made upon it at the very time when other circumstances conspired to make it less equipped to cope.

In those circumstances the neat repetition of scripture to the emotional and relational aspects of family life without reading them either in their original context or addressing them to the contemporary social context may well be further undermining family life, adding additional pressure to it, rather than strengthening it. Some evangelicals have begun to address that question[19] and to realize that a fresh understanding of biblical teaching on the family is needed to apply to the shape of family life and the meaning of marriage today. It is another example where the enduring principles of scripture constantly need fresh interpretation given the changing situation.

THE NATURE OF MISSION

The commitment to overseas mission has been characteristic of evangelicalism from the start. But again patterns are changing. At the height of the influence of the Holiness movement in evangelicalism, responding to the call to serve God in foreign parts for life was seen as the evangelical ideal of a surrendered life. Numbers of missionaries grew and all, who were not prevented by circumstances from doing so, were challenged to consider the call.

In recent days evangelicalism has demonstrated some remarkable changes in regard to mission. First there has been a dramatic decline in the number serving as missionaries. Even taking the most recent time-span for which figures are available the trend is clear.[20] The number of missionaries from the United Kingdom serving overseas fell from 5,300 in 1972 to 4,352 in 1991, a drop of nearly twenty per cent. During the same period both the number of retired missionaries and the number of office staff rose by twenty per cent.

Second, in addition to the decline in the total numbers serving there has been a rise in the number of those serving on a short-term basis. Whereas in 1976 only five per cent of Protestant missionaries were short-termers that figure had risen to thirty-two per cent in 1982 but then decreased to sixteen per cent in 1991.

Third, there has been a perceptible shift away from 'pure' missionary work to relief and development work. Whilst in general terms between 1981 and 1985 Protestant missionary societies held their own as far as fund-raising was concerned, the relief and development agencies saw their income grow in leaps and bounds from £4 million in 1981 to £34 million in 1985.[21] Although the figures are not to hand there is every reason to believe that trend has continued since.

The situation is complex and each of these factors needs interpreting carefully. With increasing nationalism and anti-colonialism some countries in the world are no longer open to missionaries and opportunities may no longer exist in the way they once did. At the same time opportunities for Christians to work and travel overseas in other employment or voluntary capacities have increased. So, more Christians might actually be serving as non-professional missionaries overseas than ever before. Also, indigenous church leadership has developed and many two-thirds world churches are sending missionaries to the West. Partnership and reverse flow is now the order of the day.

Many missionaries are not so much called to a people today as called to use particular skills and may therefore no longer be long-term career missionaries to a particular area but use their gifts short-term in one place and then transfer to another. Short-termers may either tap into a group who otherwise would not go at all or indicate a lack of commitment on the part of the younger generation. The emphasis on relief and development may either be seen as adulterating the pure work of the gospel or as discovering a wholeness in mission which evangelicals had lacked. In any case, it would be erroneous to think that earlier generations of missionaries only preached the gospel. Clearly they did not as the multitude of monuments to their educational, social, health and agricultural work show. What is more, relief and development work among evangelicals is usually channelled through existing missionary agencies and personnel. It could, therefore, be argued that such a trend is enhancing a picture that might otherwise be bleaker rather than diverting people and money from the real task.

Again, evangelicalism is in transition and people are being called to a fresh examination of the meaning of mission, a fresh appreciation of the oneness of the world church and a fresh look at what it means to respond to the call of God on their lives today. Every generation must ask itself how best it can fulfil the great commission in its own day. Old patterns may not be the only way, or the best way, of doing so.

Success or failure?

Evangelicalism is, at the moment, enjoying a period of apparent success. But the history of evangelicalism suggests that whenever success is experienced care needs to be exercised.

For the first third of the nineteenth century Anglican evangelicals had been growing in strength and influence. They approached the second third of the century in a strong position and with a confident spirit. The numbers of clergy committed to evangelicalism had grown remarkably and they were beginning to gain significant appointments in the church. Expansion was taking place in evangelical churches and institutions. They were busy. But before long they were in retreat, unable to match the new challenges which were thrown at them. It was almost a century before the tide began to come in again. For others, especially the Dissenters, growth meant a growing apart from one another. The pan-evangelicalism of the early nineteenth century gave way to a rising denominationalism and a diluting of evangelical relationships which, at times, was only barely disguised by the existence of the Evangelical Alliance after 1846. Four lessons are noteworthy:

1   Failure, when success was within their grasp, seems partly due to inadequate leadership. The men who led the Anglican evangelicals into the second third of the nineteenth century were worthy men, but not adequate for the task. They lacked the intellectual acumen and strategic skills which were needed.

2   Evangelicals were fooled by their energetic activism into thinking that much was being accomplished. With the advances of science and biblical criticism, however, the rules of the game were changing and evangelicals were so busy that they did not notice. A little less activity and a

little more energy put into the consideration of credible
defences of the faith may have led to a different scenario.
Activity is no substitute for apologetic. The same criticism
is appropriate to the fundamentalist phase of American
evangelicalism in the 1920s. There old slogans, which did
not adequately match the new situation, were propagated
feverishly. But the world rushed by with a wry smile.

3 Success meant they pulled apart when they most needed to
pull together. Evangelical ecumenism was most evident up
to 1830. After that, they believed that they did not have to
stand together so much to defend the fundamentals, so
secondary items assumed greater importance and caused
division. It started with the Bible Society, was manifest in
the controversy over baptismal regeneration, sparked off by
Spurgeon, and went on into the early twentieth century.
But while battles were being won the war was being lost.

4 Success leads to a dilution of evangelical theology, which is
not to be confused with a legitimate reinterpretation of
evangelical theology. With success, the barricades come
down, the boundaries become less clear, and being accepted
as influential in the mainstream leads to compromise. The
trend was evident from the middle of the nineteenth
century onwards but is particularly evident at the end of
the twentieth century.[22]

Positions of strength carry with them the inherent seeds of decline.
Perhaps the position of weakness is not such a bad location after all.
Evangelicalism at the turn of the twenty-first century needs to read
its history with care and take note.

Would Jesus be an evangelical today?

The question comes to the heart of the matter.[23] The loyalty of
evangelicals is, first and foremost, to Jesus Christ. If loyalty to Him
conflicts with loyalty to an evangelical party then it is time to call
the party to a halt. Sad to say, the answer to the question cannot be
an unequivocal 'yes'.

There is so much in contemporary evangelicalism with which
Christ would identify. Its commitment to Scripture derives from His
commitment to Scripture. Its emphasis on the cross is gained from
him, since his ministry was dominated by His need to go to
Jerusalem to die for our sins. The story of His death takes up a totally
disproportionate amount of space in the gospels and is spelled out

in many-splendoured detail in the epistles. Evangelicals cannot, therefore, apologize for being cross-centred. Jesus spoke of the new birth, called for conversion and, through his own person, gave people fresh beginnings and transformed lives. The desire to see people change from sin to grace-filled lives is in line with Him. The expectation of His return comes from Him. The calling of disciples to be engaged in mission and the concept of the church as a great international fellowship of believers originates with Him. He persistently demonstrated the intimate union between practical acts of compassion and the preaching of the good news. Evangelical spirituality follows the pattern and builds on the model Jesus left.

In these, as well as other ways, Jesus would be an evangelical today. Evangelicalism lays stress on what is biblical, what was originally believed and taught and on fundamental issues of the faith. Its essential principles were taught, defended and maintained by Jesus Himself.[24]

Yet, in other ways a humble caution is needed in claiming that Jesus would be an evangelical today. His freedom from the restrictive practices of Jewish culture makes one think He would not be at home in today's evangelical subculture with its emphasis on external behaviour and unimportant matters. He would burst through the bonds of the humanly-created evangelical traditions as He did the humanly-created Jewish traditions of His own day. In view of His forthright criticisms of the scribes and Pharisees one cannot help but feel He would voice similar criticisms of much that goes on within contemporary evangelicalism. Its pride, arrogance, sense that evangelicals have it right whilst others do not, its acceptance of people on the basis of their spiritual achievements, rather than out of grace, would all merit His censure. His wide embrace of others, His identification with the rejects, His associating with the immoral, His willingness to be entertained by the suspect, breathe a different atmosphere from much contemporary evangelicalism. There was, in Him, none of the rigidity and defensiveness which one can encounter in the evangelical ghetto.

So, sadly, the answer cannot be an unequivocal 'yes'. It is incumbent on evangelicals so to reform themselves and renew their faith that the answer does become an unqualified 'yes'. The call, at the end of the day, is not for them to be more evangelical, in the sense of being committed to a party, but more like Christ.

But, lest those who are not evangelicals should gloat, it is also incumbent on others to see where Christ would be at home among evangelicals today and to reform their faith and practices accordingly. Since, for all its faults, evangelicalism does seek to live by the historic Christian faith, revealed in Scripture, and to release the dynamic power of the gospel into a needy world.

SELECT LIST OF KEY EVANGELICALS AND THEIR DATES

William Booth 1829-1912
William Carey 1761-1834
John Nelson Darby 1800-1882
Jonathan Edwards 1703-1758
Charles Finney 1792-1875
Billy Graham 1918-
Carl Henry 1913-
Charles Hodge 1797-1878
Edward Irving 1792-1834
Martyn Lloyd-Jones 1899-1981
Frederick B. Meyer 1849-1929
Dwight L. Moody 1837-1899
Hannah More 1745-1833
Handley C. G. Moule 1841-1920
John Newton 1725-1807
Harold Okenga 1905-1985
James I. Packer 1926-
Phoebe Palmer 1807-1874
John C. Ryle 1816-1900
Seventh Earl of Shaftesbury 1801-1885
Charles Simeon 1759-1836
Charles H. Spurgeon 1834-1892
John Stott 1921-
Billy Sunday 1862-1935
Reuben A. Torrey 1856-1928
Benjamin B. Warfield 1851-1921
Charles Wesley 1707-1788
John Wesley 1703-1791
George Whitefield 1714-1770
William Wilberforce 1759-1833

NOTES TO CHAPTERS

With further suggested reading material

Chapter 1. Blest be the tie that binds

INTRODUCING EVANGELICALISM

For further reading: J. D. Allan, *The Evangelicals: An Illustrated History*, Baker Book House, Grand Rapids and Paternoster Press, Exeter (1989) and David L. Edwards and John Stott, *Essentials: A liberal-evangelical dialogue*, Hodder & Stoughton, London (1988).

1 Adrian Hastings, *A History of English Christianity 1920-1985*, Collins, London (1987) pp. 200ff and 219.
2 Cited in David Holloway, 'What is an Anglican Evangelical?' in Mervin Tinker (ed), *Restoring the Vision: Anglican Evangelicals Speak Out*, MARC, Eastbourne (1990) p. 16.
3 Peter Brierley (ed), *Christian England, What the 1989 English Church Census reveals*, MARC Europe, London (1991) pp. 161-167.
4 James Davison Hunter, *Evangelicalism: The Coming Generation*, Chicago University Press, Chicago and London (1987) p. 6.
5 George Marsden, 'The Evangelical Denomination', in George Marsden (ed), *Evangelicalism and Modern America*, Eerdmans, Grand Rapids (1984) p. X.
6 Donald G. Bloesch, *The Evangelical Renaissance*, Eerdmans, Grand Rapids (1973) pp. 13-18.
7 See, for example, Richard G. Hutcheson Jr., *Mainline Churches and the Evangelicals: A challenging Crisis?*, John Knox Press, Atlanta (1981).
8 Hunter, op. cit., p. 7.
9 See Steve Bruce, *Pray TV: Televangelism in America*, Routledge, London and New York (1990); J. K. Hadden and Anton Shupe, *Power and Politics in God's Frontier*, Henry Holt, New York (1988); Richard N. Ostling, 'Evangelical Publishing and Broadcasting' in Marsden (ed), *Evangelicalism and Modern America*, op. cit., pp. 46-55.
10 Hutcheson, op. cit., p. 18.
11 Hunter, op. cit., p. 6.
12 David Martin, *Tongues of Fire*, Blackwells, Oxford (1990) p. 49.
13 Bong Rin Ro, 'The Growth of the Evangelical Church in Asia' in J. D. Allan (ed), *The Evangelicals: An Illustrated History*, Baker Book

House, Grand Rapids and Paternoster Press, Exeter (1989) pp. 96–97.

14 For example, Donald W. Dayton, 'Some doubts about the usefulness of the category "Evangelical" ', in Donald W. Dayton and Robert K. Johnston, (eds) *The Variety of American Evangelicalism*, IVP, Downers Grove, Ill (1991) p. 245; John King, 'The Evangelical Party is Over', *Church of England Newspaper*, 13th November 1992, p. 7.

15 John R. W. Stott, *What is an Evangelical?* Church Pastoral Aid Society, London (1977). A fuller definition is given by D. Martyn Lloyd-Jones in *Knowing the Times: Addresses Delivered on Various Occasions 1942-1977*, Banner of Truth Trust, Edinburgh (1989) pp. 299-355, but it does not altogether avoid being too inclusive in the list it considers essential to evangelicalism.

16 Robert K. Johnston, 'American Evangelicalism: An Extended Family', in Dayton and Johnston (eds), op. cit., p. 261.

17 Randall Balmer, *Mine Eyes Have Seen the Glory: A Journey into the Evangelical Subculture in America*, Oxford University Press, New York and Oxford (1993) p. 4ff.

18 Kenneth A. Meyers, 'A Better Way: Proclamation Instead of Protest' in Michael Scott Horton (ed) *Power Religion: The Selling Out of the Evangelical Church?*, Moody Press, Chicago and Scripture Press, Amersham (1992) pp. 48-49.

19 David Bebbington, *Evangelicalism in Modern Britain: A History from the 1730s to the 1980s*, Unwin Hyman, London (1989) pp. 2-19.

20 Robert S. Michaelsen and Wade Clark Roof 'Introduction' in Robert S. Michaelsen and Wade Clark Roof (eds), *Liberal Protestantism: Realities and Possibilities* The Pilgrim Press, New York (1986) p. 3ff.

21 For a full and moden debate of the differences by a leading exponent of each side, see David L. Edwards and John R. W. Stott, *Essentials: A liberal-evangelical dialogue*, Hodder & Stoughton, London (1988). See also, Bernard L. Ramm, *The Evangelical Heritage*, Word, Waco (1973) pp. 79-85.

22 See Peter L. Berger, 'A Sociological View of the Secularisation of Theology', in *Facing Up To Modernity*, Basic Books, New York and Penguin, Harmondsworth (1977 and 1979) pp. 203-224; Steve Bruce, *Firm in the Faith*, Gower, Brookfield and Aldershot (1984) pp. 65-94; P. J. Gee, 'The Demise of liberal Christianity?' in Bryan Wilson (ed), *Religion: Contemporary Issues*, Bellew Publishing, London (1992) pp. 135-143; Dean Kelly, *Why Conservative Churches are Growing*, Harper & Row, New York (1977).

23 George Marsden, *Understanding Fundamentalism and Evangelicalism*, Eerdmans, Grand Rapids (1991) p. 1.

24 Edwards and Stott, op. cit., pp. 90-91 and Clive Calver, Ian Coffey and Peter Meadows, *Who Do Evangelicals Think They Are?* Evangelical Alliance, London p. 6. For a similar series of contrasts see, Donald G. Bloesch, *The Evangelical Renaissance*, Eerdmans, Grand Rapids (1973) pp. 143-149.

Chapter 2 Sweetly may we all agree

EVANGELICALISM'S VARIETIES AND CRITICS

For further reading: Robert E. Webber, *Common Roots: A Call to Evangelical Maturity*, Zondervan, Grand Rapids (1978); James Barr, *Fundamentalism*, SCM, London (1977); David Pawson, *Fourth Wave: Charismatics and Evangelicals are we ready to come together?*, Hodder & Stoughton, London (1993); David Wells, *No Place for Truth or Whatever Happened to Evangelical Theology?*, Eerdmans, Grand Rapids (1993).

1 Robert E. Webber, *Common Roots: A Call to Evangelical Maturity*, Zondervan, Grand Rapids (1978) p. 32.
2 Bryan Wilson, *Magic and the Millennium*, Heinemann, London (1973) pp. 18–26.
3 Richard Holloway, 'Evangelicalism: An Outsider's Perspective' in R. T. France and A. E. McGrath (eds), *Evangelical Anglicans: Their Role and Influence In The Church Today*, SPCK, London (1993) pp. 174–183.
4 —— SCM, London (1977) (2nd ed. 1981).
5 Michael Harper, *None Can Guess*, Hodder & Stoughton, London (1971).
6 Gerald Coates, *What on Earth is the Kingdom?* Kingsway, Eastbourne (1983) p. 21.
7 Arthur Wallis, *The Radical Christian*, Kingsway, Eastbourne (1981) pp. 101–121.
8 *Gospel and Spirit*, A joint statement prepared and agreed by a group nominated by the Fountain Trust and the Church of England Evangelical Council, published jointly, (1977).
9 See, for example, Tom Smail, Nigel Wright and Andrew Walker, *Charismatic Renewal: The Search for a Theology*, SPCK, London (1993).
10 David Pawson, *Fourth Wave: Charismatics and Evangelicals Are We Ready To Come Together?*, Hodder & Stoughton, London (1993).
11 John F. MacArthur, Jr., *Charismatic Chaos*, Zondervan, Grand Rapids (1992).
12 —— Jude Publications, Newcastle-upon-Tyne (1990).
13 John King, 'The Evangelical Party is Over', *Church of England Newspaper*, 13th November, 1992, p. 7.
14. —— Evangelical Press, Darlington (1992).
15 Michael Scott Horton (ed), *Power Religion: The Selling Out of the Evangelical Church?*, Moody Press, Chicago and Scripture Press, Amersham (1992).
16 David F. Wells, *No Place for Truth or Whatever Happened to Evangelical Theology?*, Eerdmans, Grand Rapids (1993).
17 C. Rene Padilla (ed), *The New Face of Evangelicalism*, Hodder & Stoughton, London (1976); Richard Quebedeaux, *The Young Evangelicals*, Harper & Row, New York (1974); Robert Webber, op.

cit.; Robert Webber and Donald Bloesch (eds) *The Orthodox Evangelicals*, Thomas Nelson, Nashville (1978).

18 Bernard L. Ramm, *The Evangelical Heritage*, Word, Waco (1973), p. 14.

Chapter 3 Rock of Ages

THE STORY OF EVANGELICALISM IN GREAT BRITAIN

For further reading: David Bebbington, *Evangelicalism in Modern Britain: A History from the 1730s to the 1980s*, Unwin Hyman, London (1989) and Kenneth Hylson-Smith, *Evangelicals in the Church of England: 1734-1984*, T & T Clark, Edinburgh (1988).

1 The story has recently been told in great detail and with expertise by David Bebbington, *Evangelicalism in Modern Britain: A History from the 1730s to the 1980s*, Unwin Hyman, London (1989), to which this chapter is greatly indebted.

2 G. R. Balleine, *A History of the Evangelical Party in the Church of England*, Longmans/Green & Co., London (1933) p. 21.

3 Kenneth Hylson-Smith, *Evangelicals in the Church of England 1734-1984*, T & T Clark, Edinburgh (1988) p. 6.

4 Balleine, op. cit., p. 18.

5 For further details see, Alan D. Gilbert, *Religion and Society in Industrial England: Church, Chapel and Social Change 1740-1914*, Longman, London and New York (1976) p. 27.

6 On John Wesley see A. Skevington Wood, *The Burning Heart, John Wesley, Evangelist*, Paternoster Press, Exeter (1967). The most recent scholarly biography is Henry Rack, *Reasonable Enthusiast*, Epworth House, London (1989).

7 On George Whitefield see, Arnold Dallimore, *George Whitefield, I & II*, Banner of Truth, Edinburgh (1970 and 1980); Harry S. Stout, *The Divine Dramatist, George Whitefield and the Rise of Modern Evangelicalism*, Eerdmans, Grand Rapids (1991). Stout argues that Whitefield's distinctive contribution was to transform the traditional sermon into 'a dramatic event capable of competing for public attention outside the arena of the churches – in fact, the market place' (p. xvi).

8 See, Deryck W. Lovegrove, *Established Church, Sectarian people: Itinerancy and the Transformation of English Dissent, 1780-1839*, Cambridge University Press, Cambridge (1988).

9 Details of these and many other stories are to be found in Balleine, op. cit., and Hylson-Smith, op. cit.

10 W. J. Limmer Sheppard, *Great Hymns and their Stories*, Lutterworth Press, Guildford & London (1974) p. 96.

11 Hugh Evan Hopkins, *Charles Simeon of Cambridge*, Hodder & Stoughton, London (1977).

12 Roger H. Martin, *Evangelicals United: Ecumenical Stirrings in Pre-Victorian Britain 1795-1830.*

13 A fuller version of this quotation is found in Hylson-Smith, op. cit., p. 23.

14 See Gilbert, op. cit., pp. 69-93.

15 Bebbington, op. cit., p. 74.

16 See, Ernest M. Howse, *Saints in Politics: The Clapham Sect and the Growth of Freedom*, Allen & Unwin, London (1953)

17 For a recent assessment of Irving see, C. G. Strachen, *The Pentecostal Theology of Edward Irving*, Darton, Longman & Todd, London (1973).

18 A classic work on this subject is, Ernest Sandeen, *The Roots of Fundamentalism: British and American Millennarianism*, Chicago University Press, Chicago and London (1970).

19 Bebbington, op. cit., p. 86ff.

20. For the course of the controversy see, Peter Toon, *Evangelical Theology, 1833-56: A Response to Tractarianism*, Marshall, Morgan & Scott, London (1979).

21 Bebbington, op. cit., p. 108.

22 G. B. A. M. Finlayson, *The Seventh Earl of Shaftesbury 1801-1885*, Eyre Methuen, London (1981).

23 For a recent assessment of their cultural impact see, James Munson, *The Nonconformists: In Search of a Lost Culture*, SPCK, London (1991).

24 *ibid.*, pp. 11, 90. See also David Bebbington, *Victorian Nonconformity*, Headstart History, Bangor (1992), pp. 23-58.

25 R. W. Dale, *The Evangelical Revival*, Hodder & Stoughton, London (1880) p. 35.

26 David M. Thompson, 'The Nonconformist Social Gospel' in Keith Robbins (ed) *Protestant Evangelicalism: Britain, Ireland, Germany and America, c. 1750-1950*, Basil Blackwell, Oxford (1990) pp. 255-280.

27 J. Edwin Orr, *The Second Evangelical Awakening in Britain*, Marshall Morgan & Scott, London (1949).

28 John Pollock, *Moody Without Sankey*, Hodder & Stoughton, London (1963).

29 For parallels see, Douglas W. Franks, *Less than Conquerors: How Evangelicals Entered the Twentieth Century*, Eerdmans, Grand Rapids (1986) pp. 124ff.

30 Oliver Barclay, *Whatever happened to the Jesus Lane lot?* IVP, Leicester (1977).

31 Randle Manwaring, *From Controversy to Co-existence: Evangelicals in the Church of England 1914-1980*, Cambridge University Press, Cambridge (1985) pp. 30-38.

32 See, Walter Hollenweger, *The Pentecostals*, SCM, London (1972) pp. 176-187, 197-208.

33 Michael Saward, *Evangelicals on the Move*, A. R. Mowbray, Oxford

(1987) pp. 29–30. Saward's book contains an incisive and witty survey of evangelical history from an Anglican standpoint.

34 William Martin, *The Billy Graham Story: A Prophet with Honour*, Heinemann, London (1992) p. 184.

35 John R. W. Stott, *Fundamentalism and Evangelicalism*, Crusade Reprint, London (1956).

36 —— IVP, London (1958).

37 For the early history of the charismatic movement see, Peter Hocken, *Streams of Renewal*, Paternoster Press, Exeter (1986).

38 For the development of restorationism see, Andrew Walker, *Restoring the Kingdom: The Radical Christianity of the House Church Movement*, Hodder & Stoughton, London (1985).

Chapter 4 Mine eyes have seen the glory

THE STORY OF EVANGELICALISM IN THE UNITED STATES

For further reading: George M. Marsden, *Understanding Fundamentalism and Evangelicalism*, Eerdmans, Grand Rapids (1991); Mark Noll, *A History of Christianity in the United States and Canada*, Eerdmans, Grand Rapids (1992).

1 William G. McLoughlin, *The American Evangelicals, 1800–1900: An Anthology*, Harper Torchbacks, New York (1968) p. 26.

2 See Iain Murray, *Jonathan Edwards, A New Biography*, Banner of Truth Trust, Edinburgh (1987).

3 Mark Noll *et al.* (eds) *Christianity in America: A Handbook*, Grand Rapids: Eerdmans & Tring: Lion (1983) p. 115. The present chapter owes much to this excellent resource.

4 Mark Noll, *A History of Christianity in the United States and Canada*, Eerdmans, Grand Rapids (1992) p. 103. This has also proved a useful guide for this chapter. It contains a great deal of evangelical history set within a wider framework.

5 See William G. McLoughlin, *Revivals, Awakenings and Reform. An Essay on Religion and Social Change in America 1607–1977*, University of Chicago Press, Chicago (1978) pp. 98–140.

6 See Keith J. Hardman, *Charles Grandison Finney, 1792–1875: Revivalist and Reformer*, Syracuse University Press, Syracuse (1987).

7 Charles G. Finney, *Lectures on Revivals of Religion*, First published 1835, Cambridge, Mass: 1960 edn, edited by William G. McLaughlin, p. 271.

8 *ibid.*, p. 108.

9 *ibid.*, p. 207.

10 *ibid.*, p. 195.

11 See McLoughlin, *Revivals, Awakening and Reform*, op. cit., pp. 141–143 where he argues it was not the third Great Awakening. Further details are given in Timothy L. Smith, *Revivalism and Social*

Reform: American Protestantism on the Eve of the Civil War, John Hopkins University Press, Baltimore and London (1980) pp. 63-79.

12 J. Edwin Orr, *The Second Evangelical Awakening in Britain*, Marshall, Morgan & Scott, London (1949) p. 37.

13 Noll, op. cit., p. 243.

14 See James Findlay, *Dwight L. Moody, American Evangelist 1837-1899*, Chicago University Press, Chicago (1969); John Pollock, *Moody without Sankey*, Hodder & Stoughton, London (1993).

15 George Marsden, *Fundamentalism and American Culture; The Shaping of Twentieth Century Evangelicalism: 1870-1925*, Oxford University Press, New York and Oxford (1980) p. 32.

16 William G. McLoughlin, *Modern Revivalism: Charles Grandison Finney to Billy Graham*, Ronald Press, New York (1959) p. 166.

17 Norris Magnuson, *Salvation in the Slums: Evangelical Social Work, 1865-1920*, ATLA Monograph Series, No. 10, Scarecrow Press & American Theological Library Association, Metuchen, NJ (1977); Noll, *History of Christianity in the United States and Canada*, op. cit., p. 306.

18 Ernest Sandeen, *The Roots of Fundamentalism: British and American Millennarianism*, University of Chicago, Chicago and London (1970).

19 Melvin E. Dieter, *The Holiness Revival of the Nineteenth Century*, The Scarecrow Press, Metuchen, NJ and London (1983).

20 The best comprehensive source of information on the Pentecostal Movement is Stanley M. Burgess and Gary B. McGee (eds), *Dictionary of Pentecostal and Charismatic Movements*, Zondervan, Grand Rapids (1988). On Parham, see pp. 660-661.

21 *ibid.*, pp. 31-36, 778-781.

22 *Christianity in America*, op. cit., p. 285.

23 A collection of his articles on the subject can be found in Benjamin B. Warfield, *The Inspiration and Authority of the Bible*, Presbyterian and Reformed, Nutley, NJ and Marshall, Morgan and Scott, London (1959).

24 The leading work on fundamentalism is George Marsden, *Fundamentalism and American Culture*, op. cit.

25 Lyle W. Dorsett, *Billy Sunday and the Redemption of Urban America*, Eerdmans, Grand Rapids (1991). For a less sympathetic portrait see Douglas W. Franks, *Less than Conquerors: How Evangelicals Entered the Twentieth Century*, Eerdmans, Grand Rapids (1986).

26 Marsden, *Fundamentalism and American Culture*, op. cit., chapter 22.

27 George Marsden (ed), *Evangelicalism and Modern America*, Eerdmans, Grand Rapids (1984) p. 10.

28 George Marsden, *Reforming Fundamentalism: Fuller Seminary and the New Evangelicalism*, Eerdmans, Grand Rapids (1987) p. 67.

29 Robert Webber and Donald Bloesch (eds), *The Orthodox Evangelicals:*

Who they are and What are they Saying, Thomas Nelson, Nashville, New York (1978).

30 There is an extensive literature on the New Christian Right. For an introduction and guide see Richard Pierard, 'The New Religious Right in American Politics,' in Marsden (ed), op. cit., pp. 161-174, 206-212.

31 For a concise history see Burgess and McGee (eds), op. cit., pp. 130-160.

32 James Davison Hunter, *American Evangelicalism: Conservative Religion and the Quandry of Modernity*, Rutgers University Press, New Brunswick (1983).

33 James Davison Hunter, *Evangelicalism: The Coming Generation*, Chicago University Press, Chicago and London (1987) pp. 19-154.

34 *ibid.*, p. 208.

Chapter 5 The Bible tells me so

EVANGELICALS AND THE BIBLE

For further reading: Andrew Green, *The Authority of Scripture*, Kingsway, Eastbourne (1990) and J. I. Packer, *God Has Spoken*, Hodder & Stoughton, London (1993).

1 The phrase is owed to Kenneth S. Kantzer, 'Unity and Diversity in Evangelical Faith,' in David Wells and John D. Woodbridge (eds), *The Evangelicals: What they believe, who they are and where they are changing*, Abingdon, Nashville (1975) p. 52.

2 The quotations are found in A. Skevington Wood, *The Burning Heart: John Wesley, Evangelist*, Paternoster Press, Exeter (1967) pp. 209-219.

3 The quotations are taken from Robert S. Dell, 'Simeon and the Bible,' in Michael Hennel and Arthur Pollard (eds), *Charles Simeon (1759-1836)*, SPCK, London (1959) pp. 29-47.

4 J. I. Packer, *Fundamentalism and the Word of God*, IVP, London (1958) p. 77.

5 David L. Edwards and John Stott, *Essentials: A liberal-evangelical dialogue*, Hodder & Stoughton, London (1988) p. 85.

6 Bernard Ramm, *Special Revelation and the Word of God*, Eerdmans, Grand Rapids (1961) p. 117.

7 Packer, op. cit., p. 79.

8 *ibid.*, pp. 81-82; I. Howard Marshall, *Biblical Inspiration*, Hodder & Stoughton, London (1982) pp. 40-45.

9 William J. Abraham, *The Divine Inspiration of the Holy Scripture*, Oxford University Press, New York and Oxford (1981). For an elaboration and development of this view see K. R. Tremblath, *Evangelical Theories of Biblical Inspiration*, Oxford University Press, New York and Oxford (1987).

10 A. Skevington Wood, op. cit., p. 214.

11 Quoted by David Bebbington, *Evangelicalism in Modern Britain: A History from the 1730s to the 1980s*, Unwin Hyman, London (1989) p. 13.

12 *ibid.*, p. 87.

13 *ibid.*, pp. 188-9; David F. Wright, 'Soundings in the Doctrine of Scripture in British Evangelicalism in the First Half of the Twentieth Century', The Tyndale Historical Lecture, 1978, *Tyndale Bulletin 31* (1980) pp. 95, 100ff.

14 Edwards and Stott, op. cit., p. 95.

15 Marshall, op. cit., pp. 54-58.

16 John Pollock, *Moody without Sankey*, Hodder & Stoughton, London (1963) pp. 256-258.

17 The case is argued by David F. Wright, op. cit.

18 Willis B. Glover, *Evangelical Nonconformists and Higher Criticism in the Nineteenth Century*, Independent Press, London (1954). Glover comments, 'In accepting the Cambridge defense against Strauss and Bauer, the evangelicals accepted higher criticism in principle without being fully aware of what they had done. They were also encouraged by the success of conservative New Testament criticism and disposed to believe that the thorough critical study of the Old Testament would likewise substantiate the main outlines of the traditional view of the Bible. They were, therefore, predisposed to give Old Testament criticism a hearing if it should ever be presented in a framework not contradictory to basic evangelical principles' (which it was after 1880). See p. 284.

19 Mark A. Noll, *Between Faith and Criticism: Evangelicals, Scholarship and the Bible* (1986 and 1991). A brief version is found in George Marsden (ed.) *Evangelicalism and Modern America*, Eerdmans, Grand Rapids (1984) pp. 103-121.

20 David W. Wright, *Themelios 3* (1978) p. 88. Quoted by Noll in Marsden (ed.) *ibid.*, p. 115.

21 R. T. France, 'Evangelical disagreements about the Bible', in *The Churchman*, 97 (1982) p. 226. Quoted by Noll, op. cit., p. 144ff.

22 Michael Green, 'Evangelical honesty and New Testament study' in John King (ed), *Evangelicals Today: Thirteen Stocktaking Essays*, Lutterworth Press, Guildford and London (1973) p. 39. Classic evangelicals introductions can be found in R. K. Harrison, *Introduction to the Old Testament*, Tyndale Press, London (1970) and Donald Guthrie, *Introduction to the New Testament*, Tyndale Press, London (rev. edn. 1970). See further, I. Howard Marshall (ed), *New Testament Interpretation: Essays in Principles and Methods*, Paternoster Press, Exeter (1977).

23 R. T. France and A. E. McGrath (eds) *Evangelical Anglicans: Their Role and Influence in the Church Today*, SPCK, London (1993) pp. 33, 42, 53.

24 A. Thiselton, 'Understanding God's Word Today', in *Obeying Christ in*

a Changing World, Fountain Books, London (1977) Vol 1, pp. 90–122. A lengthy, scholarly book was subsequently published by A. Thisleton, *The Two Horizons*, Paternoster Press, Exeter (1980).

25 John Stott, *The Contemporary Christian*, IVP, Leicester (1992) p. 193.

26 Paul Holmer, 'Contemporary Evangelical Faith', in Wells and Woodbridge (eds), op. cit., pp. 74,73.

27 John Stott, *Christ the Controversialist*, Tyndale Press, London (1970) p. 101ff.

28 Mark Noll in Marsden (ed.) op. cit., p. 111.

29 James Barr, *Fundamentalism*, SCM, London (1977) p. xiii.

30 *ibid.*, p. 341.

31 David Pawson, *Fourth Wave: Charismatics and Evangelicals – are they ready to come together?* Hodder & Stoughton, London (1993) ch. 7.

32 *ibid.*, ch. 8.

33 J. C. Ryle, *Knots Untied*, Lynn & Jarvis Ltd., London 29th edn., (1927) p. 2.

Chapter 6 The wondrous cross

EVANGELICALS AND SALVATION

For further reading: John Stott, *The Cross of Christ*, IVP, Leicester (1986) and Leon Morris, *The Atonement: Its Meaning and Significance*, IVP, Leicester (1983).

1 Quoted in David Bebbington, *Evangelicalism in Modern Britain: A History from the 1730s to the 1980s*, Unwin Hyman, London (1989) p. 14.

2 John Stott, *The Cross of Christ*, IVP, Leicester (1989) p. 7.

3 A. Skevington Wood, *The Burning Heart: John Wesley, Evangelist*, Paternoster Press, Exeter (1967) p. 237.

4 Quotations taken from *ibid.*, p. 237.

5 Bebbington, op. cit., p. 15.

6 Iain H. Murray, *D. Martyn Lloyd-Jones: The First Forty Years, 1899–1939*, Banner of Truth Trust, Edinburgh (1982) pp. 190–193; Stott, op. cit., p. 9f.

7 Bebbington, op. cit., p. 15.

8 *ibid.*, p. 145.

9 Stott, op. cit., p. 8.

10 Bebbington, op. cit., p. 208.

11 Quoted by Stott, op. cit., p. 132.

12 Quoted by H. D. MacDonald, *Forgiveness and Atonement*, Baker Book House, Grand Rapids (1984) p. 15.

13 This is what it is called by J. I. Packer in *Knowing God*, Hodder & Stoughton, London (1973) pp. 161–180.

14 See Paul S. Fiddes, *Past Event and Present Salvation: The Christian*

Idea of the Atonement, Darton, Longman & Todd, London (1989).

15 Quoted by Stott, op. cit., p. 117.

16 Jurgen Moltmann, *The Crucified God*, SCM, London (1974).

17 Stott, op. cit., p. 143.

18 Packer, op. cit., p. 163.

19 Leon Morris, *The Apostolic Preaching of the Cross*, Tyndale Press, London (3rd edn., 1965) p. 210. See also his *The Cross in the New Testament*, Paternoster Press, Exeter (1965).

20 For a sustained criticism of the evangelical view of the atonement see David L. Edwards and John Stott, *Essential: A liberal-evangelical Dialogue*, Hodder & Stoughton, London (1988), pp. 107–157. Also, Fiddes, op. cit., pp. 83–111.

21 Stott, op. cit., p. 159. Stott devotes a whole chapter to the idea of the 'self-substitution of God', pp. 133–163.

22 Fiddes, op. cit., p. 87. The issue is fully taken into account by Stephen Travis, *Christ and the Judgment of God: Divine Retribution in the New Testament*, Marshall Pickering, Basingstoke (1986), who argues that the New Testament teaching stresses judgment in relational rather than penal terms.

23 James F. Findlay Jr., *Dwight L. Moody: American Evangelist 1837-1890*, University of Chicago Press, Chicago (1969) pp. 232–234.

24 For example, Ralph Martin, *Reconciliation: A Study of Paul's Theology*, Marshall, Morgan & Scott, London (1981), who argues that reconciliation is the main interpretive key to Paul's theology.

25 Leon Morris, *The Cross of Jesus*, Eerdmans, Grand Rapids and Paternoster Press, Exeter (1988).

26 *ibid.*, pp. 27–46.

27 *ibid.*, p. 118.

28 Michael Harper, *As at the Beginning*, Hodder & Stoughton, London (1965) p. 125.

29 Tom Smail, Andrew Walker and Nigel Wright, *Charismatic Renewal: The Search for a New Theology*, SPCK, London p. 60.

30 *ibid.*, p. 68.

31 *ibid.*, p. 63.

32 Nigel Wright, *The Fair Face of Evil: Putting the Power of Darkness in its Place*, Marshall Pickering, London (1989) p. 159ff.

33 Stott, op. cit., p. 134. See further p. 245.

34 On this theme see Francis Schaeffer, *True Spirituality*, Tyndale House, Wheaton, Ill (1971) pp. 123–180.

35 See Michael Scott Horton (ed), *Power Religion: The Selling out of the Evangelical Church?*, Moody Press, Chicago and Scripture Press, Amersham (1992).

Chapter 7 O happy day

EVANGELICALS AND CONVERSION

For further reading: Peter Toon, *About Turn: The Decisive Event of Conversion,* Hodder & Stoughton, London (1987) and John Stott, *Christian Mission in the Modern World,* Falcon Books, London (1975).

1 Quoted by Iain H. Murray, *Jonathan Edwards: A New Biography,* Banner of Truth Trust, Edinburgh (1987) p. 35. See also Peter Toon, *About Turn: The Decisive Event of Conversion,* Hodder & Stoughton, London (1987) pp. 113–114.
2 Murray, *ibid.,* p. 25.
3 William Martin, *The Billy Graham Story: A Prophet with Honour,* Hutchison, London (1991) pp. 63–64.
4 When Carl Henry published a series of articles in *Christianity Today* on 'Fundamentals of the Faith' the article on the new birth was taken from Billy Graham, *World Aflame,* The World's Work, Tadworth, Surrey (1966) pp. 134–167. Page references here are to Carl Henry (ed) *Fundamentals of the Faith,* Zondervan, Grand Rapids (1969) p. 190ff.
5 *ibid.,* p. 195.
6 *ibid.,* p. 196.
7 Quoted by David Bebbington, *Evangelicalism in Modern Britain: A History from the 1730s to the 1980s* Unwin Hyman, London (1989) p. 7.
8 Henry (ed), op. cit., p. 195. On this issue see further the chapter on 'Puritan Evangelism' in J. I. Packer, *Among God's Giants: The Puritan Vision of the Christian Life,* Kingsway, Eastbourne (1991) pp. 383–407.
9 Such testimonies have been a common feature of recent mass evangelism but not always helpfully so when the superstar subsequently renounces their conversion, as has happened. There are however outstanding exceptions to that stricture and one, that of Charles Colson, former special assistant to President Nixon and Watergate conspiritor, is worth reading for its depth of description regarding conversion. Charles Colson, *Born Again,* Hodder & Stoughton, London (1976).
10 See Beverly Roberts Gaventa, *From Darkness to Light: Aspects of Conversion in the New Testament,* Fortress Press, Philadelphia (1986).
11 Quoted by James F. Findlay Jr., *Dwight L. Moody: American Evangelist, 1837–1890,* University of Chicago Press, Chicago and London (1969) p. 240.
12 Quoted by Bebbington, op. cit., p. 8.
13 John Finney, *Finding Faith Today: How Does it Happen?* British and Foreign Bible Society, Swindon (1992) p. 24.
14 See Gavin Reid, 'Evangelicals, the Evangel and Evangelism,' in Mervin Tinker (ed), *Restoring the Vision: Anglican Evangelicals Speak Out,* MARC, Eastbourne (1990) pp. 83–99.

15 See William Abraham, *The Logic of Evangelism*, Hodder & Stoughton, London (1989).

16 Henry (ed), op. cit., p. 198.

17 *ibid.*

18 J. I. Packer, *Keep in Step with the Spirit*, IVP, Leicester (1984) p. 70.

19 C. H. Spurgeon, *The Soul Winner*, Passmore & Alabaster, London (1897) p. 117. The addresses were published posthumously. See further, D. J. Tidball, 'English Nonconformist Home Missions 1796-1901,' unpublished Ph.D. thesis, University of Keele (1982) pp. 348-364.

20 See John Wimber with Kevin Springer, *Power Evangelism*, Harper & Row, San Francisco and Hodder & Stoughton, London (1985).

21 Ian Bradley, *The Call to Seriousness: The Evangelical Impact on the Victorians*, Jonathan Cape, London (1976) p. 35f.

22 Charles G. Finney, *Lectures on Revivals of Religion*, edited by W. G. McLoughlin, Cambridge, Mass: (1960) (original edition 1835), chapters 9 and 10.

23 Spurgeon, op. cit., *passim*.

24 John Finney, op. cit., pp. 36-47. Family and friends were by far the most instrumental in the leading of others to faith, followed by ministers of religion. Evangelistic events, music, drama and media had, according to this research, disappointingly low impact.

25 Bebbington, op. cit., p. 118.

26 Quoted by Bradley, op. cit., p. 42.

27 Further details are to be found *ibid.*, pp. 42-44.

28 Tidball, op. cit., pp. 243-266.

29 Bradley, op. cit., p. 50ff.

30 See Richard Carwardine, *Transatlantic Revivalism: Popular Evangelicalism in Britain and America 1790-1865*, Greenwood Press, Westport, CT (1978).

31 J. Edwin Orr, *The Light of the Nations*, Paternoster Press, Exeter (1965) p. 192. Cf. John Pollock, *Moody Without Sankey*, Hodder & Stoughton, London (1963) p. 150.

32 Brian Stanley, *The Bible and the Flag*, Apollos, Leicester (1990) p. 61.

33 Orr, op. cit., p. 174. The best general introduction remains Stephen Neill, *A History of Christian Missions*, Hodder & Stoughton, London (1964).

34 For the story of the China Inland Mission/Overseas Missionary Fellowship see Leslie T. Lyall, *A Passion for the Impossible*, OMF, London (1976). A fuller history, in seven volumes, has been written by A. J. Broomhall and published by Hodder & Stoughton, London (1981-1989).

35 See p. 41.

36 Mike Nicholls, *C. H. Spurgeon: The Pastor Evangelist*, Baptist Historical Society, Didcot (1992) pp. 122-129.

37 J. C. Ryle, *Knots Untied*, Thynne & Jarvis Ltd., London (1927, 29th edn), p. 108.

38 Findlay, op. cit., pp. 246-248.

39 William Abraham, *The Logic of Evangelism*, Hodder & Stoughton, London (1989) especially pp. 117-139.

40 Henry (ed), op. cit., p. 207.

41 John Stott, *Christian Mission in the Modern World*, Falcon, London (1975) p. 121.

42 Quoted by Bebbington, op. cit., p. 216.

43 John Stott, *The Contemporary Christian*, IVP, Leicester (1992) p. 351.

44 Jim Wallis, *The Call to Conversion*, Lion, Tring (1981) p. 5.

45 *ibid.*, p. 9.

46 See, for introductory examples, John Stott, *Christian Mission*, op. cit., especially pp. 58-82; Chris Wright, 'Inter-faith Dialogue and the Uniqueness of Christ' in Tinker (ed), op. cit., pp. 101-128.

47 The Lausanne Covenant, Clause 3, J. D. Douglas (ed), *Let the Earth Hear His Voice*, World Wide Publications, Minneapolis, Mn (1975) p. 3f.

48 The Lausanne Covenant, Clause 4, *ibid.*, p. 4.

Chapter 8 The crowning day is coming

EVANGELICALS AND THE LAST THINGS

For further reading: Stephen Travis, *I Believe in the Second Coming of Jesus*, Hodder & Stoughton, London (1982) and W. J. Grier, *The Momentous Event: A Discussion of Scripture Teaching on the Second Advent*, Banner of Truth Trust, London (1970).

1 Quoted in *Evangelical Belief: An explanation of the doctrinal basis of the Inter-Varsity Fellowship*, IVF, London (1961 3rd edn), p. 46.

2 David Bebbington, *Evangelicalism in Modern Britain: A History from the 1730s to the 1980s*, Unwin Hyman, London (1989) pp. 82-83.

3 See Robert G. Clouse (ed), *The Meaning of the Millennium: Four Views*, IVP, Downers Grove, Ill (1977).

4 This is the position documented by Iain Murray, *The Puritan Hope: Revival and the Interpretation of Prophecy*, Banner of Truth Trust, London (1971) contrary to the assertion of Timothy P. Weber, *Living in the Shadow of the Second Coming: American Premillennialism 1875-1925*, Oxford University Press, New York and Oxford (1979) p. 13. See also, W. J. Grier, *The Momentous Event: A discussion of Scripture teaching on the Second Advent*, The Banner of Truth Trust, London (1970).

5 Quoted by Weber, *ibid.*, p. 14.

6 Quoted by Iain Murray, *Jonathan Edwards: A New Biography*, Banner of Truth Trust, Edinburgh (1987) p. 296.

7 Quoted, *ibid.*, p. 297.

8 See Murray, *Hope*, op. cit., pp. 130-155.

9 George M. Marsden, *Understanding Fundamentalism and*

Evangelicalism, Eerdmans, Grand Rapids (1991) pp. 92, 112.

10 See the contributions by George Eldon Ladd and Herman A. Hoyt in Clouse (ed), op. cit., pp. 17–40, 64–92.

11 Bebbington, op. cit., p. 84.

12 The best guides are Ernest Sandeen, *The Roots of Fundamentalism: British and American Millennnarianism*, University of Chicago Press, Chicago and London (1970); George M. Marsden, *Fundamentalism and American Culture: The Shaping of Twentieth Century Evangelicalism*, Oxford University Press, New York and Oxford (1980). For a popular reflection on contemporary dispensationalism see, Randall Balmer, *Mine Eyes Have Seen the Glory: A Journey into the Evangelical Subculture in America*, Oxford University Press, New York and Oxford (1993 edn.), pp. 31-47 which concerns a visit to Dallas Theological Seminary.

13 Quotes by Weber, op. cit., p. 53. See also James F. Findlay Jr., *Dwight L. Moody: American Evangelist 1837-1890*, Chicago University Press, Chicago and London (1969) pp. 253-254.

14 This is contrary to Murray who argues that premillennialism led to an eclipse of missionary activity in *The Puritan Hope*, op. cit.

15 Quoted by Weber, op. cit., p. 75ff.

16 See Sandeen, op. cit., especially pp. 162-187 and, for a criticism of the thesis, see Marsden, *American Culture*, op. cit., pp. 5-7.

17 Quoted by Weber, op. cit., p. 29.

18 Weber, op. cit., p. 209.

19 Samuel Escobar, 'The Return of Christ', in C. Rene Padilla (ed), *The New Face of Evangelicalism: An International Symposium on the Lausanne Covenant*, Hodder & Stoughton, London (1976) p. 259.

20 Hal Lindsey with C. C. Carlson, *The Late Great Planet Earth*, Harper Paperbacks, New York (1992) p. 173.

21 William Hendriksen, *More Than Conquerors: An Interpretation of the Book of Revelation*, Tyndale Press, London (1962).

22 David L. Edwards and John Stott, *Essentials: A Liberal-evangelical Dialogue*, Hodder & Stoughton, London (1988) p. 308.

23 Quoted in Arthur Skevington Wood, *The Burning Heart: John Wesley, Evangelist*, Paternoster Press, Exeter (1967) p. 275. The comments in the text are borne out by J. I. Packer from a different perspective, 'Richard Baxter on Heaven, Hope and Holiness,' in J. I. Packer and Loren Wilkinson (eds), *Alive to God: Studies in Spirituality*, IVP, Downers Grove, Ill (1992) pp. 162-167.

24 Murray, *Edwards*, op. cit., pp. 168-169.

25 Details of quotations found in Wood, op. cit., pp. 276-278.

26 Quoted in John Wenham, *The Goodness of God*, IVP, London (1974) p. 32ff.

27 Quoted in John Blanchard, *Whatever Happened to Hell?* Evangelical Press, Darlington, Durham (1993) p. 24ff.

28 R. A. Torrey, *What the Bible Teaches*, Oliphants, London (1957 edn.) p. 313.

29 Amy Carmichael's dream is quoted in Michael Griffiths, *What On Earth Are You Doing?* IVP, Leicester (1983) p. 23. This position was certainly not adopted by all evangelical missionaries or missionary societies as is shown by Brian Stanley, *The Bible and the Flag*, Apollos, Leicester (1990) pp. 65-67. Furthermore evangelicals have been accused of being perilously close to adding to Scripture when they preached on hell, by their own number. Martyn Lloyd-Jones accuses Jonathan Edwards of doing so in *Knowing the Times*, Banner of Truth Trust, Edinburgh (1989) p. 84.

30 John Pollock, *Moody Without Sankey*, Hodder & Stoughton, London (1963) pp. 68-74. See also John Kent, *Holding the Fort: Studies in Victorian Revivalism*, Epworth, London (1978) pp. 183, 187.

31 Quoted in Blanchard, op. cit., p. 127ff.

32 Geoffrey Rowell, *Hell and the Victorians: A Study of Nineteenth Century Theological Controversies concerning Eternal Punishment and the Future Life*, Clarendon Press, Oxford (1974) pp. 123-129.

33 Blanchard, op. cit., p. 204.

34 Roger T. Forster, *Eternal Destiny: Heaven and Hell*, Ichthus Christian Fellowship, London; Clark Pinnock, 'Fire then nothing,' *Christianity Today*, 20th March 1987, pp. 40-41; Edwards and Stott, op. cit., pp. 312-320; Stephen Travis, *Christ and the Judgment of God*, Marshall Pickering, Basingstoke (1986) especially pp. 66-73, 136-140 and *I Believe in the Second Coming of Jesus*, Hodder & Stoughton, London (1982) pp. 196-199; John Wenham, op. cit., pp. 34-41. John Wenham is quoted by John Blanchard as having become more explicitly committed to the doctrine in a paper given to the Fourth Edinburgh Conference on Christian Dogmatics (1991).

35 The arguments are to be found in Edwards and Stott, op. cit., pp. 315-320.

36 Forster, op. cit., pp. 25-28.

37 Wenham, op. cit., pp. 37-39.

38 See, Blanchard, op. cit.; Murray Harris, *Raised Immortal: Resurrection and Immortality in the New Testament*, Marshall, Morgan & Scott, London (1983) pp. 180-185; Paul Helm, *The Last Things: Death, Judgment, Heaven and Hell*, Banner of Truth Trust, Edinburgh (1989); Alec Motyer, 'The Final State: Heaven and Hell' in Carl Henry (ed), *Basic Christian Doctrine*, Holt, Reinhart and Winston, New York (1962) pp. 290-297; J. I. Packer, *God's Words* IVP, Leicester (1981) pp. 206-211; David Pawson, *The Road To Hell*, Hodder & Stoughton, London (1992). Pawson deviates from the rest in also arguing that Jesus' teaching presents hell as a risk for careless believers as well as carefree sinners.

39 R. T. France, *Matthew*, Tyndale New Testament Commentaries, Eerdmans, Grand Rapids and IVP, Leicester (1985) p. 358.

40 The fate of those who have not heard the Gospel is a closely related issue for the doctrine of hell which space has prevented us from mentioning in this chapter.

41 James Davison Hunter, *Evangelicalism, The Coming Generation,* University of Chicago Press, Chicago (1987) p. 39. See pp. 34-40.

Chapter 9 Glorious things of Thee are spoken

EVANGELICALS AND THE CHURCH

For further reading: Michael Griffiths, *Cinderella with Amnesia,* IVP, Leicester (1975) and David Watson, *I Believe in the Church,* Hodder & Stoughton, London (1978).

1 Alan F. Gibson (ed) *The Church and Its Unity,* When Christians Disagree Series, IVP, Leicester (1992).

2 Peter Toon, *Evangelical Theology 1833-1856: A Response to Tractarianism,* Marshall Morgan & Scott, London (1979) p. 173.

3 Gerald Bray, 'What is the Church? An Esslesiology for Today', in Melvin Tinker (ed), *Restoring the Vision: Anglican Evangelicals Speak Out,* MARC, Eastbourne (1990) pp. 194-198.

4 Significant Bible studies will be found in John Balchin, *What the Bible Teaches about the Church,* Kingsway, Eastbourne (1979); D. A. Carson (ed) *Biblical Interpretation and the Church: Text and Context,* Paternoster Press, Exeter (1984); Michael Griffiths, *Cinderella with Amnesia,* IVP, Leicester (1975); Bruce J. Nicholls (ed) *The Church: God's Agent for Change,* Paternoster Press, Exeter (1986); Howard A. Snyder, *The Community of the King,* IVP, Downers Grove, Ill (1977); Alan Stibbs, *God's Church: A Study in the Biblical Doctrine of the People of God,* IVP, London (1959); John Stott, *One People,* Falcon Press, London (1968); David Watson, *I Believe in the Church,* Hodder & Stoughton, London (1978).

5 E. A. Litton, *The Church of Christ, in its Ideal, Attributes and Ministry,* quoted in Toon, op. cit., p. 178. Another representative expression of the same view is to be found in J. C. Ryle, *Holiness,* James Clark, Cambridge and London (1956 edn.) p. 217.

6 Bray, op. cit., pp. 194-198.

7 Martyn Lloyd-Jones, *The Basis of Christian Unity: An exposition of John 17 and Ephesians 4,* IVP, London (1962); John Stott, *The Complete Christian,* IVP, Leicester (1992) pp. 257-269.

8 Griffiths, op. cit., p. 23.

9 *ibid.,* p. 31.

10 See, Robert Webber and Donald Bloesch (eds), *The Orthodox Evangelicals,* Thomas Nelson, Nashville (1978). From a different perspective, Eddie Gibbs, *I Believe in Church Growth,* Hodder & Stoughton, London (1984), Watson, op. cit.

11 James F. Findlay Jr., *Dwight L. Moody: American Evangelist 1837-1890,* University of Chicago Press, Chicago and London (1969) pp. 246-248.

12 R. W. Dale, *The Old Evangelicalism and the New,* Hodder & Stoughton, London (1889) p. 17.

13 Pablo Perez, 'The Relationship Between Church and Para-Church: A Theological Reflection', in Nicholls, op. cit., pp. 204-214. One place in which Ralph D. Winter sets out his views succinctly is in 'The Two Structures of God's Redemptive Mission', *Missiology 2* (1974), pp. 121-139.

14 Howard A. Snyder, 'The Church as God's Agent in Evangelism', in J. D. Douglas (ed) *Let the Earth Hear His Voice*, World Wide Publications, Minneapolis (1975) pp. 327-351. The quotations are to be found on pp. 335 and 337.

15 Alister McGrath, 'A Better Way: The Priesthood of All Believers', in Michael Scott Horton (ed), *Power Religion: The Selling Out of the Evangelical Church*, Moody Press, Chicago and Scripture Press, Amersham (1992) p. 301.

16 Bray, op. cit., p. 200.

17 Jon Braun, 'A Call to Church Authority', in Webber and Bloesch (eds), op. cit., pp. 166-189.

18 Martyn Lloyd-Jones, *Knowing the Times: Addresses Delivered in Various Occasions 1942-1977*, Banner of Truth Trust, Edinburgh (1989) pp. 46-47, 185-189, 307-309. For his address on Evangelical Unity see pp. 246-258.

19 Horton, op. cit., p. 345.

20 F. Burton Nelson, 'A Call to Church Unity', in Webber and Bloesch (eds), op. cit., pp. 203-204. See also Colin Buchanan, 'The Unity of the Church', in *Obeying Christ in a Changing World: The People of God*, Fountain Books, London, Vol II (1977) pp. 122-123; Robert E. Webber, *Common Roots: A Call to Evangelical Maturity*, Zondervan, Grand Rapids (1978); Nicholls (ed) op. cit., p. 12.

21 For a forthright statement see Alec Motyer, 'The Meaning of Ministry' in Tinker (ed), op. cit., pp. 229-254; Stott, *Contemporary Christian*, op. cit., pp. 273-279.

22 McGrath, op. cit., pp. 301-313.

23 Bray, op. cit., p. 202.

24 Watson, op. cit., pp. 96-114. For an influential earlier expression see, Ray C. Stedman, *Body Life*, Regal Books, Glendale, CA (1972).

25 See, for example, Michael Green, *Evangelism through the Local Church*, Hodder & Stoughton, London (1990); Nicholls, op. cit.; Peter Savage, 'The Church and Evangelism', in C. Rene Padilla (ed), *The New Face of Evangelicalism*, Hodder & Stoughton, London (1976) pp. 105-125; Stibbs, op. cit., pp. 70-79; Stott, *Contemporary Christian*, op. cit., p. 264ff and Watson, op. cit., pp. 298-330.

26 Douglas (ed), op. cit., p. 5.

27 For example, Watson, op. cit., p. 299.

28 For ways in which participation in comprehensive denominations is justified see, David Holloway, 'The National Church', and Gordon W. Kuhrt, 'Principled Comprehensiveness', in Gibson, op. cit., pp. 21-38, 129-139; *Include Us In: the debate about evangelical presence in the main denominations*, Evangelical Alliance, London (1980).

29 J. C. Ryle, op. cit., pp. 238-239.

30 J. C. Ryle, *Warnings to the Churches*, The Banner of Truth Trust, London (1967) p. 149.

31 *ibid.*, pp. 155-156.

32 J. Gresham Machen, *Christianity and Liberalism*, London: Victory Press (1923).

33 Francis A. Schaeffer, *The Church Before the Watching World*, IVP, London (1972) p. 51. See further, Douglas (ed), op. cit., pp. 368-379.

34 James Barr, *Fundamentalism*, SCM, London (1988) pp. 328-331. The earlier phrase characterising evangelical-ecumenical relations as 'like porcupines making love' was used by Martin Wroe in an address given at the Jubilee celebrations of the London Bible College.

35 Alan F. Gibson, *Holding Hands in the Dark*, British Evangelical Council, St Albans (1988).

36 Quoted in David G. Fountain, *E. J. Poole-Connor 1872-1962: Contender for the Faith*, Henry E. Walter, Worthing (1966) p. 197. For another, less emotive, illustrative example of evangelical concern see, Donald Gillies, *Unity in the Dark*, Banner of Truth Trust, London (1964).

37 *The Nottingham Statement: The official statement of the second National Evangelical Anglican Congress held in April 1977*, Falcon, London (1977) pp. 40-43.

38 The *Chicago Call* is found in Webber and Bloesch (eds), op. cit., pp. 11-18.

39 Roger H. Martin, *Evangelicals United: Ecumenical Stirrings in Pre-Victorian Britain, 1795-1830*, Scarecrow Press, Metuchen, NJ and London (1983). The theme is further referred to in Richard Lovelace, *Dynamics of Spiritual Renewal*, IVP, Downers Grove, Ill and Paternoster Press, Exeter (1979) pp. 289-336.

40 Martin, *ibid.*, p. 43.

41 Quoted in F. Roy Coad, *A History of the Brethren Movement*, Paternoster Press, Exeter (1968) pp. 32-33.

42 Stott, *Contemporary Christian*, op. cit., p. 180.

Chapter 10 Tread all the powers of darkness down

EVANGELICALS AND SOCIAL ACTION

For further reading: Donald W. Dayton, *Discovering an Evangelical Heritage*, Harper & Row, New York (1976) and John Stott, *Issues Facing Christians Today*, Marshalls, Basingstoke (1974).

1 On the Clapham Sect see, Ernest M. Howse, *Saints in Politics: The Clapham Sect and the Growth of Freedom*, Allen & Unwin, London (1953).

2 Timothy L. Smith, *Revivalism and Social Reform: American Protestantism on the Eve of the Civil War*, John Hopkins University Press, Baltimore and London (1980 edn) pp. 149, 161.

3 Donald W. Dayton, *Discovering an Evangelical Heritage*, Harper & Row, New York (1976) p. 8ff.

4 Charles Finney, *Lectures on Revivals of Religion*, Cambridge, Mass: —— (1960 edn) William G. McLoughlin (ed.) (first published 1935) p. 288.

5 Dayton, op. cit., pp. 37–61.

6 See Smith, op. cit., especially pp. 204–224.

7 Quoted, *ibid.*, p. 206.

8 Quoted, *ibid.*, p. 154.

9 Quoted in Ian Bradley, *The Call to Seriousness: The Evangelical Impact on the Victorians*, Jonathan Cape, London (1976) p. 119.

10 See p. 41.

11 Kathleen Heasman, *Evangelicals in Action: An Appraisal of their Social Work*, Geoffrey Bles, London (1962) p. 14.

12 Bradley, op. cit., p. 122.

13 Heasman, op. cit., pp. 285–295.

14 David Bebbington, 'Evangelicals and Reform: as analysis of social and political action,' *Third Way*, 6 (1983) pp. 10–13.

15 Norris Magnuson, *Salvation in the Slums: Evangelical Social Work, 1865–1920*, ATLA, Monograph Series, No 10, Scarecros Press and American Theological Library Association, Metuchen, NJ (1977).

16 *ibid.*, p. 10.

17 According to David Moberg, *The Great Reversal: Evangelism versus Social Concern*, Scripture Union, London (1973) on which this section is dependent, the phrase was coined by Timothy Smith.

18 Quoted by Moberg, *ibid.*, p. 32.

19 Quoted by Timothy P. Weber, *Living in the Shadow of the Second Coming: American Premillennialism 1875–1925*, Oxford University Press, New York and Oxford (1979) p. 94.

20 *ibid.*, pp. 94–104.

21 For details see, Ian M. Randall, 'Spiritual Renewal and Social Reform: Attempts to Develop Social Awareness in the Early Keswick Movement,' in *Vox Evangelica*, XXIII (1993) pp. 67–86.

22 Regional conferences on evangelism were held in each continent between the Berlin Congress on Evangelism in 1966 and the Lausanne Congress in 1974. Each confronted issues of social justice. For details see, Rene Padilla and Chris Sugden (eds), *How Evangelicals Endorsed Social Responsibility: Texts on Evangelical Social Ethics 1974–1983 (ii) - A Commentary*, Grove Booklets on Ethics, Nottingham, No. 59 (1985) pp. 7–9.

23 Tom Skinner, 'The U.S. Racial Crisis and World Evangelisation,' in *Christ the Liberator*, IVP, Downers Grove, Ill and Hodder & Stoughton, London (1971 and 1972) p. 204.

24 The original paper is to be found in J. D. Douglas (ed.) *Let the Earth Hear His Voice*, World Wide Publications, Minneapolis (1974) pp. 65–78. An expanded version is found in John Stott, *Christian Mission to the Modern World*, Falcon Press, London (1975).

25 The full statement is published in J. D. Douglas, op. cit., pp. 1294-1296 and in Rene Padilla and Chris Sugden, *Texts on Evangelical Social Ethics 1974-1983 (i)*, Grove Booklets on Ethics, No. 58, Nottingham (1985) pp. 7-11.

26 Douglas, *ibid.*, p. 4ff; Padilla and Sugden, *Texts*, p. 6ff.

27 John Stott, *The Lausanne Covenant: An Exposition and Commentary*, World Wide Publications, Minneapolis (1975) pp. 25-29.

28 For example, see Arthur Johnston, *The Battle for World Evangelism*, Tyndale House, Wheaton, Ill (1978) especially pp. 291-362; Reg Burrows, *Dare to Contend*, Jude Publications, Newcastle-upon-Tyne (1990) pp. 91-100,112.

29 Padilla and Sugden, *Texts*, p. 10.

30 Evangelism and Social Responsibility: An Evangelical Commitment, in *The Grand Rapids Report*, Paternoster Press, Exeter (1982) pp. 21-24.

31 Padilla and Sugden, *Commentary*, pp. 20-22.

32 For details see, Roger Forster, 'Ichthus Christian Fellowship, London,' *Transformation*, 9/2 (1992) pp. 15-18,25.

33 Christopher J. H. Wright, *Living as the People of God: The Relevance of Old Testament Ethics*, IVP, Leicester (1983).

34 —— Lancer, Homebush West, NSW (1989).

35 —— Eerdmans, Grand Rapids (1984).

36 John Stott, *Issues Facing Christians Today*, Marshalls, Basingstoke (1984) pp. 13-25.

37 See further the comments of Rowland Croucher, *Recent Trends Among Evangelicals*, Albatross, Sutherland, NSW (1986) pp. 14,22.

Chapter 11 O for a closer walk with God

EVANGELICALS AND SPIRITUALITY

For further reading: David K. Gillett, *Trust and Obey: Explorations in Evangelical Spirituality*, Darton, Longman & Todd, London (1993); James M. Gordon, *Evangelical Spirituality: From the Wesleys to John Stott*, SPCK, London (1991).

1 Roland Croucher, *Recent Trends among Evangelicals*, Albatross Books, Sutherland, NSW (1986) p. 58; Gerald Hegarty, 'Evangelical Spirituality,' in R. T. France and A. E. McGrath (eds) *Evangelical Anglicans: Their Role and Influence in the Church Today*, SPCK, London (1993) pp. 58-59.

2 Croucher, *ibid.*, pp. 64-67; Ann Long, *Approaches to Spiritual Direction*, Grove Spirituality Series, No. 9, Nottingham (1985).

3 These are expounded by David K. Gillett, *Trust and Obey: Explorations in Evangelical Spirituality*, Darton, Longman & Todd, London (1993).

4 Quoted by James Gordon, *Evangelical Spirituality: From the Wesleys to John Stott*, SPCK, London (1991) p. 1.

5 *ibid.*, p. 162.

6 *ibid.*, p. 163.

7 *ibid.*, p. 161.

8 John Stott, *Focus on Christ*, Kingsway, Eastbourne (1979) p. 155.

9 Donald G. Bloesch, *The Future of Evangelical Christianity: A Call to Unity Amid Diversity*, Doubleday & Co., New York (1983) p. 133.

10 Quoted by Gordon, op. cit., p. 96.

11 Quoted by Gillett, op. cit., pp. 69–71.

12 Quoted by Gordon, op. cit., p. 180.

13 John Stott, *The Cross of Christ*, IVP, Leicester (1986) p. 349.

14 Gillett, op. cit., p. 13.

15 A. Skevington Wood, *The Burning Heart: John Wesley, Evangelist*, Paternoster Press, Exeter (1967) pp. 250-259; Gillett, op. cit., pp. 47-50.

16 J. C. Ryle, *Holiness*, James Clark, Cambridge (1956 edn) pp. 100-134. Ryle's other work on evangelical spirituality is *Practical Religion*, James Clark, London (1959). See also Gillett, op. cit., p. 42.

17 Gillett, *ibid.*, p. 62.

18 Ryle, op. cit., pp. 34-40.

19 J. I. Packer, *A Passion for Holiness*, Crossway Books, Cambridge (1993) also published in the USA under the title *Rediscovering Holiness*, Servant Books (1992) pp. 31-32.

20 See Melvin E. Dieter, Anthony A. Hoekema, Stanley M. Horton, J. Robertson McQuilkin and John F. Walvoord, *Five Views on Sanctification*, Zondervan, Grand Rapids (1987). The views are those of the Wesleyan, Reformed, Pentecostal, Keswick and Augustinian-Dispensational traditions.

21 See Ian S. Rennie, 'Aspects of Christian Brethren Spirituality', in J. I. Packer and Loren Wilkinson (eds.), *Alive to God: Studies in Spirituality presented to James Houston*, IVP, Downers Grove, Ill (1992) pp. 193-196.

22 Quoted by Gordon, op. cit., p. 139.

23 Quoted by Gillett, op. cit., p. 142.

24 *ibid.*, p. 213.

25 Gordon, op. cit., p. 141ff.

26 *ibid.*, p. 213.

27 James Houston, *The Transforming Friendship: A Guide to Prayer*, Lion, Oxford (1989) p. 63.

28 Richard Foster, *Prayer: Finding the Heart's True Home*, Hodder & Stoughton, London (1992).

29 Murray A. Pura and Donald M. Lewis, 'On Spiritual Symmetry: The Christian Devotion of William Wilberforce', in Packer and Wilkinson (eds), op. cit., p. 179.

30 Richard Foster, *Celebration of Discipline: The Path to Spiritual Growth*, Hodder & Stoughton, London (1980) p. 6.

31 *ibid.*, p. 164.

32 For a fuller guide see Dieter *et al*, op. cit.; Gordon, op. cit., pp.

203-228; J. I. Packer, *Keep in Step with the Spirit*, Fleming Revell, Old Tappan, NJ and IVP, Leicester (1984) pp. 121-169.

33 Ryle, op. cit., p. 21.
34 H. C. G. Moule, The Epistle to the Romans, in *The Expositor's Bible*, Hodder & Stoughton, London (1894) p. 195.
35 Packer, *Keep in Step*, op. cit., pp. 132-145.
36 Stanley M. Horton in Dieter, *et al*, op. cit., p. 183.
37 Randal Macaulay and Jerram Barrs, *Christianity with a Human Face*, IVP, Leicester (1979).
38 Gillett, op. cit., pp. 180-189. David Bebbington also comments that evangelical views on spirituality have been particularly subject to variation. *Evangelicalism in Modern Britain: A History from the 1730s to the 1980s*, Unwin Hyman, London (1989) p. 271. See also Bloesch, op. cit., pp. 131-134.
39 Wade Clark Roof, *A Generation of Seekers: The Spiritual Journeys of the Baby Boom Generation*, HarperCollins, San Francisco (1993).

Chapter 12 The Lord has yet more light and truth

EVANGELICALISM TODAY AND TOMORROW

For further reading: Donald G. Bloesch, *The Future of Evangelical Christianity: A Call to Unity Amid Diversity*, Doubleday & Co., New York (1983) and John Stott, *Christ the Controversialist*, Tyndale Press, London (1970).

1 Wade Clark Roof, *A Generation of Seekers: The Spiritual Journeys of the Baby Boom Generation*, HarperCollins, San Francisco (1993) p. 245.
2 Roger H. Martin, *Evangelicals United: Ecumenical Stirrings in Pre-Victorian Britain, 1795-1830*, Scarecrow Press, Metuchen, NJ and London (1983) p. 15.
3 Stephen Williams, 'Evangelicalism in the Nineties,' *Third Way*, 14 (1991) p. 15. The article raises questions about the character, creed and conduct of evangelicals which are pertinent to this chapter.
4 Robert Amess, *One in the Truth? Fighting the Cancer of Division in the Evangelical Church*, Kingsway, Eastbourne (1988).
5 Kenneth A. Meyers, 'A Better Way: Proclamation Instead of Protest,' in Michael Scott Horton (ed), *Power Religion: The Selling Out of the Evangelical Church?* Moody Press, Chicago and Scripture Press, Amersham (1992) p. 48.
6 Randall Balmer, *Mine Eyes Have Seen the Glory: A Journey into the Evangelical Subculture in America*, Oxford University Press, New York and Oxford (1993).
7 John Stott, *Christ the Controversialist*, Tyndale Press, London (1970) p. 32.
8 L. E. Elliot-Binns, *The Evangelical Movement in the English Church*, Methuen & Co, London (1928) p. 79.

9 James Barr, *Fundamentalism*, SCM, London (1981) p. xiii.

10 To balance John Stott's remarks about the apparent arrogance of the claim made about evangelicalism, note should be taken of his, 'Pride, Humility and God,' in J. I. Packer and Loren Wilkinson (eds), *Alive to God: Studies in Spirituality*, IVP, Downers Grove, Ill (1992) pp. 111-121.

11 The responses are spelled out in greater detail in Donald G. Bloesch, *The Future of Evangelical Christianity: A Call to Unity Amid Diversity*, Doubleday & Co., New York (1983) pp. 85-106.

12 *ibid.*, p. 92.

13 Dean M. Kelley, *Why Conservative Churches are Growing*, Harper & Row, New York (1972).

14 Paul Vitz, *Psychology as Religion*, Eerdmans, Grand Rapids (1977).

15 Stott, op. cit., pp. 37-40.

16 Olive Banks, *Faces of Feminism: A Study of Feminism as a Social Movement*, Martin Robinson, Oxford (1981) pp. 13-27.

17 Among the more important of the recent literature is: Mary Evans, *Women in the Bible*, IVP, Downers Grove, Ill and Paternoster Press, Exeter (1983); Gretchen Gaebelin Hull, *Equal to Serve: Women and Men in the Church and Home*, Fleming H. Revell, Old Tappan, NJ (1987) and Scripture Union, London (1989); James B. Hurley, *Man and Woman in Biblical Perspective*, IVP, Leicester (1981); Paul K. Jewett, *Man as Male and Female*, Eerdmans, Grand Rapids (1975); Kathy Keay (ed), *Men, Women and God*, Marshall Pickering, Basingstoke (1987); Shirley Lees (ed), *The Role of Women*, Leicester (1984); Mary Stewart van Leeuwen, *Gender and Grace: Women and Men in a Changing World*, IVP, Leicester (1990); Alvera Mickelsen (ed) *Women, Authority and the Bible*, IVP, Downers Grove, Ill (1986); Elaine Storkey, *What's Right with Feminism*, SPCK, London (1985).

18 James Davison Hunter, *Evangelicalism: The Coming Generation*, Chicago University Press, Chicago (1987) pp. 76-115.

19 See various material produced by the Jubilee Centre, 3, Hooper Street, Cambridge, CB1 2NZ.

20 Peter Brierley and David Longley (eds), *The U.K. Christian Handbook*, MARC Europe, Evangelical Alliance and Bible Society, London (1992) p. 439.

21 Peter Brierley, *Financial Trends in Christian Organisations*, MARC Europe, London (1987) *passim*.

22 See, Hunter, op. cit., and David F. Wells, *No Place for Truth or Whatever Happened to Evangelical Theology?*, Eerdmans, Grand Rapids (1993). Wells is in danger of overstating the case and of confusing reinterpretation with accommodation at times. For a historian who puts the first work in perspective, and so by implication the second, too, see George Marsden, 'Does evangelicalism have a future?' *The Reformed Journal*, 39 (1989) pp. 2-3.

23 A form of this question was posed by Martin Wroe at the Jubilee

Celebrations of the London Bible College in June 1993. He asked, 'Is there any evidence that if Jesus was alive today he would be an evangelical?' I am grateful to Martin for his provocative, but legitimate, question.

24 Stott, op. cit., p. 46.

BIBLIOGRAPHY

Abraham, William J., *The Divine Inspiration of the Holy Scripture*, Oxford University Press, New York and Oxford (1981).
  The Logic of Evangelism, Hodder & Stoughton, London (1989).
Allan, John D., *The Evangelicals: An Illustrated History*, Baker Book House, Grand Rapids and Paternoster Press, Exeter (1989).
Amess, Robert, *One in the Truth? Fighting the Cancer of Division in the Evangelical Church*, Kingsway, Eastbourne (1988).
Anderson, J. N. D., *Into the World: The Needs and Limits of Christian Involvement*, Falcon Books, London (1968).
Balchin, John, *What the Bible Teaches about the Church*, Kingsway, Eastbourne (1979).
Balleine, G. R., *A History of the Evangelical Party in the Church of England*, Longmans, Green & Co., London (1933).
Balmer, Randall, *Mine Eyes Have Seen the Glory: A Journey into the Evangelical Subculture in America*, Oxford University Press, New York and Oxford (1993).
Banks, Olive, *Faces of Feminism: A Study of Feminism as a Social Movement*, Martin Robinson, Oxford (1981).
Barclay, Oliver, *Whatever Happened to the Jesus Lane Lot?*, IVP, Leicester (1977).
Barr, James, *Fundamentalism*, SCM, London (1977).
Bebbington, David, *Evangelicalism in Modern Britain: A History from the 1730s to 1980s*, Unwin Hyman, London (1989).
  'Evangelicals and Reform: An Analysis of Social and Political Action,' *Third Way*, 6 (1983) pp. 10-13.
  Victorian Nonconformity, Headstart History, Bangor (1992).
Berger, Peter L., *Facing Up To Modernity*, Basic Books, New York and Penguin, Harmondsworth (1977 and 1979).
Blanchard, John, *Whatever Happened to Hell?* Evangelical Press, Darlington, Durham (1993).
Bloesch, Donald, *The Evangelical Renaissance*, Eerdmans, Grand Rapids (1973).
  The Future of Evangelical Christianity: A Call to Unity Amid Diversity, Doubleday & Co., New York (1983).
Bradley, Ian, *The Call to Seriousness: The Evangelical Impact on the Victorians*, Jonathan Cape, London (1976).
Braun, Jon, 'A Call to Church Authority,' in Robert Webber and Donald

Bloesch (eds), *The Orthodox Evangelicals*, Thomas Nelson, Nashville (1978).

Bray, Gerald, 'What is the Church? An Ecclesiology for Today,' in Melvin Tinker (ed), *Restoring the Vision: Anglican Evangelicals Speak Out*, MARC, Eastbourne (1990).

Brierley, Peter, (ed), *Christian England, What the English Church Census Reveals*, MARC Europe, London (1991).
Financial Trends in Christian Organisations, MARC Europe, London (1987).

Brierley, Peter and Longley, David (eds), *The U.K. Christian Handbook*, MARC Europe, Evangelical Alliance and Bible Society, London (1992).

Bruce, Steve, *Pray TV: Televangelism in America*, Routledge, London and New York (1990).
Firm in the Faith, Gower, Brookfield, Vermont and Aldershot (1984).

Buchanan, Colin, 'The Unity of the Church,' in John Stott (ed), *Obeying Christ in a Changing World*, Vol II, Fountain Books, London (1977).

Burgess, Stanley M. and McGee, Gary B., (eds), *Dictionary of Pentecostal and Charismatic Movements*, Zondervan, Grand Rapids (1988).

Burrows, Reg, *Dare to Contend: A Call to Anglican Evangelicals*, Jude Publications, Newcastle-upon-Tyne (1990).

Calver, Clive; Coffey, Ian and Meadows, Peter, *Who Do Evangelicals Think They Are?* Evangelical Alliance, London

Carson, D. A. (ed), *Biblical Interpretation and the Church: Text and Context*, Paternoster Press, Exeter (1984).

Carwardine, Richard, *Transatlantic Revivalism: Popular Evangelicalism in Britain and America 1790-1865*, Greenwood Press, Westport, CT (1978).

Catherwood, Sir Frederick, *A Better Way*, IVP, London (1975).
The Christian in Industrial Society, Tyndale Press, London (1974).

Clouse, Robert G. (ed), *The Meaning of the Millennium: Four Views*, IVP, Downers Grove, Ill (1977).

Coad, F. Roy, *A History of the Brethren Movement*, Paternoster Press, Exeter (1968).

Coates, Gerald, *What on Earth is the Kingdom?*, Kingsway, Eastbourne (1983).

Colson, Charles, *Born Again*, Hodder & Stoughton, London (1976).

Croucher, Rowland, *Recent Trends Among Evangelicals*, Albatross, Sutherland, NSW (1986).

Dale, R. W., *The Atonement*, Congregational Union, London (1894).
The Evangelical Revival, Hodder & Stoughton, London (1880).
The Old Evangelicalism and the New, Hodder & Stoughton, London (1889).

Dallimore, Arnold, *George Whitefield*, 2 vols, Banner of Truth Trust, Edinburgh (1970 and 1980).

Dayton, Donald W., *Discovering an Evangelical Heritage*, Harper & Row, New York (1976).

Dayton, Donald W. and Johnston, Robert K., *The Variety of American Evangelicalism*, IVP, Downers Grove, Ill (1991).

Denny, James, *The Death of Christ*, Tyndale Press, London (first published 1902) 1951 edn, edited by R. V. G. Tasker.

Dieter, Melvin E., *The Holiness Revival of the Nineteenth Century*, The Scarecrow Press, Metuchen, NJ and London (1983).

Dieter, Melvin E., Hoekema, Anthony A., Horton, Stanley M., McQuilkin, J. Robertson and Walvoord, John F., *Five Views on Sanctification*, Eerdmans, Grand Rapids (1987).

Dorsett, Lyle W., *Billy Sunday and the Redemption of Urban America*, Eerdmans, Grand Rapids (1991).

Douglas, J. D., (ed), *Let the Earth Hear His Voice*, World Wide Publications, Minneapolis, Mn (1975).

Edwards, David L. and Stott, John, *Essentials: A Liberal-Evangelical Dialogue*, Hodder & Stoughton, London (1988).

Elliot-Binns, L. E., *The Evangelical Movement in the English Church*, Methuen & Co., London (1928).

Escobar, Samuel, 'The Return of Christ,' in C. Rene Padilla (ed), *The New Face of Evangelicalism: An International Symposium on the Lausanne Covenant*, Hodder & Stoughton, London (1976).

Evangelical Belief: An Explanation of the Doctrinal Basis of the Inter-Varsity Fellowship, IVP, London (3rd edn) (1961).

Evangelism and Social Responsibility: An Evangelical Commitment, The Grand Rapids Report, Paternoster Press, Exeter (1982).

Evans, Mary, *Women in the Bible*, IVP, Downers Grove, Ill and Paternoster Press, Exeter (1983).

Fiddes, Paul, *Past Event and Present Salvation: The Christian Idea of the Atonement*, Darton, Longman & Todd, London (1989).

Findlay, James, *Dwight L. Moody, American Evangelist 1837-1899*, Chicago University Press, Chicago (1969).

Finlayson, G. B. A. M., *The Seventh Earl of Shaftesbury 1801-1885*, Eyre Methuen, London (1981).

Finney, Charles G., *Lectures on Revivals of Religion*, Cambridge, Mass: (first published 1835) 1960 edn, edited by William G. McLoughlin.

Finney, John, *Finding Faith Today: How Does it Happen?* British and Foreign Bible Society, Swindon (1992).

Forster, Roger T., *Eternal Destiny: Heaven and Hell*, Ichthus Christian Fellowship, London (n.d.).

'Ichthus Christian Fellowship, London,' in *Transformation*, 9 (1992) pp. 15-18,25.

Forsyth, P. T., *The Cruciality of the Cross*, Hodder & Stoughton, London (1909).

Foster, Richard, *Celebration of Discipline: The Path to Spiritual Growth*, Hodder & Stoughton, London (1980).

Prayer: Finding the Heart's True Home, Hodder & Stoughton, London (1992).

Fountain, David G., *E. J. Poole-Connor 1872-1962: Contender for the*

Faith, Henry E. Walter, Worthing (1966).

France, R. T., 'Evangelical Disagreements about the Bible,' *The Churchman*, 97 (1982), pp. 226-240.

Matthew, Tyndale New Testament Commentaries, Eerdmans, Grand Rapids and IVP, Leicester (1985).

France, R. T. and McGrath, A. E., (eds), *Evangelical Anglicans: Their Role and Influence in the Church Today*, SPCK, London (1993).

Franks, Douglas W., *Less than Conquerors: How Evangelicals Entered the Twentieth Century*, Eerdmans, Grand Rapids (1986).

The Fundamentals, 4 Vols, Baker Book House, Grand Rapids (first published 1910-1915) (1972).

Gaventa, Beverley Roberts, *From Darkness to Light: Aspects of Conversion in the New Testament*, Fortress Press, Philadelphia (1986).

Gibbs, Eddie, *I Believe in Church Growth*, Hodder & Stoughton, London (1984).

Gibson, Alan F. (ed), *The Church and its Unity*, IVP, Leicester (1992).

Holding Hands in the Dark, British Evangelical Council, St Albans (1988).

Gilbert, Alan D., *Religion and Society in Industrial England: Church, Chapel and Social Change 1740-1914*, Longman, London and New York (1976).

Gill, Athol, *Life on the Road*, Lancer, Homebush West, NSW (1989).

Gilles, Donald, *Unity in the Dark*, Banner of Truth Trust, London (1964).

Gillett, David K., *Trust and Obey: Explorations in Evangelical Spirituality*, Darton, Longman & Todd (1993).

Glover, Willis B., *Evangelical Nonconformists and Higher Criticism in the Nineteenth Century*, Independent Press, London (1954).

Gordon, James M., *Evangelical Spirituality: From the Wesleys to John Stott*, SPCK, London (1991).

Gospel and Spirit, A Joint Statement prepared and agreed by a group nominated by the Fountain Trust and the Church of England Evangelical Council, published jointly, 1977.

Graham, Billy, *World Aflame*, The World's Work, Tadworth, Surrey (1966).

Green, Michael, *The Empty Cross of Jesus*, Hodder & Stoughton, London (1984).

Evangelism through the Local Church, Hodder & Stoughton, London (1990).

Griffiths, Michael, *Cinderella With Amnesia*, IVP, Leicester (1985).

What On Earth Are You Doing?, IVP, Leicester (1983).

Grier, W. J., *The Momentous Event: A Discussion of Scriptural Teaching on the Second Advent*, Banner of Truth Trust, London (1970).

Guthrie, Donald, *Introduction to the New Testament*, Tyndale Press, London, rev. edn (1970).

Hadden, J. K. and Shupe, Anton, *Power and Politics in God's Frontier*, Henry Holt, New York (1988).

Hammond, T. C., *In Understanding Be Men*, IVP, London (1936).
  Perfect Freedom, IVP, London (1938).
Hardman, Keith J., *Charles Granidson Finney, 1792-1875: Revivalist and Reformer*, Syracuse University Press, Syracuse (1987).
Harper, Michael, *As at the Beginning*, Hodder & Stoughton, London (1965).
  None Can Guess, Hodder & Stoughton, London (1965).
Harris, Murray, *Raised Immortal: Resurrection and Immortality in the New Testament*, Marshall, Morgan and Scott, London (1983).
Harrison, R. K., *Introduction to the Old Testament*, Tyndale Press, London (1970).
Hastings, Adrian, *A History of English Christianity 1920-1985*, Collins, London (1987).
Heasman, Kathleen, *Evangelicals in Action: An Appraisal of their Social Work*, Geoffrey Bles, London (1962).
Helm, Paul, *The Last Things: Death, Judgment, Heaven and Hell*, Banner of Truth Trust, Edinburgh (1989).
Hendricksen, William, *More Than Conquerors: An Interpretation of the Book of Revelation*, Tyndale Press, London (1962).
Hennell, Michael and Pollard, Arthur (eds), *Charles Simeon (1759-1836)*, SPCK, London (1959).
Henry, Carl, *Aspects of Christian Social Ethics*, Eerdmans, Grand Rapids (1964).
  The Uneasy Conscience of Modern Fundamentalism, Eerdmans, Grand Rapids (1947).
Henry, Carl (ed), *Basic Christian Doctrine*, Holt, Reinhart and Winston, New York (1962).
  Fundamentals of the Faith, Zondervan, Grand Rapids (1969).
Hocken, Peter, *Streams of Renewal*, Paternoster Press, Exeter (1986).
Hollenweger, *The Pentecostals*, SCM, London (1972).
Holloway, David, 'The National Church', in Alan F. Gibson (ed), *The Church and its Unity*, IVP, Leicester (1992).
  'What is an Anglican Evangelical?' in Melvin Tinker (ed), *Restoring the Vision: Anglican Evangelicals Speak Out*, MARC, Eastbourne (1990).
Hopkins, Hugh Evan, *Charles Simeon of Cambridge*, Hodder & Stoughton, London (1977).
Horton, Michael Scott (ed), *Power Religion: The Selling Out of the Evangelical Church?* Moody Press, Chicago and Scripture Press, Amersham (1992).
Houston, James, *The Transforming Friendship: A Guide to Prayer*, Lion, Oxford (1989).
Howse, Ernest M., *Saints in Politics: The Clapham Sect and the Growth of Freedom*, Allen & Unwin, London (1953).
Hoyt, Herman A., 'Dispensational Premillennialism', in Robert G. Clouse, *The Meaning of the Millennium: Four Views*, IVP, Downers Grove, Ill (1977).

Hull, Gretchen Gaebelin, *Equal to Serve: Women and Men in the Church and at Home,* Fleming H. Revell, Old Tappan, NJ and Scripture Union, London (1989).

Hurley, James B., *Man and Woman in Biblical Perspective,* IVP, Leicester (1981).

Hutcheson, Richard G. Jr., *Mainline Churches and the Evangelicals: A Challenging Crisis?* John Knox Press, Atlanta (1981).

Hunter, James Davison, *American Evangelicalism: Conservative Religion and the Quandary of Modernity,* Rutgers University Press, New Brunswick (1983).

Evangelicalism: The Coming Generation, Chicago University Press, Chicago and London (1987).

Include Us In: The Debate About Evangelical Presence in the Main Denominations, Evangelical Alliance, London (1980).

Jewett, Paul K., *Man as Male and Female,* Eerdmans, Grand Rapids (1975).

Johnston, Arthur, *The Battle for World Evangelism,* Tyndale House, Wheaton, Ill (1978).

Keay, Kathy (ed), *Men, Women and God,* Marshall Pickering, Basingstoke (1987).

Kelley, Dean, *Why Conservative Churches Are Growing,* Harper & Row, New York (1977).

King, John, 'The Evangelical Party is Over', *Church of England Newspaper,* 13th November 1992.

King, John (ed), *Evangelicals Today: Thirteen Stocktaking Essays,* Lutterworth Press, Guildford and London (1973).

Kuhrt, Gordon W., 'Principled Comprehensiveness', in Alan F. Gibson (ed), *The Church and its Unity,* IVP, Leicester (1992).

Ladd, George Eldon, 'Historic Premillennialism', in Robert G. Clouse (ed), *The Meaning of the Millennium: Four Views,* IVP, Downers Grove, Ill (1977).

Lees, Shirley (ed), *The Role of Women,* When Christians Disagree Series, IVP, Leicester (1984).

van Leeuwen, Mary Stewart, *Gender and Grace: Women and Men in a Changing World,* IVP, Leicester (1990).

Lindsey, Hal with Carlson, C. C., *The Late Great Planet Earth,* Harper Paperbacks, New York (first published 1970) (1992).

Lloyd-Jones, D. Martyn, *The Basis of Christian Unity: An Exposition of John 17 and Ephesians 4,* IVP, London (1962).

Knowing the Times: Addresses Delivered on Various Occasions 1942-1977, Banner of Truth Trust, Edinburgh (1989).

Long, Ann, *Approaches to Spiritual Direction,* Grove Books, Nottingham, Spirituality Series, No 9 (1985).

Longenecker, Richard, *New Testament Social Ethics for Today,* Eerdmans, Grand Rapids (1984).

Lovegrove, Deryck W., *Established Church, Sectarian People: Itinerancy and the Transformation of English Dissent 1780-1839,* Cambridge

University Press, Cambridge (1988).

Lovelace, Richard, *Dynamics of Spiritual Renewal*, IVP, Downers Grove, Ill and Paternoster Press, Exeter (1979).

Lyle, Leslie T., *A Passion for the Impossible*, OMF, London (1976).

MacArthur, John F., *Charismatic Chaos*, Zondervan, Grand Rapids (1992).

Macaulay, Randal and Barrs, Jerram, *Christianity with a Human Face*, IVP, Leicester (1979).

MacDonald, H. D., *Forgiveness and Atonement*, Baker Book House, Grand Rapids (1984).

Machen, J. Gresham, *Christianity and Liberalism*, Victory Press, London (1923).

Magnuson, Norris, *Salvation in the Slums: Evangelical Social Work 1865-1920*, ATLA Monograph Series, No 10, Scarecrow Press and American Theological Library Associations, Metuchen, NJ (1977).

Manwaring, Randle, *From Controversy to Co-Existence: Evangelicals in the Church of England 1914-1980*, Cambridge University Press, Cambridge (1985).

Marsden, George, 'Does Evangelicalism Have a Future?' in *The Reformed Journal*, 39 (1989), pp. 2-3.

Fundamentalism and American Culture; the Shaping of Twentieth Century Evangelicalism: 1870-1925, Oxford University Press, New York and Oxford (1980).

Reforming Fundamentalism: Fuller Seminary and the New Evangelicalism, Eerdmans, Grand Rapids (1987).

Understanding Fundamentalism and Evangelicalism, Eerdmans, Grand Rapids (1991).

Marsden, George (ed), *Evangelicals and Modern America*, Eerdmans, Grand Rapids (1984).

Marshall, I. Howard, *Biblical Inspiration*, Hodder & Stoughton, London (1982).

Marshall, I. Howard (ed), *New Testament Interpretation: Essays in Principles and Methods*, Paternoster Press, Exeter (1977).

Martin, David, *Tongues of Fire*, Blackwells, Oxford (1990).

Martin, Ralph, *Reconciliation: A Study in Paul's Theology*, Marshall, Morgan & Scott, London (1981).

Martin, Roger H., *Evangelicals United: Ecumenical Stirrings in Pre-Victorian Britain 1795-1830*, Scarecrow Press, Metuchen, NJ and London (1983).

Martin, Walter, *The Billy Graham Story: A Prophet with Honour*, Heinemann, London (1992).

McGrath, Alister, 'A Better Way: the Priesthood of All Believers,' in Michael Scott Horton (ed), *Power Religion: The Selling Out of the Evangelical Church*, Moody Press, Chicago and Scripture Press, Amersham (1992).

McLoughlin, William G., *The American Evangelicals, 1800-1900: An Anthology*, Harper Torchbacks, New York (1968).

Modern Revivalism: Charles Grandison Finney to Billy Graham, Ronald Press, New York (1959).

Revivals, Awakenings and Reform; an Essay on Religion and Social Change in America 1607-1977, University of Chicago Press, Chicago (1978).

Meyers, Kenneth A., 'A Better Way: Proclamation instead of Protest', in Michael Scott Horton (ed), *Power Religion: the Selling Out of the Evangelical Church*, Moody Press, Chicago and Scripture Press, Amersham (1992).

Michaelsen, Robert S. and Roof, Wade Clark, (eds), *Liberal Protestantism: Realities and Possibilities*, The Pilgrim Press, New York (1986).

Mickelsen, Alvera (ed), *Women, Authority and the Bible*, IVP, Downers Grove, Ill (1986).

Moberg, David, *The Great Reversal: Evangelism versus Social Concern*, Scripture Union, London (1973).

Inasmuch: Christian Social Responsibility in the Twentieth Century, Eerdmans, Grand Rapids (1965).

Moltmann, Jurgen, *The Crucified God*, SCM, London (1974).

Morris, Leon, *The Apostolic Preaching of the Cross*, Tyndale Press, London, 3rd edn (1965).

The Atonement: Its Meaning and Significance, IVP, Leicester (1983).

The Cross in the New Testament, Eerdmans, Grand Rapids and Paternoster Press, Exeter (1965).

The Cross of Jesus, Eerdmans, Grand Rapids and Paternoster Press, Exeter (1988).

Motyer, Alec, 'The Final State: Heaven and Hell', in Carl Henry (ed), *Basic Christian Doctrine*, Holt, Reinhart & Winston, New York (1962).

'The Meaning of the Ministry', in Melvin Tinker (ed), *Restoring the Vision: Anglican Evangelicals Speak Out*, MARC, Eastbourne (1990).

Moule, H. C. G., *The Epistle to the Romans*, The Expositor's Bible, Hodder & Stoughton, London (1984).

Munson, James, *The Nonconformists: In Search of a Lost Culture*, SPCK, London (1991).

Murray, Iain, *D. Martyn Lloyd-Jones: The First Forty Years, 1899-1939*, Banner of Truth Trust, Edinburgh (1982).

Jonathan Edwards, A New Biography, Banner of Truth Trust, Edinburgh (1987).

The Puritan Hope: Revival and the Interpretation of Prophecy, Banner of Truth Trust, London (1970).

Neill, Stephen, *A History of Christian Missions*, Hodder & Stoughton, London (1964).

Nelson, F. Burton, 'A Call to Church Unity', in Robert Webber and Donald Bloesch (eds), *The Orthodox Evangelicals*, Thomas Nelson, Nashville (1978).

Nicholls, Bruce J. (ed), *The Church: God's Agent for Change*, Paternoster Press, Exeter (1986).

Nicholls, Mike, *C. H. Spurgeon: The Pastor Evangelist*, Baptist Historical Society, Didcot (1992).

Noll, Mark, *A History of Christianity in the United States and Canada*, Eerdmans, Grand Rapids (1992).

Between Faith and Criticism: Evangelicals, Scholarship and the Bible, Harper & Row, New York and Apollos, Leicester (1986 and 1991).

Noll, Mark, Hatch, Nathan O., Marsden, George M., Wells, David F. and Woodbridge, John D., (eds), *Christianity in America: A Handbook*, Eerdmans, Grand Rapids and Lion, Tring (1983).

The Nottingham Statement: The Official Statement of the Second National Evangelical Anglical Congress held in April 1977, Falcon, London (1977).

Orr, J. Edwin, *The Light of the Nations*, Paternoster Press, Exeter (1985).

The Second Evangelical Awakening in Britain, Marshall, Morgan & Scott, London (1949).

Ostling, Richard, 'Evangelical Publishing and Broadcasting', in George Marsden (ed), *Evangelicalism and Modern America*, Eerdmans, Grand Rapids (1984).

Packer, James I., *A Passion for Holiness*, Crossway Books, Cambridge (1993).

Among God's Giants: The Puritan Vision of the Christian Life, Kingsway, Eastbourne (1991).

Fundamentalism and the Word of God, IVP, London (1958).

God Has Spoken, Hodder & Stoughton, London (1993).

God's Words, IVP, Leicester (1981).

Keep in Step with the Spirit, IVP, Leicester (1984).

Knowing God, Hodder & Stoughton, London (1973).

Packer, James I. and Wilkinson, Loren (eds), *Alive to God: Studies in Spirituality*, IVP, Downers Grove, Ill (1992).

Padilla, C. Rene (ed), *The New Face of Evangelicalism: An International Symposium on the Lausanne Covenant*, Hodder & Stoughton, London (1976).

Padilla, C. Rene and Sugden, Chris (eds), *How Evangelicals Endorsed Social Responsibility: Texts on Evangelical Social Ethics 1974-1983 (ii) - A Commentary*, Grove Booklets on Ethics, Nottingham, No. 59 (1985).

Texts on Evangelical Social Ethics 1974-1983 (i), Grove Booklets on Ethics, Nottingham, No. 58 (1985).

Pawson, David, *Fourth Wave: Charismatics and Evangelicals, are we Ready to Come Together?* Hodder & Stoughton, London (1993).

The Road to Hell, Hodder & Stoughton, London (1992).

Perez, Pablo, 'The Relationship between Church and Para-Church', in Bruce J. Nicholls (ed), *The Church: God's Agent for Change*, Paternoster Press, Exeter (1986).

Pinnock, Clark, 'Fire then Nothing', *Christianity Today*, 20th March 1987.

Pollock, John, *Moody Without Sankey*, Hodder & Stoughton, London (1963).

Pura, Murray A., and Lewis, Donald M., 'On Spiritual Symmetry: The Christian Devotion of William Wilberforce,' in J. I. Packer and Loren Wilkinson (eds), *Alive to God: Studies in Spirituality*, IVP, Downers Grove, Ill (1992).

Quebedeaux, Richard, *The Young Evangelicals*, Harper & Row, New York (1974).

Rack, Henry, *Reasonable Enthusiast*, Epworth Press, London (1989).

Ramm, Bernard, *The Evangelical Heritage*, Word, Waco (1973).
  Special Revelation and the Word of God, Eerdmans, Grand Rapids (1961).

Randall, Ian M., 'Spiritual Renewal and Social Reform: Attempts to Develop Social Awareness in the Early Keswick Movement,' *Vox Evangelica*, XXIII (1993), pp. 67–86.

Reid, Gavin, 'Evangelicals, the Evangel and Evangelism,' in Mervin Tinker (ed), *Restoring the Vision: Anglican Evangelicals Speak Out*, MARC, Eastbourne (1990).

Rennie, Ian S., 'Aspects of Christian Brethren Spirituality,' in J. I. Packer and Loren Wilkinson (eds), *Alive to God: Studies in Spirituality*, IVP, Downers Grove, Ill (1992).

Robbins, Keith (ed), *Protestant Evangelicalism: Britain, Ireland, Germany and America, c.1750–1950*, Basil Blackwell, Oxford (1990).

Roof, Wade Clark, *A Generation of Seekers: The Spiritual Journeys of the Baby Boom Generation*, HarperCollins, San Francisco (1993).

Rowell, Geoffrey, *Hell and the Victorians: A Study of Nineteenth Century Theological Controversies Concerning the Eternal Punishment and the Future Life*, Clarendon Press, Oxford (1974).

Ryle, John C., *Holiness*, James Clark & Co., Cambridge (1956).
  Knots Untied, Lynn & Jarvis Ltd., London, 2nd edn, (1927).
  Practical Religion, James Clark & Co., London (1959).
  Warnings to the Churches, Banner of Truth Trust, London (1967).

Samuel, Leith, *Time to Wake Up! Evangelical Fantasy vs Biblical Realism*, Evangelical Press, Darlington (1992).

Sandeen, Ernest, *The Roots of Fundamentalism: British and American Millennarianism*, Chicago University Press, Chicago and London (1970).

Saward, Michael, *Evangelicals on the Move*, A & R Mowbray, Oxford (1987).

Schaeffer, Francis, *The Church Before a Watching World*, IVP, London (1972).
  True Spirituality, Tyndale House, Wheaton, Ill (1971).

Sheppard, David, *Built As a City*, Hodder & Stoughton, London (1974).

Sheppard, W. J. Limmer, *Great Hymns and their Stories*, Lutterworth Press, Guildford and London (1974).

Skinner, Tom, 'The US Racial Crisis and World Evangelisation,' in *Christ the Liberator*, IVP, Downers Grove, Ill and Hodder & Stoughton, London (1971 and 1972).

Smail, Tom, Wright, Nigel and Walker, Andrew, *Charismatic Renewal:*

The Search for a Theology, SPCK, London (1993).

Smith, Kenneth Hylson, *Evangelicals in the Church of England: 1734-1984*, T & T Clark, Edinburgh (1988).

Smith, Timothy L., *Revivalism and Social Reform: American Protestantism on the Eve of the Civil War*, John Hopkins University Press, Baltimore and London (1980).

Snyder, Howard A., 'The Church as God's Agent in Evangelism,' in J. D. Douglas (ed), *Let The Earth Hear His Voice*, World Wide Publications, Minneapolis (1975).

The Community of the King, IVP, Downers Grove, Ill (1977).

Spurgeon, C. H., *The Soul Winner*, Passmore & Alabaster, London (1897).

Stanley, Brian, *The Bible and the Flag*, Apollos, Leicester (1990).

Stedman, Ray C. *Body Life*, Regal Books, Glendale, Ca (1972).

Stibbs, Alan, *God's Church: A Study in the Biblical Doctrine of the People of God*, IVP, London (1959).

Storkey, Elaine, *What's Right with Feminism?*, SPCK, London (1985).

Stott, John, *Christ the Controversialist*, Tyndale Press, London (1970).

Christian Mission in the Modern World, Falcon Books, London (1975).

The Contemporary Christian, IVP, Leicester (1992).

The Cross of Christ, IVP, Leicester (1986).

Focus on Christ, Kingsway, Eastbourne (1979).

Fundamentalism and Evangelicalism, Crusade Reprint, London (1956).

Issues Facing Christians Today, Marshall, Basingstoke (1977).

The Lausanne Covenant: An Exposition and Commentary, World Wide Publications, Minneapolis (1975).

One People, Falcon Press, London (1968).

What is an Evangelical? Church Pastoral Aid Society, London (1977).

Stott, John (ed), *Obeying Christ in a Changing World*, Vols 1 and 2, Fountain Books, London (1977).

Stout, Harry S., *The Divine Dramatist, George Whitefield and the Rise of Modern Evangelicalism*, Eerdmans, Grand Rapids (1991).

Strachen, C. G., *The Pentecostal Theology of Edward Irving*, Darton, Longman & Todd, London (1973).

Thiselton, Anthony, *The Two Horizons*, Paternoster Press, Exeter (1980).

'Understanding God's Word Today,' in John Stott (ed), *Obeying Christ in the Changing World*, Vol 1, Fountain Books, London (1977).

Tinker, Mervin (ed), *Restoring the Vision: Anglican Evangelicals Speak Out*, MARC, Eastbourne (1990).

Tidball, Derek J., 'English Nonconformist Home Missions 1796-1901,' unpublished Ph.D. Thesis, University of Keele (1982).

Toon, Peter, *About Turn: The Decisive Event of Conversion*, Hodder & Stoughton, London (1987).

Evangelical Theology 1833-1856: A Response to Tractarianism, Marshall, Morgan & Scott, London (1979).

Torrey, R. A., *What the Bible Teaches*, Oliphants, London (1957).

Travis, Stephen, *Christ and the Judgment of God: Divine Retribution in the New Testament*, Marshall Pickering, Basingstoke (1986).

I Believe in the Second Coming of Jesus, Hodder & Stoughton, London (1982).

Tremblath, K. R., *Evangelical Theories of Biblical Inspiration*, Oxford University Press, New York and Oxford (1987).

Vitz, Paul, *Psychology as Religion*, Eerdmans, Grand Rapids (1977).

Walker, Andrew, *Restoring the Kingdom: The Radical Christianity of the House Church Movement*, Hodder & Stoughton, London (1985).

Wallis, Arthur, *The Radical Christian*, Kingsway, Eastbourne (1981).

Wallis, Jim, *The Call to Conversion*, Lion, Tring (1981).

Warfield, Benjamin B., *The Inspiration and Authority of the Bible*, Presbyterian and Reformed Publishing Company, Nutley, NJ and Marshall, Morgan and Scott, London (1959).

Watson, David, *I Believe in the Church*, Hodder & Stoughton, London (1978).

Webber, Robert E., *Common Roots: A Call to Evangelical Maturity*, Zondervan, Grand Rapids (1978).

Webber, Robert and Bloesch, Donald (eds), *The Orthodox Evangelicals*, Thomas Nelson, Nashville (1978).

Weber, Timothy P., *Living in the Shadow of the Second Coming: American Premillennialism 1875-1925*, Oxford University Press, New York and Oxford (1979).

Wells, David, *No Place for Truth or Whatever Happened to Evangelical Theology?* Eerdmans, Grand Rapids (1993).

Wells, David and Woodbridge, John D., (eds), *The Evangelicals: What they Believe, Why they Are and Where they are Changing*, Abingdon, Nashville (1975).

Wenham, John, *The Goodness of God*, IVP, London (1974).

Williams, Stephen, 'Evangelicalism in the Nineties,' *Third Way*, 14 (1991), p. 14-17.

Wilson, Bryan, *Magic and the Millennium*, Heinemann, London (1973).

Wilson, Bryan (ed), *Religion: Contemporary Issues*, Bellew Publishing, London (1992).

Wimber, John with Springer, Kevin, *Power Evangelism*, Harper & Row, San Francisco and Hodder & Stoughton, London (1985).

Winter, Ralph D., 'The Two Structures of God's Redemptive Mission,' *Missiology*, 2 (1974), pp. 121-139.

Wirt, Sherwood E., *The Social Conscience of an Evangelical*, Harper & Row, New York (1968).

Wood, A. Skevington, *The Burning Heart, John Wesley, Evangelist*, Paternoster Press, Exeter (1967).

Wright, Christopher J., 'Inter-faith Dialogue and the Uniqueness in Christ,' in Mervin Tinker (ed), *Restoring the Vision: Anglican Evangelicals Speak Out*, MARC, Eastbourne (1990).

Living as the People of God: The Relevance of Old Testament Ethics, IVP, Leicester (1983).

Wright, David F., 'Soundings in the Doctrine of Scripture in British

Evangelicalism in the First Half of the Twentieth Century; The Tyndale Historical Lecture, 1978, *Tyndale Bulletin*, 31 (1980), pp. 87–106.

Wright, Nigel, *The Fair Face of Evil: Putting the Power of Darkness in its Place*, Marshall Pickering, London (1989).

Additional note

A number of significant books came to hand too late to be referred to by the author but should be noted.

Cameron, Nigel, *Complete in Christ, Rediscovering Jesus and Ourselves*, Marshall Pickering, London, 1989.

—— *Universalism and the Doctrine of Hell*, Paternoster, Exeter, 1993.

Chester, Tim, *Awakening to a World of Need: The recovery of Evangelical Social Concern*, IVP, Leicester, 1993.

Grenz, Stanley, *Revisioning Evangelical Theology*, IVP, Downers Grove, Ill, 1993.

Kantzer, Kenneth and Henry, Carl, *Evangelical Affirmations*, Zondervan, Grand Rapids, 1990.

INDEX